THE
EVERYTHING
GUIDE TO
WINE

Dear Reader,

When I first went to work for a winery in its hospitality department, I had a wine certification under my belt and a desire to help visitors understand and enjoy wine as much as I did. Then one day a guest asked me a question about our vineyard I could not answer. I apologized profusely, but the guest simply smiled encouragingly, patted me on the back, and we continued our tour.

The guest turned out to be an established winemaker from Germany, someone who knew much more about wine than I did. The way he responded to my ignorance taught me something valuable about the wine industry as a whole: Wine and generosity of spirit seem to go hand in hand. Those who work in the industry bring great passion to their professions as well as a desire to share what they know with others.

This book is a product of that spirit. After reading it, I hope you become inspired to ask questions, taste something unfamiliar, and share your newfound knowledge with others. Even if you don't work in the wine industry itself, you can embody everything it stands for.

Cheers!

Peter Alig

Welcome to the EVERYTHING® Series!

These handy, accessible books give you all you need to tackle a difficult project, gain a new hobby, comprehend a fascinating topic, prepare for an exam, or even brush up on something you learned back in school but have since forgotten.

You can choose to read an *Everything*® book from cover to cover or just pick out the information you want from our four useful boxes: e-questions, e-facts, e-alerts, and e-ssentials.

We give you everything you need to know on the subject, but throw in a lot of fun stuff along the way, too.

We now have more than 400 *Everything*® books in print, spanning such wide-ranging categories as weddings, pregnancy, cooking, music instruction, foreign language, crafts, pets, New Age, and so much more. When you're done reading them all, you can finally say you know *Everything*®!

Vino Veritas

Connoisseur's class notes

Message in a Bottle

The sommelier speaks

Savvy Sipping

Tasting tips and tricks

The Ripe Stuff

Facts for wine lovers

PUBLISHER Karen Cooper

DIRECTOR OF ACQUISITIONS AND INNOVATION Paula Munier

MANAGING EDITOR, EVERYTHING® SERIES Lisa Laing

COPY CHIEF Casey Ebert

ACQUISITIONS EDITOR Katrina Schroeder

SENIOR DEVELOPMENT EDITOR Brett Palana-Shanahan

EDITORIAL ASSISTANT Ross Weisman

EVERYTHING® SERIES COVER DESIGNER Erin Alexander

LAYOUT DESIGNERS Colleen Cunningham, Elisabeth Lariviere, Ashley Vierra, Denise Wallace

Visit the entire Everything® series at *www.everything.com*

THE
EVERYTHING.
GUIDE TO
WINE

All you need to know about buying, storing, serving,
and enjoying the world's most remarkable wines

Peter Alig

Wine Educator at Robert Mondavi Winery

Avon, Massachusetts

An Everything® Series Book.
Everything® and everything.com® are registered trademarks of F+W Media, Inc.

Published by Adams Media, a division of F+W Media, Inc.
57 Littlefield Street, Avon, MA 02322 U.S.A.
www.adamsmedia.com

ISBN 10: 1-4405-0748-1
ISBN 13: 978-1-4405-0748-9
eISBN 10: 1-4405-0749-X
eISBN 13: 978-1-4405-0749-6

Printed in the United States of America.

10 9 8 7 6 5 4 3 2 1

Library of Congress Cataloging-in-Publication Data
is available from the publisher.

This publication is designed to provide accurate and authoritative information with regard to the subject matter covered. It is sold with the understanding that the publisher is not engaged in rendering legal, accounting, or other professional advice. If legal advice or other expert assistance is required, the services of a competent professional person should be sought.

—From a *Declaration of Principles* jointly adopted by a Committee of the American Bar Association and a Committee of Publishers and Associations

Many of the designations used by manufacturers and sellers to distinguish their products are claimed as trademarks. Where those designations appear in this book and Adams Media was aware of a trademark claim, the designations have been printed with initial capital letters.

Contains material adapted and abridged from *The Everything® Wine Book, 2nd Edition*, by Barbara Nowak and Beverly Wichman, copyright © 1997, 2005 by F+W Media, Inc, ISBN 10: 1-59337-357-0, ISBN 13: 978-1-59337-357-3.

Sidebar wine bottle, wine glass, and grape art © istockphoto / aerobaby
Sidebar corkscrew art © istockphoto / fckuen

This book is available at quantity discounts for bulk purchases.
For information, please call 1-800-289-0963.

Contents

Acknowledgments

My greatest thanks go to the people of Robert Mondavi Winery, especially Jocelyn Hoar, Anne LeBlanc, Sanda Manuila, Inger Shiffler, and Dana Andrus, who continue to inspire me with their passion and commitment to excellence. I am also indebted to the insights of my teachers along the way: Paul Wagner of Balzac Communications, Paul Mabray of Vintank, Bryan Avila of Nappa Valley College, and Karen MacNeil of the Culinary Institute of America.

Special thanks are also in order for my dear family, who gave me their blessing to go west to play the game of wine. Cheers to you all!

Top 10 Wine Myths

1. Aged wine is better than young wine.
   Not all wines need aging. Generally speaking, red wines—particularly those high in tannins—require more aging than whites.

2. Red wine should never be chilled.
   Some light reds, like Beaujolais, benefit from chilling.

3. "Reserve" wines are top of the line.
   "Reserve" on American wine labels has no legal meaning. Winemakers can use the term at their whim.

4. Wines with sulfites will give you a headache.
   Sulfites are the cause of headaches in only about 1 percent of the population—mostly asthmatics.

5. All German wines are sweet.
   German wines come in all degrees of sweetness—from dry to very, very sweet. "Trocken" on a German wine label means "dry."

6. Screw tops are a sign of cheap wine.
   Au contraire! Increasingly, top winemakers are using screw tops to avoid cork contamination of their wines.

7. Wines should always breathe.
   In general, breathing is only necessary for wines that need further aging.

8. All wines have the same amount of alcohol.
   The level of alcohol depends on the amount of sugar that has been converted during fermentation.

9. The more a wine costs, the better it is.
   Price is related to many factors: the cost of the vineyard land, the type of grapes used, whether it's aged in oak barrels, and—most of all—the reputation of the winery or winemaker.

10. Zinfandel is a pink wine.
    Zinfandel is a red grape, but it can be made into a red wine or a blush wine.

Introduction

THE GREAT BRITISH WINE writer Hugh Johnson, in the preface to his memoir *A Life Uncorked*, writes, "Wine is first and foremost a social game; only secondarily an interest like music or collecting. It is about human relations, hospitality, bonding, ritual . . . all the maneuvers of social life—and all under the influence, however mild and benign, of alcohol."

In these beautiful, perfectly chosen words, Johnson conveys two important ideas. First, wine is indeed a big subject that touches on many dimensions of human life, and second, wine is supposed to be, well, fun! If you find wine to be a bit intimidating at this point, then try not to think of it as an "interest" or a subject to be mastered. Think of wine first as a "game," a beverage that enhances the dynamics of a meal or social event, and the rest will eventually fall into place.

If you are just beginning to play the game of wine, *The Everything® Guide to Wine* is for you. If your number-one fear in life is ordering a bottle of wine at a restaurant, this book will help you breathe easier. If you wish you could give words to the aromas you experience in your favorite Chardonnay, this book will give you those tools. If you are not really sure what "Chardonnay" means, read on.

If you enjoy the game of wine and wish to expand your knowledge of this fascinating drink, this book includes information on wine regions just beginning to make a splash on the world scene. If you are seriously considering a career in the wine industry or want to make wine at home, again, you have come to the right place.

The great thing about wine is that the more you learn and taste, the more you want to learn and taste. Given the ever-changing, ever-growing world of wine, there is always a new game to play.

CHAPTER 1

A Brief History of Wine

The discovery of wine was probably an accident. It didn't have to be "invented," because wine can happen all by itself. It's safe to assume that, way back, people learned to store their fruits of summer for the bleak winters ahead. More than likely, they put their grapes into a hollow in a rock, where nature took over, and fermentation turned the grapes into a bubbling liquid, which we now call wine.

Wine in the Ancient World

We may not know how humans were first introduced to wine, but we do know that people have been imbibing since at least 4000 BC, perhaps as far back as 6000 BC, and maybe even further back than that. Mesopotamia (Persia), near present-day Iran and Egypt—the end-points of the Fertile Crescent—seem to be the birthplace of ancient winemaking, and recent discoveries point to winemaking in China during the same period.

A Persian fable has it that an ancient king kept his beloved grapes in an earthen jar labeled "poison." A discontented member of his harem drank juice from the jar in a suicide attempt, but instead of dying, she found her spirits quite rejuvenated. She shared the drink with her king, who took her into his favor and decreed that, henceforth, grapes would be allowed to ferment.

Ancient Persia was truly wine country. Not only did the Persians give toasts to their gods with wine, they also paid salaries in wine. Men earned ten to twenty quarts a month, and women earned ten. The grape varieties they used to make wine are believed to be the precursors of those used today.

The ancient Egyptians cultivated grapes and made wine in a surprisingly modern fashion. They developed the first arbors and pruning methods, and their grapes were stomped and fermented in large wooden vats. The wine was mostly sweet white wine, probably made from the grape now known as the Muscat of Alexandria. As a matter of respect to the gods, the Egyptians used wine in their funeral rites. Depending on the status held by the deceased, his body and belongings were anointed with wine prior to being entombed.

Message in a Bottle

Most of the Muscat of Alexandria cultivated today ends up as table grapes or raisins. But you can find modern wines using the grape in Spain's Moscatel de Málaga, which is heavy, sweet, and golden brown, or in Portugal's Moscatel de Setúbal, which is a sweet fortified wine.

Situated between Egypt and Mesopotamia along the Fertile Crescent were the Phoenicians, who sailed the Mediterranean from what is now the coast of Lebanon. Thus the grapevine—and wine—found its way to Greece, Sicily, and north-central Italy.

During ancient times, everyone drank wine and beer, even children. That's not as decadent as it might sound. Frankly, drinking the water was hazardous to one's health, and wine was a good substitute thirst-quencher. If you sipped one of those old-style wines today, you would probably notice that it tastes more like vinegar with a hint of cider, and possesses a fairly low alcohol content. It was certainly better than the water that was available. While wine was a staple of daily life, it was consumed mostly by the rich and powerful. Beer was the drink of the common folk.

Greeks Democratize Wine

Greeks embraced wine drinking more enthusiastically than any culture before them. Wine became a drink not just for the elite, but for everyone. It is said that of all the vessels Greeks used daily, more than half related to the consumption of wine. Wine was considered to be a gift from Dionysus, the patron god and symbol of wine, and it was used in religious rituals. Greek doctors, including Hippocrates, even prescribed it for their patients.

Savvy Sipping

Retsina is a traditional wine of Greece with a long history and the distinctive taste of pine resin. The taste that permeated the wine in ancient times became so accepted that long after resin-caulked containers were discontinued, chunks of resin were added to the wine during fermentation to reproduce the flavor. Most people who have tried Retsina—Greeks included—say it's an acquired taste.

Greeks considered it barbaric to drink wine straight, so they diluted it in varying proportions with water. They also learned to add herbs and spices to mask spoilage. Another addition to this delicious taste profile was the flavor of pine resin. Greeks typically stored their wine in porous clay jugs, which had to be sealed to preserve the wine. They caulked the jugs with the resin of pine trees, which imparted its unique essence.

Wine was important to the economies of Greek cities. It was traded within Greece and exported throughout the Mediterranean world. As

Greece began to colonize the western Mediterranean, the Greeks took their grapevines and winemaking technology with them.

Romans Advance Winemaking

The Roman Empire covered, at its greatest outward expansion, most of the Mediterranean lands and a good part of Europe. The Romans found grapes already under cultivation in many of their conquered lands, the wine culture having been widely distributed by their Greek and Phoenician predecessors. The Romans, too, loved wine and fostered its development throughout the empire.

By about 1000 BC, Romans were classifying grape varieties, charting ripening characteristics, identifying diseases, and increasing yields through irrigation and fertilization. They developed wooden barrels to store the wines in place of the skins and jars previously used. The Romans may have been the first ones to put wine into glass containers.

By the first century CE, Rome was awash with wine. Each person in the city of Rome drank on average half a liter each day. Winemaking techniques had spread from Italy to Spain, Germany, England, and France, and those regions developed their own vineyards. You could certainly call this the world's first wine boom. Corner bars popped up all over cities such as Pompeii. The supply (or oversupply) of wine drove down the prices, so much so that Emperor Domitian ordered the great vineyards of France be uprooted to eliminate the competition of French wines with the local Italian wines. Fortunately that order wasn't fully executed, and it was rescinded two centuries later.

Wine in Europe

Wine and its extraordinary properties have always been associated with spirituality and religion. While most of the religions practiced in the eastern Mediterranean incorporated wine in their rituals, it was the spread of Christianity in the fourth century that ensured the survival of viticulture and winemaking after the collapse of the Roman Empire. Because wine was such an integral part in the celebration of the Eucharist, the monasteries and cathedrals that sprang up across Europe took up winemaking and amassed substantial vineyard holdings. The monks—who had the education, the financial resources of the Catholic Church, and the requisite time for cultivating land and trying new techniques—became some of the most important winemakers of the Middle Ages.

Monastic wineries established extensive vineyards across Europe—and especially in Burgundy, Bordeaux, Champagne, the Loire Valley, and the Rhone Valley. During this time France emerged as the preeminent wine-making region in the world.

Wine and War Don't Mix

In 1152 Henry II of England married France's Eleanor of Aquitaine, whose dowry included the vineyard areas of Bordeaux and neighboring Gascony. The light red wine produced there gained favor in England and came to be called claret. By 1350, the port city of Bordeaux was shipping a million cases of claret a year, but the sporadic fighting between the kings of England and France—known as the Hundred Years' War (1337–1453)—put an end to England's access to her much-loved wine. Any ship transporting the wine faced piracy, and protecting the ships became prohibitively expensive. England had to look beyond western France for wine imports.

A trading friendship with Portugal began that led, ultimately, to the creation of port wine. The journey by sea from Portugal to England was hard on wine. The shippers in Oporto, the port city, began adding buckets of brandy to the wine to stabilize it so it would arrive in good condition. They started adding the brandy earlier and earlier until they were adding it during fermentation. This wine became known as, quite appropriately, porto—or port.

Inventions Spur Change

Even though the Romans may have used blown-glass containers to serve wine, pottery and stoneware jugs were the norm—that is, until the seventeenth century and the advent of commercial glass making. The first glass bottles were onion-shaped but eventually evolved into cylindrical bottles that could be stacked on their sides. Needless to say, there could be no sideways stacking without an effective bottle stopper. Enter the cork.

Originally corks were tapered so they could fit a bottle with any size neck and could be manually removed. But with the production of mold-made bottles and horizontal stacking, a standard cylindrical cork was developed that could be driven into the bottle for maximum wine containment.

Now a special tool was required to remove the cork. Corkscrews of all kinds were introduced, and continue to be introduced to this day.

Reaching Out to the New World

With the discovery and colonization of new lands, emigrating Europeans took their vines and their winemaking knowledge elsewhere. Exploration and settlement brought wine to the Americas and South Africa in the 1500s and 1600s and to Australia in the 1700s. The wine history of Europe thus became intertwined—for better and for worse—with that of the New World.

Wine in the Americas

The wine-guzzling conquistadors who arrived in South and Central America from Spain in the 1500s were responsible—directly or indirectly—for introducing winemaking to those lands. Hernando Cortés, perhaps the most successful of the conquistadors and later governor of Mexico, defeated the Aztecs in 1521. After much celebration, he and his soldiers were out of wine. One of his first orders of business was to direct all new Spanish settlers to plant vines on the land they'd been granted. Winemaking flourished. In fact, it flourished to such an extent that the settlers needed to import less and less wine from Spain.

Vino Veritas

Mexico is home to the oldest commercial winery in the Americas. The first wine was produced there in 1596. The winery was known as "Santa Maria de las Parras"—or Holy Mary of the Vines. It still operates today as Casa Madero in the Parras Valley.

The king of Spain, who wanted a captive market for Spanish goods, wasn't happy about this. He levied heavy taxes and ordered vineyards destroyed in all of Spain's new colonies. The edict was enforced most aggressively in Mexico, and the growth of the burgeoning wine industry there came to an abrupt halt.

The church was the sole exception to the king's edict. Just like in Europe, vineyards survived under the care of the church. Missions—

particularly Jesuit missions—were established early in Chile, Argentina, Peru, and Mexico. Later, a series of missions along the Pacific Coast would bring winemaking to California.

Colonial Experiments in North America

Early settlers brought with them a mighty thirst for wine. Imagine their delight when they found a landscape practically smothered by grapevines. Upon closer inspection, however, they found vines unlike any they were familiar with back in Europe. Being the pioneers they were, they forged ahead and fermented anyway. The first wine from native American grapes was made in Jamestown in 1609, and it paled to what they had consumed in Europe.

The colonists' next step was to import vine cuttings of *Vitis vinifera* from Europe so they could grow familiar varieties such as Cabernet Sauvignon, Merlot, Chardonnay. All up and down the Atlantic coast settlers planted vines from every great European wine region. Even Thomas Jefferson planted vines at Monticello. No one succeeded. Each vineyard would die off after only two or three years. It was thought that the extremes of weather were the reason for failure, or that indigenous diseases were at fault.

Even though the *vinifera* vines failed, the side effect of these experiments was the emergence in the 1800s of new American hybrid varieties. These hybrids became the foundation for the wine industry in the eastern United States. Winemaking centers emerged in Ohio, Missouri, on the shores of Lake Erie, and in the Finger Lakes region of upstate New York. The American wine industry was on its way.

California Dreamin'

Beginning around 1770, Franciscan monks established missions—and planted vineyards—up the coast of what would become California. Father Junípero Serra led the way when he planted the first vineyard at Mission San Diego. He traveled north and established eight more missions. His work gave him the name "the father of California wine."

The Gold Rush of 1849 brought frenzied growth, both in terms of population and vineyards. By this time Sonoma had 22,000 acres under vine, and Napa had 18,000. The Santa Clara Valley and Livermore Valley were widely planted and had numerous wineries at this same time. Many pioneer vintners settled south and east of the San Francisco Bay where most of the bottling plants were located. Railroads arrived, and now California wines were available in eastern markets and shipped around the world. By the end of the century, all of the state's winemaking regions were producing wine. California had become the premier wine-growing region in the country.

An International Wine Crisis

In 1863 an unidentified vine disease was being talked about in France's Rhone Valley. By 1865 the disease had spread to Provence. By the late 1860s vine growers all over France were watching their vineyards die before their very eyes. Over the next twenty years it decimated nearly all the vineyards of Europe. The scourge was phylloxera, an insect indigenous to the eastern United States. European *Vitis vinifera* vines had no evolutionary protection against it.

Vino Veritas

How did phylloxera get to Europe?
It was popular in nineteenth-century Europe to import living plants. Between 1858 and 1862 large numbers of rooted American vines were sent to Bordeaux, England, Ireland, Alsace, Germany, and Portugal. Phylloxera came along too.

The parasite spread and affected vines in Australia, New Zealand, and South Africa. For a while, eradicating phylloxera seemed hopeless. Eventually a solution presented itself: graft vinifera vines to pest-resistant American rootstocks. It worked, but it was a long and laborious undertaking to graft and replant each and every vine in Europe.

There's been some debate that the quality of wine declined in the post-phylloxera era. No one will ever know for sure. But if you want to try a wine from *Vitis vinifera* vines grown on their own roots, try a Chilean wine. Chile is the only wine-producing country in the world that escaped phylloxera.

Prohibition Wipes Out an Industry

The winemaking business had its ups and downs, sometimes due to insects and other times to economics. In 1920 however, it crashed and burned because of politics. The Eighteenth Amendment to the U.S. Constitution made Prohibition the law of the land. The Prohibition movement in America was not a sudden twentieth-century phenomenon. It started small, but soon became a national obsession.

In 1816 Indiana forbade Sunday sales of alcohol. In the 1840s "dry" towns and counties emerged in seven states. In 1851 Maine outlawed the manufacture and sale of alcohol. By 1855, New Hampshire, Vermont, Delaware, Michigan, Indiana, Iowa, Minnesota, Nebraska, Connecticut, Rhode Island, Massachusetts, and New York had followed suit. At the outbreak of World War I, thirty-three states had gone dry.

The Eighteenth Amendment was ratified on January 29, 1919, and one year later Prohibition began, making virtually all alcoholic beverages illegal. Even after ratification by the states, the amendment still needed an act of Congress to make it enforceable. That came in the form of the Volstead Act, spearheaded by the Minnesota congressman of the same name. Many supporters of the Eighteenth Amendment had assumed that the "intoxicating liquors" to be banned were the high-alcohol distilled spirits, with 40 percent alcohol. Sadly, Volstead defined intoxicating liquors as any beverage containing more than one-half of 1 percent alcohol, thus including beer, with its 3 to 7 percent alcohol, and wine, with its less than 13 percent alcohol.

Lasting Effects

The almost immediate result of these acts was the decimation of the American wine industry. Vineyards were uprooted. Equipment was abandoned. Growers and producers—if they didn't go completely under—had to find creative ways to stay in business. Cooking wine could still be produced, as long as it was salted and undrinkable. Sacramental and religious wines were still allowed, even wine made for medicinal purposes. Home producers were permitted to make up to 200 gallons of wine a year.

Prohibition's damage to the wine industry was far more than economic; it was cultural. The art of winemaking, which had been practiced for centuries, became illegal. People who had invested their lives and savings in research and equipment had their investments wiped out. Thousands of workers involved in making, bottling, distributing, serving, and selling wine were out of jobs. In 1919 the United States produced 55 million gallons of wine. In 1925 it was 3.5 million gallons.

By 1933, when the Twenty-first Amendment repealed Prohibition, the damage had been done. The country had lost its winemakers and an entire generation of wine drinkers. Other effects of this "Noble Experiment" exist to this day in the form of direct-shipping and distribution laws. By 1936 fifteen states had laws that created state monopolies on wine sales and prevented free-market competition. Other states, while allowing hotels and restaurants to serve wine, banned bars and "liquor by the drink." The aftermath of Prohibition resulted in a hodgepodge of alcohol laws that vary from state to state and community to community.

Vino Veritas

Ingenious California grape growers introduced a product they named Vine-Glo. While they weren't permitted to make wine, the growers could still make grape juice. They sold their juice with instructional material telling consumers what not to do, lest their juice turn to wine in sixty days.

The Wine Boom in the United States

When Prohibition was repealed, the wine industry was slow to recover. In the early days following Repeal, the quality of wine was poor, in part because California grape growers were raising grapes that shipped well, rather than grapes that made fine wine. Wineries mostly sold their wines to wholesalers who bottled them under their own brands and then, in turn, sold them under generic names like Chablis and Burgundy. In 1940 Americans were drinking one gallon of wine a year per person compared to the French, who were consuming forty gallons. Nevertheless, the American wine industry did recover.

A major development that helped this process was the introduction of French hybrids. French hybrids crossed American and European vines to resist phylloxera. They were hardy enough to withstand a northeastern winter, yet yielded good-quality wine without the "grapey" taste of native varieties.

JFK and Julia Child Join Forces

The American wine boom really began with the affluence of the late 1950s. Wine was attractive to educated suburbanites, especially those wealthy enough to travel abroad. Wine, which to most of the wine-drinking world is a simple beverage, had become a status symbol in the United States.

A few role models helped. When John F. Kennedy was sworn in he brought with him, among other things, a new sense of internationalism. His lovely wife, Jackie, adored all things French. French restaurants—and French wines—became very trendy, and from a kitchen in a Boston television studio, Julia Child taught a generation of Americans how to prepare French cuisine and how to match it with French wine.

New products appeared in wine stores to meet the growing demand. Portuguese rosé in the form of Mateus and Lancer's hit the shelves. They were sweet and slightly fizzy, but fruity. Their Europe provenance gave them cachet. West Germany contributed Liebfraumilch, a flowery, fruity, and slightly sweet blend of Riesling and other lesser grape varieties.

Meanwhile, California's reputation for world-class fine wines rapidly grew. In the early 1970s resourceful winemakers, many educated in their craft at the University of California at Davis, finally established California as a world-class wine region. In a blind tasting that pitted several California wines against top French wines in 1976, the American wines—Stag's Leap Wine Cellars Cabernet Sauvignon and Château Montelena Chardonnay— won. The decision, by a panel of all French judges, shocked the world.

Varietals Take Over

American winemakers soon began the practice of labeling their wines according to the grape varieties used to make them. This was in direct contrast to the European custom of labeling wines according to place of origin. Ordering a glass of "white wine" was replaced with ordering a glass of "Chardonnay."

Americans became attached to their new varietals. One California variety, however, wasn't having as much success in the 1970s: Zinfandel. Unfortunately, many growers had acre upon acre of Zinfandel vines whose grapes matured effortlessly in the California sunshine. The growers might have replanted their vineyards with other varieties had it not been for Bob Trinchero, owner of Sutter Home Winery, who was the first to make a fruity, pink, slightly sweet rosé from this red wine grape. It was an instant and enormous success in the American market. Its popularity helped to drive yearly wine consumption in the United States up to two gallons per person.

The Last Twenty Years

Wine-drinking Americans are continuing to upgrade their taste in wines. The proliferation of wine classes, tastings, dinners, and publications has certainly been beneficial. While White Zinfandel is still a staple for millions, there's an enthusiasm for venturing beyond those pink borders. The White Zin craze morphed into a Chardonnay trend and Merlot fad. That fad is largely shifting toward Pinot Grigio and Shiraz. There will always be new wines in vogue.

Message in a Bottle

Gewürztraminer, pronounced "guh-VURTS-trah-mee-ner," is lately in vogue. If you like White Zinfandel, chances are you'll enjoy a glass of Gewürztraminer, particularly if it's a German Gewürztraminer. It's a fragrant white wine with a hint of sweetness. Drier versions are produced in Alsace, California, and Oregon.

California has taken up growing more Old World grapes. So-called "Cal-Ital" varieties like Barbera and Sangiovese are popular. As are Syrah and Grenache—the traditional grapes of the Rhone Valley of France.

International collaboration as well as international competition have picked up. Famous names in wine—Mondavi, Lafite Rothschild, Lapostolle—have invested heavily in land and facilities in places like South America to produce high-quality wines. On the other hand, Australian wineries have been able to give American producers a run for their money with well-made inexpensive wines. They've been so successful that some U.S. wineries are labeling their bottles of Syrah with the Aussie name, Shiraz.

Another recent trend has been the consolidation in the wine industry, with larger wine companies buying up smaller brands. This consolidation has enabled one producer to market many brands and gain shelf space in retail stores. For consumers, the positive effect of consolidation is lower prices and ease of purchase; the downside is reduced exposure to smaller but equally good producers. This should not be a serious cause of alarm, however, because as the number of educated wine drinkers grows, the demand for choice in the wine market will doubtless make the wines of boutique producers more accessible.

CHAPTER 2

Categories of Wine: More Than Red, White, and Pink

One of the most remarkable features of wine is that nature wants to make it. If a grape in the vineyard is bruised, and sugars in the grape juice happen to touch the yeast clinging to the grape skins, wine is the result. However, this wine would not remind you of the $30 Chardonnay you just bought at the store for dinner. That bottle's color, clarity, and much of its flavor profile is due to the watchful eye of the winemaker.

How Wine Is Made

Winemaking begins in the vineyard. Without ripe grapes, there is not much a winemaker can do to create a fine bottle of wine. The next step is to get the juice out of the grapes under controlled conditions. These days, that will not involve the use of feet, but the use of sanitary equipment. Once the juice has been exposed, the winemaker can allow the natural yeast clinging to the grape skins to turn the sugars in the juice into alcohol and carbon dioxide, or she can neutralize the native yeast and add her own strain. The process of converting sugars into alcohol and carbon dioxide with the aid of yeast is called fermentation.

When nature is in balance, all goes according to plan. The reality, of course, is that nature can be annoyingly unpredictable, and a winemaker can run into a plethora of problems in the quest to produce an outstanding bottle of wine. Fortunately, technology has come to the aid of winemakers in an activity that is a careful balance of art and science.

There are many technological options available to the modern winemaker. But—whether the end product is red, white, or pink, or whether it's cheap or expensive—there are several principles common to all winemaking.

Harvesting and Preparing the Grapes

In order to make the best wine possible, the grapes must be picked at just the right moment of ripeness. As grapes ripen, their sugar content increases. At the same time, their acidity declines. The trick is to harvest them when the sugar and acid levels are in balance. This is always a subjective judgment by the winemaker and is based on what style of wine he is producing.

During harvest it is crucial that the grape skins not be split open prematurely. The winemaker does not want fermentation to begin before the grapes enter the winery. While handpicking is the most gentle, mechanical harvesting machines can handle grape bunches with some care. Handpicking, incidentally, is more expensive for a winery than mechanical picking.

Inside the winery, crushing the grapes produces a combination of juice, skins, and seeds called the must. If red wine is the goal, the must will go into a tank for fermentation. If white wine is the goal, the seeds and skins will be separated from the juice as soon as possible, and only the juice will go into the tank or barrel for fermentation.

Fermenting the Juice

Winemakers can "manage" fermentation to enhance the resulting wine. Fermentation usually takes place in large stainless steel tanks, but winemakers can choose to ferment in large oak tanks to add complexity and to refine the wine's texture or mouthfeel. Many white wines are fermented in smaller, sixty-gallon oak barrels to add richness and a toasty character.

In addition to alcohol and carbon dioxide, fermentation generates heat, and high temperatures kill yeast cells. Therefore, fermentation tanks usually have sensors installed that alert winemakers if temperatures approach the danger zone. At the flip of a switch, winemakers can activate cooling systems also installed in the tanks to bring the temperatures down to a more safe level.

Vino Veritas

Grape skins rise to the top of the fermenting must, forming a "cap" over the juice. This cap needs to be broken up and mixed back in to extract the desirable qualities from the skins. The cap is pumped or manually punched back with a paddle. Manual punching can release more tannin from the skin and add to a wine's structure or backbone.

Winemakers also have options when it comes to yeast. Instead of relying solely on naturally occurring yeasts, they can add cultured yeasts to the juice that are better suited to the kind of wine they're producing. Natural yeasts often produce off-aromas and flavors in wine, so cultured yeasts can yield more predictable results. Some yeasts strains have better alcohol tolerances, and still other strains can help add a flowery perfume to white wines.

When fermentation has ended, the winemaker does not always remove the wine from the tank or barrel immediately. For many red wines, the winemaker will leave the new wine in contact with its skins for several more days or even weeks. This allows more color to be extracted from the skins and gives the wine time to soften. This process is called maceration. White wines fermented in small oak barrels will often stay in contact with the lees—dead yeast cells and bits of grape matter left over from fermentation—for several days for the sake of a fuller, richer texture.

Aging the Wine

After fermentation, some wines are ready for immediate bottling. Rosés, many whites, and light reds are bottled soon after fermentation and should be drunk while still young. Others will be aged—either in stainless steel or oak—for several months or up to several years. Fine red wines, in particular, need to age in oak to reach their full potential. This aging often takes place in sixty-gallon barrels and allows the wines to soften and absorb some of the wood's flavors and tannins. Winemakers must be careful, however: Too much time in oak overpowers the wine with the wood flavor and astringency. Additional aging can take place in the bottle.

When the wine moves from fermentation tank to barrel, it is cloudy because of the dead yeast and tiny particulate matter, or lees. Over time, the lees settle at the bottom of the barrel. At this point the winemaker can begin clarifying the wine. Using special equipment, the clearer wine can be pulled or "racked" off the lees and the barrel flushed out. The wine is then returned to the barrel to continue its aging. Racking is frequently done more than once before the wine moves to bottle.

Savvy Sipping

Some winemakers think that fining and filtering remove too much flavor and body from the wine, and forego those processes. The resultant wines (sometimes labeled "unfined" and "unfiltered") may have a small amount of sediment in the bottle, but the winemakers believe a fuller flavor will more than offset any inconvenience to the consumer.

As the wine gets closer to bottling, the wine can be clarified on a more microscopic level using a process called fining. When fining agents—such as charcoal, bentonite clay, casein (milk protein), or egg whites—are added to the wine, they grab onto the solid particles and drag them, over a period of days, to the bottom of the tank. The wine can then be separated from the sediment and fining agents by racking. Some winemakers will further clarify the wine right before bottling by filtering it through layers of paper filters or synthetic fiber mesh.

Sometimes during aging, a winemaker will add special bacteria to encourage a process called malolactic or secondary fermentation (ML or

MLF, for short). This process converts the sharper malic acid in the wine into the softer lactic acid. In terms of what you sense in your mouth, imagine a Granny Smith apple at one end of the spectrum and milk at the other. Most reds and some whites undergo ML.

If a white or red wine is a blend, this combining of several grape varieties in distinct proportions often happens during aging. For example, many Cabernet Sauvignon wines contain dashes of Merlot, which can add a softer, fruitier note to the Cabernet's muscular tannins.

Bottling the Wine

When a wine is ready for release, it's bottled in a highly mechanized process that keeps the wine from contact with the air, germs, and impurities. Many wineries have elaborate bottling lines that fill, cork, cap, and label spotless wine bottles with little human intervention. For the finest wines it is often advantageous for the winery to keep the bottles in storage for two or more years. This makes for better wine when it finally reaches the market and, in many cases, substantially increases its value.

Red Wine

The major thing separating red wine from white wine is the presence of the grape skins in the fermentation tank. Red skins add red color to otherwise clear grape juice. It is possible, then, to make white wine from red grapes, although most white wines you buy are made from white grapes.

When fermentation and, if necessary, maceration end, the wine is drained from the tank. This first run of juice, called free-run juice, comes forth voluntarily. Afterward, the mixture is pressed, yielding press wine, which is darker and more tannic. The winemaker may, at this point, choose to blend the two in order to adjust the tannin level and color. Now the wine moves either to oak barrels for aging or to stainless steel vats for holding in an oxygen-free environment.

Aging in Barrels and Bottles

Prolonged barrel aging before bottling is desirable for most types of red wine to allow all the flavor components time to harmonize. The oak barrel imparts flavor to the wine, sometimes reminiscent of vanilla, spice, chocolate, or wood. The barrel also allows a very slight and controlled exposure to oxygen. Winemakers usually try to avoid exposing their wines to the air, but this low-level oxidation is actually beneficial to the structure and character of the wine.

Savvy Sipping

Oak barrels are expensive and usually reserved for premium wines. But wineries sometimes use less-expensive techniques for their cheaper wines, like adding oak chips to the wine in the tanks. The results, however, aren't usually as good. Wines that sell for less than $10 probably did not spend time in oak barrels.

Some wines improve with further aging in the bottle, particularly fine reds that begin life high in tannins. They include California Cabernet Sauvignon, French Bordeaux and Italian Barolo—and they can continue to improve after many years and, sometimes, even decades. Their harsh tannins soften, their aromas become more complex, and their textures become silky.

White Wine

Most white wines come from "white" grapes, which are actually greenish, greenish yellow, golden yellow, or pinkish yellow. Regardless of the actual color of the skins, the juice for white wine is fermented without the skins and seeds. The result is no tannin and little color. White wines can take on a pale straw color or greenish to deep gold tones, depending on the grape variety and aging treatment.

Vino Veritas

White wines have a propensity to produce tartaric acid crystals known as "wine diamonds." They're harmless—but a nuisance. They form when wine gets too cold. Many winemakers force crystals to form under extremely cold conditions during fermentation so they can remove them. The process is called cold stabilization.

Unlike red wines, winemakers can choose whether to put their white wines through malolactic fermentation. When you peruse wine shelves, you'll be able to find clean, crisp whites that have not undergone any MLF, full-bodied whites that have undergone full MLF, and whites somewhere in the middle.

Aging in Barrels or Bottles

Winemakers have similar decisions to make regarding aging white wines in oak barrels. Chardonnay, for example, is fairly neutral in flavor on its own and can benefit from oak. Others, such as Riesling and Sauvignon Blanc, are less likely to be oak-aged.

Most white wines are meant to be drunk young, but there are exceptions. Some whites with aging potential in bottle include white Burgundies and German Rieslings.

Rosé Wine

Rosé is French for "pink." Rosés are made from red grapes, but the juice and skins are only in contact for a short time (anywhere from a few hours to several days) before the juice is separated. When the winemaker is happy with the color, the winemaking process continues as it would for white wine. Rosés are rarely aged in oak.

Message in a Bottle

Even though a rosé has acidity and tannins acquired from the grape skins, its fruit flavor disappears quickly, which is why you should always buy the most recent vintage available. Like a white wine, a rosé should be served well chilled.

Rosés have always been drunk in southern France. Originally they were made from leftover grapes that didn't make it into the local red wine. The winemaking philosophy has changed, and rosés are now being made on purpose and have acquired respect. They're made in a dry style.

Some of the best rosés come from France—from Tavel (which makes only rosé wines) in the Rhone region and Anjou in the Loire Valley. Back in the 1960s, rosés were quite popular in the United States but fell out of fashion. Then white Zinfandel hit the market in the '80s and the blush wine category was born. White Zinfandel is sweet and low in alcohol, and due to its massive popularity, many consumers now believe that all rosés are sweet. In fact, many are dry and off-dry.

Rosé wines can be found with names. Rosado is a rosé from Spain. Rosato is a rosé from Italy. Vin Gris ("gray wine"), from France, is a very pale rosé made from very lightly pressed red grapes.

Sparkling Wine

What a difference a few bubbles make! Sparkling wine starts out as still wine and then undergoes a second fermentation. More carbon dioxide is formed—but this time, it's captured and not allowed to escape.

There are many sparkling wines: Cava (from Spain); Prosecco and Asti (from Italy); Sekt (from Germany); blanc de noir (from the Pinot Noir grape); blanc de blanc (from the Chardonnay grape)—and, the most famous, Champagne. Not all sparkling wines are Champagne. In order to legitimately be called Champagne, a sparkling wine must meet the following criteria. It must:

- Be produced in the Champagne district of France.
- Be produced from the Chardonnay, Pinot Noir, and/or Pinot Meunier grapes grown there.
- Get its bubbles via the *méthode champenoise* (Champagne method).

The Champagne method is an expensive and labor-intensive means of naturally carbonating a wine. First, wine is made from local grapes. This is no easy feat. The vineyards of Champagne lie so far north that ripeness is an issue in most years. After clarification and a measure of aging, the wine is put into thick Champagne bottles, along with enough yeast and sugar to initiate a second fermentation. It is this second fermentation in the tightly sealed bottle that puts the bubbles in the bubbly. The carbon dioxide can't get out, so it's dissolved in the wine.

The wine is aged—sometimes for years—along with the dead yeast that accumulates as sediment. The trick is to get rid of the sediment without losing all the bubbles. By gradually tilting the bottle a little bit each day until it is inverted, the dead yeast is coaxed into the neck of the bottle where it can quickly be removed. At that time, the bottle is topped off and adjusted for sweetness and then immediately corked so that the wine doesn't lose its effervescence. The Champagne method, because it's so time-consuming and labor-intensive, is expensive—one reason for the high price tag of good Champagne. Sparkling wines that are carbonated in other, cheaper ways can be sold for much less.

Fortified Wine

Fortified means that extra alcohol has been added to a wine. In the beginning it was done to preserve the wine for shipping, but fortified wines have become specialties to be enjoyed on their own terms.

If you were making regular table wine, you would crush the grapes and let fermentation take its course. You would end up with a dry wine with about 12 percent alcohol. For a fortified wine you would add a brandy (usually made from the same grape as the wine) or a neutral spirit. If you add the brandy after fermentation, the fortified wine is dry, with no residual sugar. If it is added before fermentation is complete—before all the natural fruit sugar is consumed—the alcohol stops the yeast from converting the sugars, and you have a sweet fortified wine.

There are four primary types of fortified wines: port, sherry, Madeira, and Marsala. The popular drinking wines are port and sherry. Madeira and Marsala are better known as cooking wines, but there are good bottles of each for drinking. Here is a quick look at each:

- **Port** is sweet and is most often served after a meal. True port comes from the Douro Valley in Portugal.
- **Sherry,** from the vineyards of southern Spain, can range from dry to sweet. Pale, dry sherry is served chilled as an apéritif. Darker, sweet sherry is usually enjoyed as an after-dinner drink.
- **Madeira** is named after its birthplace, a Portuguese island off the coast of Africa. Unlike other fortified wines, Madeira is heated in its production. It can be sweet or dry.
- **Marsala,** named for the town on the western tip of Sicily, comes both dry and sweet. Of all the fortified wines, Marsala is the least distinctive as a beverage and is mostly used for cooking.

Dessert Wine

Dessert wines are called "dessert" because, obviously, they're sweet. They're served either with dessert or as dessert. The most popular dessert wines are frequently called late harvest wines, because the grapes are left on the vine through late autumn until they are practically bursting with sugar. Because of the high concentration of sugar, not all of it converts to alcohol during fermentation. The result is an extremely sweet wine. Most late harvest wines are produced from grapes that have been affected by a mold called *Botrytis cinerea.*

The most noble late harvest, Botrytis-affected wines are German Rieslings that say Beerenauslese or Trockenbeerenauslese on the bottle. Others include the French Sauternes and Barsac, and the Hungarian Tokay.

Another popular dessert wine in Canada, Germany, and Austria is eiswein, or icewine. Grapes are left on the vine so long they freeze when winter arrives! The ultra-sweet grapes are picked and pressed before they can thaw, separating out the frozen water and leaving concentrated juice. The yeasts work as hard as they can, but the amount of sugar wears them out, and the resulting wine is beyond decadent.

Kosher Wine

Wine has played an important part in Jewish tradition and rituals for thousands of years. Most important religious ceremonies begin with the Kiddush, the prayer over the wine. During Passover, celebrants drink four cups of wine to symbolize the four dimensions of freedom. In ancient times, before the Roman conquest drove the Jewish inhabitants out of what is now Israel, vineyards and winemaking were common. Because tradition mandated the drinking of wine, Jewish winemakers took their skills with them into exile. When Jewish immigrants settled in the northeastern United States a century ago, the only grapes available to them were the native American Concord grapes. The wines made from these grapes had a musty character, often referred to as "foxy." In order to make them palatable, the wines had to be heavily sweetened. This heavy and cloyingly sweet style became synonymous with kosher wine. Since the mid-1980s kosher winemaking has changed. Kosher wines are often dry and made from popular grape varietals such as Chardonnay, Merlot, and Cabernet Sauvignon.

What Makes Wine Kosher?

Kosher wines are produced under the strict supervision of a rabbi. To qualify as kosher, certain regulations have to be followed. Because the Holy Land has such a sanctified status in Judaism, some practices are mandated for wineries in Israel but not for those outside of Israel.

Vino Veritas

What does *kosher* mean?
It's Hebrew for good, fitting, or proper. According to Jewish dietary code, foods can be naturally kosher (fruits and vegetables); not kosher but with the potential to be made so by special processing; or not kosher—without the possibility of becoming kosher (pork and shellfish).

Qualifying for kosher status extends from the vineyard to the table:

- The vines have to be at least four years old before the grapes can be made into wine. (In Israel, this applies both to grapes grown in one's own vineyard and to purchased grapes.)
- For wineries in Israel, the vineyard must be left fallow every seventh year, and the growing of other fruits or vegetables in the vineyard is prohibited.
- Only Sabbath observant workers are allowed to take part in making the wine. Even after the wine has gone into barrels and been given a rabbinical seal, a shomer—or watchman—has to guard it. And none of the work can be done on a holy day.
- All of the equipment, tools, materials, and storage facilities may be used only for making kosher products.
- No animal products may be used to produce kosher wine. Instead of using gelatin or egg whites in the fining process, nonanimal fining agents (such as bentonite clay) or kosher fish gelatin are used.
- No leavens are permitted. While yeasts are part of winemaking, they must be certified kosher.
- In Israel, 1 percent of the finished wine has to be discarded. This practice commemorates the time before the Roman conquest when tithing was mandatory.

Two Types of Kosher Wine

For observant Jewish people, kosher wine is holy in nature. And to retain its "kosherness," it must be opened and poured by equally observant Jewish individuals. In answer to the social and economic limitations this poses—to restaurants, for example—there is mevushal wine. It undergoes an additional process to retain its religious purity no matter who opens and pours it. In a sense it's super-kosher.

Mevushal means "boiled." In reality, the wine isn't boiled; it's subjected to flash pasteurization. Wines are pasteurized by heating them to about 185°F for one minute—or flash pasteurized by heating them to 203°F for a few seconds—followed by rapid cooling.

Vino Veritas

A wine's label tells you if a wine is kosher. You'll see an O with a U inside of it with a P near it—a sign that the world's largest kosher certification organization has approved it. A wine label that reads "Made from grapes that are not orlah" indicates that the winery observed the age rule—that the vines were at least four years old.

Who Makes Kosher Wines?

In the United States, the largest producer and importer of kosher wine is the Herzog family, whose labels include Baron Herzog, Herzog Wine Cellars, and Weinstock Cellars. In Europe, a number of well-known wineries have set aside a portion of their production for kosher wines. And in Israel, a new generation of winemakers is producing outstanding wines. Here are just a few of the high-quality kosher wine producers:

- Hagafen Cellars, California
- Gan Eden Winery, California
- Château Sarget de Gruaud Larose, France
- Barkan, Israel
- Gamla, Israel
- Bartenura, Italy
- Ramon Cardova, Spain
- Hafner Koscher Wein, Austria
- Backsberg, South Africa
- Teal Lake, Australia
- Alfasi, Chile

Organic Wine

It was only a matter of time before the organic movement reached the vineyards. Most winemakers are farmers. The wines they produce will be only as good as the grapes they grow. So they have a natural interest in growing the best-tasting fruit and maintaining the health of the land for years to come.

Conventional Versus Organic Farming

All grape growers face the same natural obstacles: weather, pests, disease, and weeds. Conventional techniques adopted over the last fifty years to meet nature's challenges have come from man's own inventions—insecticides, chemical fertilizers, fumigants, and herbicides.

Organic farming forsakes chemicals in favor of more "natural" techniques. From a practical viewpoint this means that organic farmers will:

- Fertilize using composted animal manure or algae.
- Combat weeds by mowing them periodically and allowing them to rot back into the ground, providing organic fertilizer.
- Get rid of insects by growing other plants in the vineyard to attract "beneficial" bugs to act as predators.

Organic farming is as much philosophy as practice. The objective is balance in nature and the long-term health of the soil, the plants and, ultimately, the wine drinker. Grapes grown in this fashion can be government certified as organic grapes. The wine can then be advertised as wine from "organically grown grapes." The irony is that many producers are using organic techniques because they make good sense—but not seeking certification because of the rigidity of government oversight.

Conventional Versus Organic Winemaking

The term organic—or, more precisely, the government certification of a wine as "organic"—doesn't stop at the harvest. Organic winemakers have to use only approved organic methods in cellar operations as well. The subject of organic has been muddied over the practice of adding sulfur dioxide (sulfites), which is the main ingredient wineries use to extend the shelf life of wine.

The health effects of sulfites are negligible except for a small percentage of people who have a sensitivity. It's difficult to make a wine that will keep for any length of time without adding some sulfites to those that are naturally produced by the yeasts during fermentation. But to be able to call a wine "organic," the winemaker has to abide by strict, government-mandated sulfite rules.

How to Know You're Getting "Organic"

Organic claims on store shelves are just plain confusing. When you want an organic alternative to conventional wine, who and what should you believe? The answer is on the label—if you understand what the terms mean. There are four categories that organic wines can claim:

- **100 Percent Organic.** The wine must be from 100 percent organically produced ingredients. There can be no added sulfites. It can have naturally occurring sulfites from fermentation, but they have to measure less than 100 parts per million.
- **Organic.** The wine must be from 95 percent organic ingredients. The nonorganic 5 percent has to be either an agricultural ingredient that's not organically available or another substance like added yeast. There can be no added sulfites, but naturally occurring sulfites can measure up to 100 parts per million.
- **Made with Organic Ingredients/Organic Grapes/Organically Grown Grapes.** The wine must be from 70 percent organic ingredients. Sulfites have to measure below 100 parts per million.
- **Some Organic Ingredients.** The wine has less than 70 percent organic ingredients. The label can't have any information about a certifying agency or any other reference to organic content.

Simply put, "organic" wines are made from certified organic grapes and contain no additives such as sulfites. Wineries that use organic grapes but add sulfites or other additives can only be labeled "made with organically grown grapes." To give you a leg up on your next organic wine-buying expedition, here are some wineries that produce certified organic wines:

- Frey Vineyards, California
- Badger Mountain Vineyard, Washington

- Bonterra Vineyards, California
- Cooper Mountain Vineyards, Oregon
- Organic Wine Works, California

Vegetarian and Vegan Wine

Winemakers—both organic and nonorganic—often use animal-based products in the fining process to clarify the wine. The fining agents act as magnets to attract the unwanted material, which falls to the bottom of the tank. The clear wine is siphoned off, but trace amounts of the fining agent may linger in the finished wine.

Wines suitable for vegans use earth-based fining agents such as bentonite clay, diatomaceous earth, carbon, and kaolin (similar to bentonite). But the fining agents aren't listed on the label, and you have to do some investigating. It's not that vegan wines are scarce. There are lots of them. They're just not always advertised as vegan. However, as veganism gains popularity some wineries are making it clear that their wines don't use animal products. A quick Internet search for "vegan wine" will bring up various sites which list wines suitable for vegans.

A word to the wise vegan: A suitable wine in one vintage may not be suitable in the next. Winemakers can change their fining agents from one year to the next. You might have to make a call to the producer or exporter to find out. A simpler solution to finding a vegan-friendly wine is to look for wines labeled "unfined."

Filtering is another process to remove impurities. A wine can be both fined and filtered, it can undergo one process without the other, or it can undergo neither. "Unfined" on the label means that no clarifying agent has been used.

CHAPTER 3

Great Wine Begins in the Vineyard

All great wines have great winemakers behind them. Great wines are also inseparable from great vineyards. In other words, if a winemaker does not have quality fruit at her disposal, then it is unlikely that she can create a memorable bottle of wine. A great vineyard is the product of more than ideal weather; it is also the product of proper farming, matching the correct vine with the correct soil, and responding to threats in a way that preserves the vineyard's long-term health.

Getting to Know the Vine

In broadest terms, the grapevine is a weak-stemmed, fruit-bearing plant that grows most successfully between 30 and 50 degrees north latitude and between 30 and 40 degrees south latitude. Because of its weak stem, you can find wild grapevines climbing up neighboring trees for support. If you visit a commercial vineyard, you will find grapevines tied to a stake or anchored on a trellis.

Vitis Who?

All grapevines are members of the plant genus *Vitis*. Some *Vitis* grapevines produce awful wine, but not *vinifera*, the species to which Cabernet Sauvignon, Chardonnay, Merlot, Riesling, and many other familiar ones belong. *Vitis vinifera* is indigenous to west Asia and Europe. Scholars are fairly certain that the first *Vitis vinifera* vines were cultivated in what is now Turkey in approximately 4000 BC. It took thousands of years for the various *vinifera* "cultivars"—Merlot, Gamay, Sauvignon Blanc, etc.—to develop and spread throughout Western Europe.

The Ripe Stuff

How many different cultivars of *Vitis vinifera* are there in the world? There are between 5,000 and 10,000 different cultivars. Only a fraction of those are used by winemakers.

Many species of *Vitis* are native to North America, and some of them have vast commercial importance. The major one is *Vitis labrusca*, which counts among its cultivars Concord, Niagara, and Catawba. Welch's grape juice, for example, is made from the unfermented juice of the Concord grape. Other North American *Vitis* species, such as *berlandieri, riparia,* and *rupestris,* would not have achieved superstardom were it not for a pesky insect called phylloxera, the greatest scourge in the history of the wine industry.

North American *Vitis* versus Phylloxera

Phylloxera was to the grapevine what the Black Death was to the population of Europe in the fourteenth century. Phylloxera is native to the United States, and no one really knew it was here until *Vitis vinifera* vines began to be planted in mass quantities. Phylloxera loves to feed on the root systems of *vinifera* vines, and soon U.S. vineyards planted with French vines began to die agonizing deaths. North American *Vitis* grapevines are resistant to the effects of phylloxera. To make matters ten times worse, when American vines were sent to France in the 1860s, phylloxera was sent along with them and proceeded to wipe out most of the vineyards of Europe.

It was an American, T. V. Munson of Texas, who in the 1870s solved the problem by grafting (connecting) *vinifera* vines onto American *Vitis* rootstocks. Amazingly, growers could preserve the characteristics of the *vinifera* vines they loved so much while eradicating phylloxera at the same time.

Things slowly returned to normal, until a new biotype of phylloxera was discovered in the Napa Valley in 1983. Vines once again began to die, because many of the rootstocks in use were the now-infamous AxR1, a cross between an American *Vitis* grapevine and a European *vinifera* grapevine. AxR1 was not strong enough to repel this new biotype, and replanting began again. The AxR1 rootstocks were replaced with stocks having as their basis *Vitis riparia, rupestris,* and *berlandieri* vines, which don't make the best wine on their own, but which now allow more appealing vines to share their bounty with the world.

Phylloxera's Unexpected Gift

Even though phylloxera was a costly fix in California and the rest of the world, the prospect of replanting thousands of vineyard acres gave growers the chance to step back and determine whether they had been planting vines and using rootstocks best suited to their respective locales. If growers had not been getting the most quality out of their vineyards, they now had the opportunity to try new things.

For example, what if a grower has the perfect climate for red grapes, but his vineyard soil is so deep and fertile that the *vinifera* vine he wants to plant, say, Merlot, grows so full and dense that leaves block the grapes from the sun and inhibit ripening? The grower could graft Merlot vines onto

Vitis riparia rootstocks, which don't penetrate the soil too deeply. The result is that the rootstock keeps the Merlot vine in check by denying it the full extent of the soil's nutrients. This holds the vine back and promotes lower yields and higher quality.

Message in a Bottle

When the new biotype of phylloxera emerged in the Napa Valley in 1983, more than 16,000 acres of vines in Napa and Sonoma counties were replanted at a cost of $1.2 billion. Much more money was lost as vintners waited for newly planted vineyards to become productive.

Grafting Was Just the Beginning

When growers responded to the phylloxera epidemic by grafting *Vitis vinifera* vines onto the rootstocks of American *Vitis* vines, they realized that grapevines are adaptable. Growers then had the means to retain preferred characteristics in vines and even create new characteristics that suited their needs. For example, when growers took cuttings from well-performing vines to create new vines, they ended up propagating clones. The Pinot Noir grape, for example, has dozens of clones, all of which are more alike than different, but their differences can influence a grower's decision to plant them. Popular clones of Pinot Noir include Mt. Eden and Dijon.

Speaking of Pinot Noir, it is one of most genetically unstable vines. It practically wants to become something else. Pinot Grigio and Pinot Blanc, for example, are natural mutations of Pinot Noir. Think of clones as products of genetic changes so small that the vine retains its identity, whereas mutations are products of genetic changes so big that they affect all structures and functions of the vines. Pinot Noir ceases to be Pinot Noir and becomes Pinot Grigio.

Sometimes, new varieties of vines can arise from existing varieties without mutations taking place. Cabernet Sauvignon, for example, the noblest red grape variety in the world, is the offspring of a cross between Sauvignon Blanc and Cabernet Franc, both *Vitis vinifera* varieties.

It is also possible for different species of grapevine to cross and form new varieties. These new varieties are not called crosses, but hybrids. For example, if Cabernet Sauvignon (*Vitis vinifera*) were crossed with Concord (*Vitis labrusca*), the resulting vine would be a hybrid, not a cross. Crosses occur within species; hybrids occur when two different species come together.

The Annual Growth Cycle of the Vine

Whether the vine is a clone, a cross, a mutation, or a hybrid, it follows a certain annual growth pattern.

- If you visit Napa Valley in **February**, the vines are somewhat unexciting—no grapes, no leaves—but the vines are by no means inactive. Spring has almost arrived, and as the soil temperature begins to rise, the roots begin absorbing water from the soil. This activity pushes sap through the vines, and you can often see this sap oozing out of what is left of the pruned canes from the previous year. Certain soil types warm up faster than others, and this can influence when the vine begin to weep, or push sap.
- About a month after the vine begins to weep, roughly the end of **March** or early **April**, the buds open. When the previous year's fruiting canes are pruned off, a remnant of that cane is left behind, and on that remnant are buds, which form the foundation of the following year's crop. Bud break signals the beginning of the new vintage.
- By the month of **May** in the northern hemisphere, you can see embryo bunches on the canes that have emerged from the buds. These are the grapevine flowers. When they bloom and self-pollinate, the grapes begin to emerge. Growers have a general idea of how large the crop will be at this point. Frost is a major threat.
- It is now late **May** to early **June**. The vine has flowered and fertilization has taken place. This can be stressful time for the grower, because steady temperatures in the high 60s to low 70s are necessary for the vine to flower successfully. If it is windy, cold, or excessively damp, the vines will flower unevenly, which can affect the quality of the grape clusters. Frost is still a factor.
- Before **June** is over, the grapes themselves will have set. At this point you can see actual clusters of grapes begin to take shape on the

vine. Different varieties of grapes, such as Riesling and Cabernet Sauvignon, vary in terms of the number of grapes each embryo bunch produces.

- As the grapes ripen, red grapes take on their color (white grapes more or less keep theirs), and grape acidity levels drop and sugar levels rise. This process is called verasion. By **August** this is well underway.
- Harvest in places such as Napa Valley can begin in late **August**. Grapes such as Sauvignon Blanc and Pinot Noir will start arriving at the winery. Grapes such as Cabernet Sauvignon ripen later due to their thick skins, but usually all grapes are off the vines by the end of **October**. The danger here is for an early rain shower to douse the grapes and cause rot, so growers must be very careful.
- After harvest, the vines slip into dormancy, and growers prune off the fruiting canes to make room for new ones. Pruning also helps maintain the vines' shape and preserves their precious supply of resources. The whole cycle then repeats!

Growing the Perfect Grape

Nature and the grape grower work hand in hand to grow high-quality grapes. Obviously, the location of the vineyard is hugely important (try growing Cabernet Sauvignon in Alaska!), but a savvy grower can make the most of a harvest even when nature throws some curveballs her way. If the following things are in place, however, a grower's job becomes a little easier.

Heat

If a region's spring and summer temperatures never top 50 degrees, the vine will never wake up from winter, much less bear quality wine grapes. Even if the region is sunny, you need heat.

During the growing season itself, if temperatures hover below 50 degrees or above 95 degrees, photosynthesis virtually stops. Photosynthesis is the process by which energy from sunlight allows for the manufacture of sugars in green plants, including grapevines. A vine without these sugars is like a car without tires—useless. Excessive heat or cold can frustrate this process.

Some grapes can tolerate warmer temperatures, such as the thick-skinned Cabernet Sauvignon grape, but more delicate grapes such as Pinot Noir and Riesling like cooler weather. If you attempted to grow Pinot Noir in the hotter northern regions of the Napa Valley, for example, grape acid levels would be difficult to maintain and the grapes themselves could dehydrate and shrivel into raisins. Good for eating; bad for winemaking.

Vino Veritas

Why is it so important to maintain good levels of acidity in wine grapes?
Think of Coca-Cola without the carbonation. It is flat and syrupy. Wine made from grapes harvested with low acid levels is flabby, noticeably alcoholic, and lacks spark.

Sunshine

Sunshine is necessary for photosynthesis to occur. Even in areas with stretches of cloudy days in the summer, grapevines can usually get the light they need. Excessive cloudiness becomes problematic if rain begins to fall from them, especially during fertilization or harvest.

Sunshine is also important for color development in grapes, especially red grapes. One of the reasons that a glass of Shiraz is dark as ink is because growers allowed their grapes sufficient sun exposure. Growers may have to remove leaves from around their grape clusters so that the sun can have this effect on the fruit. Excessive sun, of course, leads to raisins.

Water

Grapevines do need a certain amount of water to live, much less bear grapes. If that water reaches the vines in the form of rain, then approximately twenty-seven inches of it should fall per year, although some vines get by with less. As important as rain is, however, if it falls at the wrong time of the year, such as during fertilization or right before harvest, it is problematic.

The ideal time for rain to fall is in the winter and early spring when the vines are dormant. If it falls during fertilization in late May or early June, then grape-cluster development will be affected. If it falls too close to harvest, then it can literally dilute the wine and rob it of its intensity. If the rain is particularly hard, then the grapes can get knocked off the vine or the grape skins can be punctured, causing rot.

Many wine regions depend on irrigation to make up for a lack of rainfall. For example, the Swan District in Western Australia, quite possibly the hottest grape growing region in the world, would not be on the wine map without irrigation. The desert-like wine regions of Eastern Washington State also depend heavily on irrigation.

Soil

If you have the ideal levels of heat, light, and water for grapevines but not the proper soil, then you might be in for a short career as a grape farmer. Here are just a few of the questions you need to ask yourself about your soil before you charge ahead with planting grapes: Is it shallow or deep? Is it rocky or clay-heavy? Is the soil acidic? Answers to these questions can make or break your vineyard plans.

First of all, grapevines need three major nutrients (nitrogen, phosphorus, and potassium) and six minor nutrients (magnesium, manganese, iron, zinc, copper, and boron) to live. If a soil's pH is too low (acidic) or too high (alkaline or basic), then the availability of these nutrients, along with the vine's capacity to absorb them, will be affected. In addition, if your soil has an excess of limestone, for example, then the vine will not be able to absorb iron, leading to a nasty condition called chlorosis.

Second, if you know about phylloxera, you know that you need rootstocks for your *Vitis vinifera* vines. Not all rootstocks, however, are created equal. If your vineyard is near a river, drought is probably not your foremost concern, as your soil will be moist. Using a rootstock that reaches deep into that wet soil will deliver an excess of water to your vine, causing it to grow so vigorously that grape quality might be affected. Using the American *Vitis riparia* would be a good move in this case, as its roots are shallow, thus managing the vines' water intake. On the other hand, if your vineyard has a rocky soil and barely gets the necessary amount of rainfall, then you should plant your Cabernet Sauvignon vines on *Vitis rupestris* stocks, as these reach much deeper into the soil than *Vitis riparia*, thereby snatching up precious extra drops of moisture.

Finally, soil content determines how growers train their vines. If the soil has a high composition of gravel, sand, and loam, and the climate is hot, then the grower should train his vines such that the grapes do not develop too close to the ground. The heat absorbed by gravel, sand, and loam rises up from the ground and ripens the grapes much faster than the grower might prefer. Conversely, if the soil has a high concentration of clay and the climate is somewhat cool, then grapes should be closer to the ground, as clay does not absorb as much heat as gravel, sand, and loam, and some extra heat might be needed to get riper fruit.

Savvy Sipping

Napa Valley has more than thirty distinct soil types, which, combined with variations in climate from north to south, produce a wide variety of wine styles.

Farming for Success

Even if you understand your vineyard down to the last microbe, you must still decide how you plan to farm your vineyard. Farming methods vary, but the three most important for grape growers are organic, biodynamic, and sustainable approaches.

Organic

As discussed in Chapter 2, the organic approach, at its most basic level, shuns the use of any synthetic insecticides, fungicides, and fertilizers in the cultivation of a vineyard. Philosophically, organic growers seek to preserve the delicate ecosystem of which they are stewards, safeguarding the health of the land as well as the health of consumers. As such, organic growers only use compost and cover crops to fertilize. In order to maintain an ecological balance in the vineyard, spiders and ladybugs manage pests; owls and hawks manage grape-hungry birds, such as starlings. However, growers are still free to use fungicides based in copper and sulfur if they deem them appropriate.

Wines labeled organic have been certified by a government body, and what constitutes an organic wine varies from country to country. For example, a wine labeled organic in the United States cannot contain added sulfites. Wines that do have some added sulfites but were otherwise farmed organically can be labeled as "wine made from organic grapes."

Biodynamic

This is the most spiritual of the farming approaches covered in this chapter. Biodynamic growers attempt to understand the biological rhythms of the earth and apply such understanding to vineyard operations. For example, much like lunar forces control the tides of the ocean, these same forces exert an influence over grapevine physiology. At Grgich Hills Estate in Napa Valley, harvest is halted on days when these lunar forces pull water up into the vine, diluting the grapes.

Like organic farmers, biodynamic farmers can combat fungus and nurture healthy soil by applying sprays and compost, but these must be provided by the Josephine Porter Institute in Virginia (*www.jpibiodynamics.org*). Hawks and owls are also the friends of biodynamic farmers. Biodynamic certifications are available, though not by any government agency.

Sustainable

Practitioners of sustainable agriculture have goals virtually identical to those of organic and biodynamic farmers. The key difference is that sustainable farmers have no guidelines to follow. They can literally assess every farming technique on its own terms. They might choose to have goats eat the nitrogen-generating cover crops between the vines, not because they must, but because they have decided that the exhaust generated by using mechanical mowers is too damaging to the ecosystem they are trying to keep in balance.

CHAPTER 4

A Primer on Red Grape Varieties

All wine grapes impart their distinctive characteristics to the wines made from them: body, flavor, texture—and, in the case of red wine grapes, color and tannins. Regardless of the winemaker's unique touch, the personality of the grape will be imprinted on the wine. You may not always see the grape names on the label, but each variety has contributed something special to the blend.

Cabernet Sauvignon

For a wine that has consistently captivated audiences around the world, you would expect Cabernet Sauvignon (Cab, for short) to have a long, illustrious history. Quite the opposite is true. In fact, the grape has been around for fewer than six hundred years, which, in wine terms, is not long. Recent genetic studies have revealed that Cabernet Sauvignon is really the offspring of the much older Cabernet Franc and Sauvignon Blanc varieties.

One Tough Customer

Cabernet Sauvignon grapes are small, black, and very tough-skinned. The thick skins make Cabernet grapes fairly resistant to disease and capable of withstanding hard autumn rains, which is a good thing because the grapes ripen late. The skins are also what give the wine its hard tannins. Cab grapes are adaptable and can grow in almost any climate that's not too cool. They grow in most major wine-producing regions of the world. Even in Spain and Italy, where local grapes have dominated the landscape for centuries, Cabernet is being planted and used in nontraditional blends.

Message in a Bottle

Some Napa Valley Cabernets have reached "cult" status. They're made in extremely small quantities and are sold almost exclusively by mailing list. When you find one for resale on the open market, you can pay thousands. Some of these elite wineries are Harlan Estate, Screaming Eagle, Grace Family Vineyard, Dalla Valle Vineyards, Bryant Family Vineyard, Araujo Estate Wines, and Colgin Cellars.

The planting of Cabernet Sauvignon got a real jump-start in the late 1800s when it was used to replant the vineyards of Europe that had been ravaged by phylloxera. It became the primary grape of the famous Bordeaux blends from the Médoc, but its popularity has spread around the world. California is particularly suited to the grape, and its Cabs can command enormous prices.

The Wines

Because of their often harsh tannins, young Cabernets require quite a bit of aging, first in oak barrels and later in bottles. Cabernets reward patience with velvety tannins and extraordinary complexity. Serious Cabs can age for fifteen years or more. Typical tasting notes on young Cabernets praise their black currant, dark berry, chocolate, and spice flavors. Older vintages are often described as having a taste of tobacco, cedar, smoke, and earth.

While 100 percent Cabernet wines are made (many in California), the trend seems to be toward blending. Bordeaux has always blended its Cabernet wine with Merlot, Cabernet Franc, Petit Verdot, and/or Malbec. Merlot and Cabernet Franc, in particular, add a soft fruit finish.

In Australia, Shiraz is added to the Cabernet, giving the wine a somewhat peppery flavor. In Italy winemakers have introduced Cabernet to their Sangiovese-based wines, producing a new breed of wine referred to as "Super Tuscans." In Spain Cabernet is blended with the native Tempranillo.

A SAMPLING OF GREAT CABERNET SAUVIGNONS
- Bodegas Catena Zapata Cabernet Sauvignon (Mendoza, Argentina)
- HdV "La Belle Cousine" Cabernet Sauvignon-Merlot (Napa Valley, California)
- Chateau Lynch-Bages, (Pauillac, Bordeaux France)

Merlot

The 1990s thrust Merlot into the spotlight, as it became the easy-drinking red varietal of choice. In winemaking circles though, Merlot didn't always have star status. It was relegated to the role of blending grape. But its mass-market appeal led to mass plantings around the world. In California alone, Merlot acreage went from 2,000 acres in 1985 to 50,000 in 2003.

Second Fiddle, No More

Merlot's small, dark blue grapes do not have skins as thick as those of Cabernet Sauvignon, which equates to earlier ripening and softer tannins. The Merlot grape can be traced back to first-century France, but it wasn't named as a distinct variety until the 1800s.

While Cabernet gained recognition in Bordeaux's Médoc district, Merlot became prominent in the Right Bank Bordeaux districts of Pomerol and Saint-Emilion. Merlot is the third most planted red grape in France. Besides France, Merlot is important in California, Washington, New York's Long Island district, northeastern Italy, and Chile.

Savvy Sipping

When Merlot is good, It's really good. The famous Château Pétrus in Pomerol makes possibly the world's most expensive Merlot. Its 1990 bottling earned a perfect score of 100 from *Wine Spectator* magazine.

Merlot has a reputation for relatively low acidity and softness. It makes beautiful wines all by itself or blended with others. With its soaring popularity, however, came overproduction in some areas and a tarnished image for many undistinguished wines that were shaped more by market forces than by the winemaker's art.

Most American Merlots do not benefit much from bottle aging. It's a "drink now" wine. Typical descriptions of Merlot flavors are plum, black cherry, spice, blueberry, and chocolate.

MERLOT WITH DISTINCTION
- Swanson Merlot (Oakville, Napa Valley, California)
- Leonetti Merlot (Walla Walla, Washington)
- Ferrero Merlot Maremma Toscana "Me" (Tuscany, Italy)

Pinot Noir

Pinot Noir has been frustrating winemakers since the ancient Romans. It's recognized worldwide as a premier grape, but it presents obstacles to winemaking every step of the way, from its propagation to bottle aging.

Pinot Noir first earned its reputation for making the magnificent wines of the Burgundy region of France—and, more specifically, the two-mile-wide stretch called the Côte d'Or. Pinot Noir is also grown in the Champagne region, where it is one of the three grape varieties allowed to be used in its sparkling wine.

A Handful of Trouble

How difficult can Pinot Noir be? Let's count some of the ways. It's finicky about where it's planted and requires a long, cool growing season. Because it is so sensitive to place, you can practically taste its "terroir" when you open a bottle. The vine is genetically unstable, making the fruit from parent and offspring vines inconsistent. Its buds open early in warmer areas such as Carneros in the Napa Valley, making it susceptible to spring frosts. In addition, its skins are so thin that a heat spike in July can easily dehydrate the grape and produce raisins.

Message in a Bottle

Pinots have a huge family tree. Due to its genetic instability, it has given rise to grapes such as Pinot Blanc, Pinot Gris, and Pinot Meunier.

Pinot Noir produces the best wines when grown in limestone soil and relatively cool climates. Outside of France it's grown in such areas as Germany, Switzerland, Australia, New Zealand, and the United States. It emerged in California in the 1930s and has gained prominence farther north in Oregon.

You might wonder, with all its difficulties, why anyone would go to all the trouble of producing a wine from Pinot Noir. One sip will give you the answer. Pinot Noir has been described as liquid silk. The texture is soft and velvety. Because the grape is less pigmented than other red wine grapes, the wine is lighter in color too. When it is full-bodied, it's not heavy as well. It can be ripened to high alcohol levels without the sting of tannins and acidity. Typical Pinot Noir flavors are raspberries, cherries, and smoke.

PICKING THE PERFECT PINOT
- Saintsbury Brown Ranch Pinot Noir (Carneros, California)
- Patz & Hall Hyde Vineyard Pinot Noir (Carneros, California)
- Domaine Serene "Evenstad Reserve" Pinot Noir (Willamette Valley, Oregon)
- Faiveley, Les Cazetiers, Gevrey-Chambertin (Burgundy, France)

Syrah/Shiraz

It's called Shiraz in Australia, but everywhere else the grape is known as Syrah. It has grown in France's Rhone Valley since Roman times. The grape arrived in Australia in the 1800s and became one of the most widely planted varieties in the country. Not too long after that, Syrah arrived in the United States, but only in the last ten years or so has the grape become very fashionable.

Syrah has all sorts of legends attached to it. One has it that Syrah was brought by the Crusaders from Shiraz, Persia, to the Rhone. Another says the ancient Romans brought it from Syracuse in Sicily. But DNA testing has shown that Syrah is really a native of the Rhone Valley.

Syrah the Survivor

The Syrah grape is black, thick-skinned, and can survive almost anywhere. That's why you'll find Syrah in places as diverse as France, Australia, California, Washington, and South Africa. Even within those areas, Syrah thrives both in cool climates and in warm and sunny conditions.

In the northern Rhone, Syrah is used in the wines from Cornas, Côte Rôtie, Hermitage, and Crozes-Hermitage. The Syrah is rarely blended there. When young, the wines are deeply colored and tannic with a distinct spiciness. As they age, they ease into flavors of blackberries, plums, and smoke. In the southern Rhone, Syrah is blended with other varietals to produce such well-known wines as Châteauneuf-du-Pape. Australia mainly produces big, rich, tannic Shiraz wines.

A SAMPLING OF SYRAH
- Spice Route "Chakalaka" Swartland (South Africa)
- d'Arenberg McLaren Vale "The Dead Arm" Shiraz (Australia)
- Arnot-Roberts, Alder Springs Vineyard Syrah (Mendocino County, California)

Sangiovese

Sangiovese is one of Italy's oldest red varieties and is said to have been cultivated by the Etruscans, the early inhabitants of the Italian peninsula. It wasn't until about 1600 that Sangiovese finally got its name. It comes from the Latin *sanguis jovis*, which means "blood of Jupiter." Sangiovese grows all over its native Italy, but its real home base is in Tuscany. It's only recently that the grape's popularity has risen dramatically in the United States.

All in the Family

Sangiovese is the main component of Chianti. Like Pinot Noir, Sangiovese has several clones. Both Vino Nobile de Montepulciano and the long-lived Brunello di Montalcino are made from them. For the most part, wines made with Sangiovese have moderate tannins and high acidity—but not great depth of color. In the 1960s Italian winemakers began producing 100 percent Sangiovese wines and also blending the grape with Cabernet Sauvignon and Merlot—wines that became known as "Super Tuscans."

SAMPLING SANGIOVESE
- Altesino "Montosoli" Brunello di Montalcino (Italy)
- Ruffino Riserva Ducale Oro Chianti Classico Riserva DOCG (Italy)
- Benessere Vineyards Sangiovese (Napa Valley, California)
- Masciarelli Montepulciano d'Abruzzo (Italy)

Tempranillo

Tempranillo has been called Spain's answer to Cabernet Sauvignon. It's the country's most important red grape variety and is the main grape in Rioja wines. It was once rarely used outside of Spain except for blending. Today it is making itself known in California, Australia, and South America. It can be somewhat unexciting when young, but with age it can develop notes of leather and wood. In Spain it is aged in more aggressive American oak to add more character.

The Name Game

Tempranillo (from the Spanish word *temprano*) means "early"—so named because it ripens earlier than most red varieties. Tempranillo has a bewildering array of aliases. Inside Spain it goes by Cencibel, Ojo de Liebre ("eye of the hare"), Tinto del Pais, Tinto Fino, Tinto de Toro, and Aragonez.

In Portugal It's known as Tinta Roriz. It's also been grown in California for grape juice and jug wines and called Valdepeñas.

Savvy Sipping

When young, Tempranillo is more mellow and easy to drink than Cabernet Sauvignon. Yet, like Cabernet, it has the alcohol and tannins to age well. In Spain's Rioja region, Tempranillo is often blended with the Grenache, Graciano and Mazuela grapes.

TEMPRANILLO WINES TO TRY
- Bodegas Muga Rioja Torre Muga (Spain)
- Marques de Riscal Rioja Gran Reserva (Spain)
- Viader DARE Tempranillo (Napa Valley, California)
- Tandem Ars Nova Navarra Tempranillo-Cabernet Sauvignon-Merlot (Spain)

Zinfandel

The reputation of the United States' wine industry is based largely on the ability of European grape varieties to grow well here. Zinfandel became a particular source of pride in the nineteenth and twentieth centuries because it was considered the only indigenous American grape variety to produce wines that Europeans could respect. However, thanks to genetic testing courtesy of the University of California at Davis, Zinfandel was determined to be identical to the Croatian grape Crljenak Kastelanski. No one truly knows how the grape arrived in America, but the reputation of American Zinfandel wines is secure.

Vino Veritas

Many Zinfandels are labeled "old vines." As vines age, they produce fewer grapes and—as the theory goes—more flavorful and intense grapes. This is obviously good for the wine. The term "old vines," however, is not regulated, so it can mean different things to different producers.

One Grape, Two Very Different Wines

Zinfandel would probably not occupy as much California vineyard land as it does today were it not for the success of White Zinfandel in the 1980s. Zinfandel is a red grape, but when it is crushed and the skins are left to soak in its juice for a few hours, the juice turns pink. Quick removal and partial fermentation results in a sweet, pink, fruity wine that has captivated wine drinkers in the United States.

Red Zinfandel is a completely different story. Zinfandel can ripen to high sugar levels, creating high-alcohol wines with a pronounced viscosity and raspberry, peppery aromas and flavors. Growing Zinfandel requires skill as its large grape bunches often do not ripen evenly.

BLOCKBUSTER ZINS
- Storybook Mountain Vineyards Estate Mayacamas Range Zinfandel (Napa Valley, California)
- Ravenswood Zinfandel (Sonoma County, California)
- Rosenblum Cellars Monte Rosso Vineyard Reserve Zinfandel (Sonoma Valley, California)

Malbec

Bordeaux's loss is Argentina's gain. While the fifth of the five noble Bordeaux varieties (six, if you count the minor grape Carmenère) still has a home in its native land, its susceptibility to many grape maladies has discouraged its planting. In warmer areas such as Mendoza, Argentina, the grape thrives and is commanding higher and higher prices internationally. Known for its density, dark fruit, and backbone of tannins, Argentine Malbec is giving California reds some fierce competition. While Malbec is grown to some scale in California, it is mainly used as a blending grape, adding color to Merlot and Cabernet Sauvignon.

MALBECS TO KNOW
- Achaval Ferrer "Finca Bella Vista" Malbec (Mendoza, Argentina)
- Antigal "1" Malbec (Mendoza, Argentina)
- Ladera Vineyards Malbec (Napa Valley, California)

Other Red Grape Varieties

Each variety of *Vitis vinifera* has something unique to bring to a wine. More often than not, wines are blended so that the final product—the sum of all the parts—is greater than any single wine by itself. Perhaps a wine's contribution is acid, maybe texture, maybe tannins. Here are some other red grape varieties that put their distinctive mark on wines.

Barbera

Barbera is an Italian grape that contributes deep garnet colors, medium to full body, and light tannin levels. In warmer growing areas, it develops high sugar levels and, consequently, high alcohol levels. Barbera makes Italy's Barbera d'Asti, Barbera d'Alba, and Barbera del Monferrato.

Message in a Bottle

Barbera d'Alba and Barbera d'Asti are neighbors to Barolo and Barbaresco in Italy's Piedmont region, but they're miles apart in taste. The Barberas are like the people's wine because they're easy-drinking and go well with "peasant" food. Their light tannins mean that they aren't meant for long aging. In contrast, Barolo and Barbaresco are big and brawny.

Carignan

Originally from northern Spain, this high-yielding vine grows extensively in France and around the Mediterranean. It is popular as a blending grape because it brings red fruit characteristics, deep purple color, strong tannin structure, and high levels of alcohol. Carignan is also known as Carignane, Carignano, Carinena, Mazuelo, and Monestel.

Carmenère

A historic variety once heavily planted in Bordeaux, Carmenère was one of the six varieties allowed for use in making red Bordeaux wines. Because of low yields and ripening problems, it was almost completely abandoned in Bordeaux, but it has found a new home in Chile. It was imported there in 1850 but mislabeled as Merlot. In 1991 its true identity was discovered. Carmenère produces deeply colored, full-bodied wines.

Gamay

Gamay is the French variety solely responsible for the distinctive wines of Beaujolais, which are light-to-medium bodied, high in acid, low in tannins, and meant to be drunk young. Beaujolais Nouveau is a special category of "new" Gamay wine (seven-to-nine weeks old) that is released on the third Thursday of each November.

Vino Veritas

Beaujolais Nouveau is the first wine made from each year's harvest. Originally, it was made for the winery workers, but its popularity quickly spread to local bistros and beyond. Today, festivals around the world celebrate the wine's release the third Thursday in November.

Grenache

Grenache is a grape that can produce wines with 15 or 16 percent alcohol because of its high sugar level. It's one of the official blending partners in Châteauneuf-du-Pape. In Spain it's known as Garnacha, where it can be blended with Tempranillo to produce the red Rioja wines.

Nebbiolo

A thick-skinned grape grown mainly in Italy's Piedmont region, Nebbiolo produces wines high in acid, tannin and alcohol—perfect for aging. It is most famous for making two of Italy's great reds: Barolo and Barbaresco. It generally needs long aging in wood and in bottle to soften. When ready, the wines exhibit unique aromas of truffles and roses.

Pinotage

A uniquely South African grape created in the 1920s by crossing Pinot Noir and Cinsault, Pinotage has a distinct spicy and peppery flavor. Although winemakers elsewhere have been experimenting with Pinotage, it remains primarily a product of South Africa.

CHAPTER 5

A Primer on White Grape Varieties

White wines often don't get the respect they deserve. Many wine lovers believe that only red wines have the capacity to become "great." It is true that white wines, without the tannins and alcohol contents that many red wines possess, do not age as long or as well as many red wines do, but this does not mean that great white wines do not exist. The greatest white wines are the products of a select few white grapes.

Chardonnay

Chardonnay is undoubtedly the noblest white grape in the world. It can produce the greatest variety of wines in the greatest variety of areas. DNA profiling has concluded that Chardonnay is a cross between the notoriously unstable Pinot Noir and an ancient, and almost extinct, variety called Gouais Blanc. Burgundy claims the title of Chardonnay's birthplace, and there is little to dispute that claim.

The Chameleon

Chardonnay is fairly low in varietal character, meaning that it is not terribly impressive on its own, or vastly distinguishable from other white grape varieties. Much of what determines the personality of a Chardonnay is what the winemaker does to the grapes. Using oak to ferment and/or age the wine produces vanilla flavors, while adding richness. Leaving the wine on the spent yeast cells, or lees, adds complexity and a toasty note. Conducting malolactic fermentation reduces the overall acidity and produces a softer, creamier wine. None of this is derived from the grapes themselves.

Location, Location, Location

Chardonnay is hardy and versatile and can grow successfully in all but the most extreme wine regions around the world. It can make great—though somewhat different—wines almost anywhere it's reasonably comfortable. Cool climate Chardonnays tend toward a dry crispness and clean fruit flavors. Warmer climate Chardonnays lean toward richer honey and butterscotch flavors.

In Burgundy, Chardonnay goes into all the region's white wines, such as Montrachet, Meursault, Pouilly-Fuissé, and Chablis. It's one of the three grapes—along with Pinot Noir and Pinot Meunier—allowed in Champagne and the only grape in *blanc de blancs*.

One Grape, Many Styles

Chardonnay is ubiquitous. Some would say boring. Chardonnay is particularly compatible with oak, and many wine connoisseurs have criticized producers, especially in the New World, for over-oaking their Chardonnays.

Recently, a series of unoaked Chardonnays have entered the arena and are gaining momentum. Traditionally, famed unoaked styles have come from northern Italy, Chablis, and Burgundy's Mâconnais district.

Chardonnay's versatility is the main reason why it has become one of the most recognized wines in the world. You can expect a tremendous variety of flavors, medium to high acidity, medium to full body, and minimal fruit to tropical fruit. And you can count on a wine that's dry.

BIG, OAKY, AND CREAMY CHARDONNAYS
- Lewis Cellars Reserve Chardonnay (Napa Valley, California)
- Rombauer Chardonnay (Carneros, Napa Valley, California)
- Château Potelle Winery "VGS" Chardonnay (Napa Valley, California)

UNOAKED CHARDONNAYS
- Kim Crawford Unoaked Chardonnay (Marlborough, New Zealand)
- Jermann Chardonnay (Friuli, Italy)
- Scarpantoni Estate Wines Unwooded Chardonnay (McLaren Vale, Australia)

Chenin Blanc

The traditional home of Chenin Blanc is the Loire Valley of France, where It's been cultivated among picturesque châteaux since the Middle Ages. Chenin Blanc is a sturdy grape with high natural acidity and the versatility to produce crisp, dry table wines, sparkling wines, and sweet dessert wines. From France you'll find dry Chenin Blancs from Saumur and Savennières, off-dry wines from Vouvray and Anjou, dessert wines from Coteaux du Layon, and sparkling wines labeled Crémant de Loire.

Message in a Bottle

If you've ever tasted a Vouvray, you know that it can be dry or it can be sweet, but there's nothing stated on the label that tells you in advance what to expect. As a general rule, as Vouvray moves up in price, the sweeter it gets.

Outside of France Chenin Blanc is often used as a blending grape, with only a small percentage of it going into varietal bottlings. However, South Africa produces the full range of Chenin Blanc wines, referring to the grape as Steen. It's even used in their fortified wines and spirits.

The Model of Cooperation

Chenin Blanc is a cooperative sort of grape. It ripens in the middle of the season so that no extraordinary harvesting measures have to be taken. Because of its compact clusters, it's easy to pick. The grapes have tough skins that minimize damage as they make their way to the crusher, and their natural acidity helps the aging process. A number of California producers make the classic dry style of Chenin Blanc that typifies the Loire.

EXCELLENT AND RELIABLE CHENIN BLANC PRODUCERS
- Chalone Vineyard Chenin Blanc (Monterey County, California)
- Pine Ridge Chenin Blanc-Viognier (Napa Valley, California)
- Casa Nuestra Dry Chenin Blanc (Napa Valley, California)

Gewürztraminer

Gewürztraminer is an extremely difficult wine to perfect, which is why so many people either love it or hate it. If the grapes are picked too late, the wines will lack acidity, making them seem flabby and boring as a result. In their greatest expressions, Gewürztraminers can complement highly seasoned food and spicy Asian and Mexican dishes or be enjoyed on their own.

Vino Veritas

In 1968 Cornell University first planted a new grape variety called Traminette, a cross of Gewürztraminer and the hardier Joannes Seyve. Traminette has the same floral aroma and spicy flavor, but can withstand the harsh winters and unpredictable temperature swings of cold-weather climates like that of New York State. Traminette is being successfully produced in the Finger Lakes region with both dry and sweet examples.

Gewürztraminer traces its origin to the Tyrol grape of Italy. Because of its taste, the word *gewürz* (meaning "spicy") was attached to it by Alsatians in the nineteenth century. The name caught on, but it wasn't until 1973 that the term Gewürztraminer was officially adopted.

Sweet 'n' Spicy

The first thing you'll notice is that Gewürztraminer smells like flowers and exotic spice. Many wine connoisseurs assume that all Gewürztraminers are sweet, and while sweet examples exist, many are bone dry.

Alsace, on the French-German border, has had arguably the most success with dry Gewürztraminer. The grape also grows widely in Germany and Austria. It has had more limited success in North America.

FINE EXAMPLES OF GEWÜRZTRAMINER
- Trimbach Gewürztraminer (Alsace, France)
- Chateau St. Jean Gewürztraminer (Sonoma County, California)
- Corazón Gewürztraminer (Anderson Valley, California)

Muscat

Muscat is the world's oldest known grape variety. It grows in Old World and New World regions alike. One of the earliest recorded Muscat wines hails from the port of Frontignan in southwest France. Actually, Muscat is a family of grapes with more than two hundred varieties. The grapes range from white to almost black, and the wines vary from fine and light—even sparkling—to deep, dark, and sweet. The following are the most familiar of the Muscat varieties:

- **Muscat Blanc à Petits Grains.** Considered the noblest of the Muscats, it is responsible for the sweet, fortified Muscat de Beaumes-de-Venise; for Italy's sparkling Asti; and for Clairette de Die. The grape is also known as Muscat Blanc, Muscat Canelli, Moscat d'Alsace, and Moscatel rosé, among others.
- **Muscat of Alexandria.** This version dates back to the ancient Egyptians. Today Spain grows a lot of it—they call it Moscatel—and it is

one of the three varieties permitted in making sherry. The grape also goes by Moscatel de Málaga, Moscatel, Moscatel Romano, Moscatel Gordo, and Gordo Blanc, among others.

- **Muscat Ottonel.** The palest of all the Muscats, both in color and character, this grape can be found in dry and sweet wines originating from Alsace, Austria, Hungary, and Romania.
- **Muscat Hamburg.** This Muscat is more of a table grape than a wine grape, but eastern European winemakers produce thin red wines from it.

Savvy Sipping

With all the variations of Muscat, it's easy to assume Muscadine is one of them. But Muscadine is a grape family that's native to the southern United States. It's usually grown for use as table grapes, but some goes into limited quantities of wine.

Pinot Gris

The French call it Pinot Gris. The Italians call it Pinot Grigio. Americans produce both and drink a ton of it. The Pinot Gris grape exhibits a range of colors from grayish blue to brownish pink. It's in the same family as Pinot Noir and Pinot Blanc but has a character all its own. Pinot Gris (meaning "gray") has been known to produce wines that range from white to light-tinged pink.

Pinot Gris is thought by many to reach its pinnacle in Alsace, where it's called Tokay-Pinot Gris or Tokay d'Alsace. Alsatian Pinot Gris grapes show up in dry, acidic wines or decadent late harvest styles. Just across the border in Germany, Pinot Gris goes by the name Grau Burgunder and produces full-bodies white wines.

That's a far cry from what most people know as Italy's Pinot Grigio—often a light (some might say thin), pale, and herbal wine for easy quaffing. Some of the best Pinot Grigios come from the Friuli region of Italy, where leading producers show full, rounded versions.

The current hot spot for Pinot Gris is Oregon. It was introduced there in 1966 and has become the state's premier white grape. Oregon producers prefer the name Pinot Gris to Pinot Grigio, although there's no single style of wine made. Some winemakers use oak. Others use only stainless steel. Most produce a completely dry wine. Some leave a little residual sugar.

Message in a Bottle

Pinot Grigio has been called the "new Chardonnay" because of its soaring popularity among both casual drinkers and serious wine enthusiasts. Santa Margherita was the first winery to make its mark as an import to the United States in 1979. In the last five years, small growers all over Italy's northeast have been planting Pinot Grigio to take advantage of the demand.

Riesling

If Riesling were one of the grapes in Champagne, it would undoubtedly be the world's noblest white grape, supplanting Chardonnay for the title. In the nineteenth century, Riesling was considered the best white grape variety because it produced wine of such "elegance." The physical and spiritual home of Riesling is Germany, where it's been grown for at least five hundred years and possibly as long as 2,000 years. It thrives in the coldest vine-growing climates and has found excellent homes in Alsace, Austria, Canada, and in the northern United States, in areas of New York, Washington, Oregon, and Michigan.

A Grape in No Need of Blending

Riesling is rarely blended with other grapes. It doesn't need to be. It produces wines that run the gamut from bone dry and crisp to ultra-sweet and complex. Riesling is one of the few whites that have a long aging capacity. The finest will last for twenty years or more. Unlike Chardonnay, which relies on winemaker interventions for its style, Riesling relies on nature for its diversity. The winemaker really has only two decisions to make: when to pick the grapes and how long to ferment the juice.

The ripeness level of the Riesling grape at harvest drastically conditions the personality of the finished wine. In Germany, where ripeness levels vary from year to year, a system was developed to convey that ripeness level to consumers. Germany's Riesling's can de designated "Kabinett" (least ripe) all the way to "Trockenbeerenauslese" (ripest, late harvest).

"Dry" Riesling

Riesling is the favored grape for the sweet and acclaimed late harvest wines and for some ice wines. However, for table wines the preference in recent years has been for dry wines. Producers have been deliberately making Rieslings in a dry style, which means crisp and lower in alcohol. In Germany, dry Rieslings will have the terms "Trocken" (dry), "Classic," or "Selection" on the label.

In Alsace, the French wine region across the Rhine from Germany, Rieslings are usually fermented bone dry. Compared to a dry German Kabinett Riesling with an alcohol content as low as 10 percent, an Alsatian Riesling will have at least 12 percent alcohol.

Riesling is sometimes labeled as Johannisberg Riesling, Rhine Riesling, or White Riesling.

RIESLINGS WORTH TRYING
- Dr. Konstantin Frank Johannisberg Riesling (Finger Lakes, New York)
- Pewsey Vale Riesling (Eden Valley, South Australia)
- Dr. Burklin-Wolf Estate Riesling (Pfalz, Germany)

Sauvignon Blanc

Sauvignon Blanc is widely cultivated in France and California. The Loire Valley produces wines that are 100 percent Sauvignon Blanc, most notably the crisp, tart examples of Sancerre and Pouilly-Fumé. Dry white Bordeaux wines are usually Sauvignon Blanc blended with Sémillon and aged in oak. While not the primary grape, Sauvignon Blanc plays an important part in the sweet and revered dessert wines of Sauternes.

Sauvignon Blanc is also produced successfully in Italy, Australia, South America, and—met with much recent acclaim—in New Zealand.

Historians believe that a Frenchman named Louis Mel first brought Sauvignon Blanc cuttings to California in the 1870s. His cuttings were not just any cuttings; they came from the world-famous Chateau d'Yquem vineyards, source of a magisterial dessert wine. He planted them in an area of the Livermore Valley now home to Wente Vineyards. Needless to say, the vines grew so successfully they spread to other parts of California, such as Napa Valley, where a vintner named Robert Mondavi was beginning to make a name for himself in the 1960s.

Vino Veritas

How did Louis Mel acquire such prized Sauvignon Blanc cuttings? Louis Mel happened to be married to the niece of the Marquis de Lur Saluces, owner of Chateau d'Yquem. The sweet wines of d'Yquem are so famous that even Thomas Jefferson asked to buy some back in 1787. The d'Yquem property is only 20 percent Sauvignon Blanc (the rest is Semillon), making the cuttings Mel acquired even more prestigious.

Sauvignon Blanc's Alias

Back in the 1960s when Robert Mondavi introduced a dry style of Sauvignon Blanc, he wanted to distinguish it from the sweeter, blander versions coming out of California. He called the new wine Fumé Blanc. Rather than trademark the name for his exclusive use, he permitted other winemakers to use it. Many American wineries label their Sauvignon Blanc wines Fumé Blanc. The variations in labeling can be confusing, but today Sauvignon Blanc and Fumé Blanc are the same wine.

Whatever the particular style, you can recognize a Sauvignon Blanc by its distinctive aromas and flavors. Wines from cooler climates have been described as grassy or herbaceous; from warmer climates they develop citrus and tropical characteristics; and in the late harvest style they take on notes of honey and roasted nuts.

SOME SAUVIGNON SAMPLINGS
- Pascal Jolivet Pouilly-Fumé (Loire Valley, France)
- Warwick Estate Sauvignon Blanc (South Africa)
- Spy Valley Sauvignon Blanc (New Zealand)
- Casa Lapostolle Classic Sauvignon Blanc (Chile)
- Louis Mel, Wente Vineyards Sauvignon Blanc (Livermore Valley, California)

Semillon

Semillon is one of the easiest grapes to grow. It produces abundant grapes, flowers later in the spring thus avoiding frost, and resists many diseases. Very little of it is planted in North America, which is why you might be surprised to see this grape in this list. As a dry wine, it is fairly unimpressive in its youth. Aged versions are more interesting, yielding aromas that might remind you of lanolin and nuts.

Semillon's greatest expression—and the reason it is on this list—can be found in the Sauternes sub-region of Bordeaux, where it makes late-harvest dessert wines prized as far away as the Russian imperial court.

The Gift of Thin Skins

Semillon is susceptible to one grave disease, but it's a disease growers want the vine to get. The condition is Botrytis bunch rot, and if your goal is a dry wine, this is devastating, but if your goal is something sweet, Botrytis bunch rot is a godsend. Because Semillon has such thin skins, in damp conditions it succumbs easily to the fungus Botrytis, which shrivels the grapes and concentrates both the sugars and the flavors. These Botrytis-infected grapes produce precious little juice, and the winemakers want every last drop. The resulting wine is sweet, rich, and lasts forever. Chateau d'Yquem is the most famous and most expensive of the Sauternes Semillon wines, but fortunately there are others for mere mortals to enjoy.

DRY AND SWEET SEMILLONS
- Plantagenet "Hazard Hill" Semillon-Sauvignon Blanc; dry (Western Australia)
- Chateau Sigalas Rabaud; sweet (Sauternes Bordeaux, France)
- Far Niente "Dolce"; sweet (Napa Valley)

Viognier

Viognier is no easy grape to grow. The plants are susceptible to all kinds of diseases, such as powdery mildew. Yields can be extremely low, due in no small part to uneven ripening. To make matters worse, if growers pick the grapes too late, the acidity will be so low they might as well make brandy out of them.

This may be why the grape was headed toward extinction. In 1965 only a few acres of Viognier remained under cultivation in Condrieu, in the grape's Rhone Valley homeland. Since then, Viognier has been making a comeback—first in Condrieu and then in the south of France in Languedoc-Roussillon and Provence. Later, the plantings spread to California and Australia. To give you an idea of the escalation: In 1993 California crushed 231 tons of Viognier grapes. Ten years later that increased to 9,800 tons.

A Gift of Flowers and Perfume

When Viognier prospers it produces arguably the most aromatic wines in the world, replete with vibrant floral qualities. The classic Old World style of Viognier is crisp, dry, and intense. As winemakers around the world craft their own Viogniers, more style variations appear. While cooler regions of California produce a style closer to the French classic, wines from warmer areas are richer and fuller.

Vino Veritas

It's rare for France to permit the use of a white wine grape in a high-quality red wine. But in an unusual twist in the vineyards of the Côte Rôtie, Viognier vines are planted among Syrah vines. The white and red grapes are harvested and vinified together to produce the highly regarded Côte Rôtie red wines.

A FEW VIOGNIER SELECTIONS
- Alban Vineyards Viognier (Arroyo Grande, California)
- Château de Campuget Viognier (France)
- Yalumba Viognier (Australia)
- Pride Mountain Viognier (Spring Mountain, Napa Valley, California)

Up-and-Comers

Grape varieties go in and out of fashion. They might be popular in one part of the world and then catch on elsewhere. As wine lovers tire of ordering the same old familiar varietals, they are always on the lookout for "new" grapes.

Grüner Veltliner

Austria has jumped onto the American scene with its dry, crisp Grüner Veltliner. It is the most extensively grown grape variety in Austria, accounting for 37 percent of all vine plantings. The wine has different expressions depending on how the grapes are grown and how they're treated by the winemaker.

Grüner Veltliner used to be treated as a high-production commercial grape. The high-yield grapes produced light and refreshing sippers that were popular in Austria's heurigen (wine taverns). In the 1980s Austria's wine industry made a conscious step toward higher quality. With lower yields and higher ripeness, the resulting wines are more complex and fuller-flavored. The wines have a peppery quality and naturally high acidity. The best bottles of Grüner Veltliner have potential for some aging.

A TASTE OF AUSTRIAN WINES
- Pfaffl, Grüner Veltliner Hundsleiten Sandtal (Austria)
- Leopold Sommer Grüner Veltliner (Austria)
- Weingut Bründlmayer Grüner Veltliner Berg Vogelsang (Austria)

Fiano

In Italy's Campania wine region, the area around Naples and Mount Vesuvius, Fiano is the popular grape. Hardly "new," Fiano's history—and popularity—date back to ancient Rome. While the origin of the word is the subject of conjecture, Fiano may have come from "apiano" because the ripe grapes attracted bees (apis in Latin).

The towns of Avellino and Lapio and their surrounding areas are the primary growing centers. Hence, the wines are called Fiano di Avellino and Fiano di Lapio. They can be fairly light and dry with a creamy texture or (when the grapes are harvested late and fully fermented) full-bodied and ripe.

A TASTE OF FIANO WINES
- Villa Raiano, Fiano di Avellino "Ripa Alta" (Campania, Italy)
- I Favati, Fiano di Avellino Pietramara (Campania, Italy)
- Feudi di San Gregorio, Fiano di Avellino (Campania, Italy)

Albariño

Albariño presents certain roadblocks to its producers. The vine produces high-quality grapes; they just don't produce that many. The grape skins are so thick that only a small amount of juice can be squeezed out. Albariño's scarcity made it one of Spain's most expensive wine grapes.

In the mid-1980s only five commercial wineries existed in the Rias Baixas region of northwest Spain where Albariño is produced, so very little Albariño was made. Since then, the number of wineries has multiplied to more than one hundred—with a positive (if not overwhelming) effect on production. Albariño is produced across the border in Portugal, where it's called Alvarinho.

A TASTE OF ALBARIÑO/ALVARINHO WINES

- Morgadío Albariño (Spain)
- Valminor Albariño (Spain)
- Varanda do Conde Vino Verde Alvarinho (Portugal)

The wine has a creamy texture with complex flavors of apricots, peaches, and citrus. Albariño is rarely barrel fermented, so the flavors are clean and vibrant. In spite of its high acidity, Albariño doesn't age well and should be consumed within the first two years.

CHAPTER 6

Wine Regions of the "Old World"

Europe and the Mediterranean basin are called the "Old World," not because their wines are stale and forgettable but because they have a centuries-old winemaking tradition. Many Old World winemakers use cutting-edge techniques, but their fame comes from their commitment to preserving terroir ("the soil") in their wines, the sense that the land and the climate should have more influence on the nature of the wine than the winemaker.

France

As Julius Caesar concluded two thousand years ago, France is a pretty good place to grow wine grapes. Through trial and error, and after centuries of careful cultivation and meticulous record-keeping, the French learned how to make excellent wine. Even their indigenous grapes—Cabernet Sauvignon, Sauvignon Blanc, Pinot Noir, Merlot, Chardonnay—have been exported to all corners of the world. Wine connoisseurs generally accept that France produces many "best of" types:

- Champagnes are the best sparkling wines.
- Alsace produces the ultimate Gewürztraminer.
- The Pauillac and Margaux districts of Bordeaux produce the finest Cabernet Sauvignon–based wines.
- Merlot best displays its qualities in the Bordeaux regions of Saint-Emilion and Pomerol.
- The grand cru vineyards of the Côte de Beaune produce the finest Chardonnays.
- Some of the most refined Sauvignon Blanc–based wines come from Sancerre.
- Chenin Blanc is in its glory along the Loire River.
- Sauternes is widely acclaimed as the world's finest dessert wine.
- The prototype of Pinot Noir comes from the vineyards of Côte de Nuits in Burgundy.

The list above is hardly exhaustive. Other French wine regions may not have the cachet of those listed above, but their wines are equally coveted and can offer real bargains for wine lovers.

French Wine Law

If you purchase a bottle of wine in the United States, your first thought is the grape. If you purchase a bottle of wine in France, your first thought is the region. If the average American wine consumer wants a Chardonnay, it doesn't matter whether it comes from Santa Barbara County or Mendocino County, but for the average French consumer, a Corton-Charlemagne is more highly prized than a Pouilly-Fuissé. Both of these are Chardonnay wines, by the way, and both are technically from Burgundy. The Corton-Charlemagne, however, is from a very small grand cru vineyard recognized for its outstanding quality. Pouilly-Fuissé wines come from decent vineyards, but not grand cru vineyards, which give the wines less caché. This cultural feature should be no surprise, since regional terroir is the most important consideration for both a French winery and a French wine consumer.

Given the way French wine law is enforced by the Institut National des Appellations d'Origine (INAO), a government agency, the gold standard for a French estate is to be able to call its wine AOC (Appellation d'Origine Controllee). An AOC wine must originate from vineyards located in a precisely demarcated area and meet the most stringent government quality standards not limited to the following:

- The grape variety or varieties that can be used to make the wines
- Grape sugar levels at harvest or date of harvest
- The maximum weight of grapes that can be harvested per unit area
- How vineyards are planted and managed
- How the wine is made
- Minimum and/or maximum alcoholic strength of the wine

If an estate falls outside an AOC, it is not necessarily the end of the world. The quality perception of the estate's wines may diminish, but there are three other quality categories that may apply to the wine.

- **Vins Délimité de Qualité Supérieure (VDQS)**—a second set of standards for wines in areas not covered by AOC law. Although a notch down in quality, VDQS is still a reliable government guarantee of quality.
- **Vin de pays**—a third, and slightly more relaxed set of rules that regulate country wines. The phrase is always followed by a place name—be it larger (region) or smaller (community).
- **Vin de table or vin ordinaire**—table wines whose place names are "France." This is the lowest category of wine in the French system. These wines are rarely sold commercially.

Within France, each region has its own system of organization and classification, and each region is known for producing specific wines.

Bordeaux

Bordeaux, an industrial city in southwestern France, is the center of the world's most famous wine region. Several types of wine are produced there:

- Dry white wines—blends of Sauvignon Blanc and Sémillon
- Sweet dessert wines—blends of Sauvignon Blanc, Sémillon, and Muscadelle afflicted with *Botrytis cinerea* (noble rot)
- Medium-bodied red wines—blends of Cabernet Sauvignon, Merlot, Cabernet Franc, Malbec, and Petit Verdot (Some subregions produce wine made primarily from Cabernet, while Merlot is the dominant grape in other areas.)

The most important subregions of Bordeaux are Sauternes (famous for its dessert wines), Pomerol (known for Merlot-dominant reds), Saint-Émilion (more Merlot-based reds), Entre-Deux-Mers (light whites), Graves (home of both fine dry whites and Cabernet-based reds), and Médoc (Cabernet-based reds). Médoc is probably the most famous of the Bordeaux subregions and has communes within its borders that also qualify for village appellation status: Saint-Estèphe, Saint-Julien, Margaux, Pauillac, Listrac, and Moulis.

The 1855 Classification

Back in 1855 Napoleon III went to the wine brokers of Bordeaux and asked them to rate the red wines of Médoc. This they did by looking at the price history of the wines—the operating theory being that the most expensive wines would be the best. The brokers came up with the sixty "best" wine estates in the Médoc plus one in Graves and then assessed their quality on a scale of one through five, with one being the highest rank. The four chateaux initially granted top status were dubbed premier crus, or "first growths." This ranking became known as the 1855 Classification.

Vino Veritas

The châteaux of Sauternes were also ranked in the classification of 1855. Eleven châteaux have the premier cru designation, with one additional producer being given "super" status. Château d'Yquem was designated premier cru supérieur ("superior first growth").

The four châteaux that were first awarded this classification are Lafite Rothschild, Latour, Margaux, and Haut-Brion. In 1973 Château Mouton-Rothschild was upgraded to premier cru status. You'll see "Premier Grand Cru Classé" on their labels.

With a total of only sixty-one châteaux listed in the original classification, thousands of other producers in Médoc were left out. In 1932 another classification, cru bourgeois, was created to include the best of them. Later, the Bordeaux appellations of St. Emilion and Graves created their own hierarchies to showcase the quality of their wines.

Burgundy

In Bordeaux, the wine estates are called châteaux. In Burgundy, They're called domaines. That's just your first clue that the two regions are figuratively (and geographically) miles apart. While Bordeaux is dominated by large producers, Burgundy has thousands of small growers who often own only very small pieces of vineyard land. For example, the famous 125-acre Clos de Vougeot vineyard has more than eighty owners.

If anything is certain in Burgundy, it is that red wines are made from the Pinot Noir grape and white wines are made from Chardonnay. One wrinkle is Beaujolais in the southern part of the region, which is known for light and fruity reds made from the Gamay grape.

Savvy Sipping

The French love for classifying wines is supremely evident in Burgundy. Whereas premier cru is top dog in Bordeaux, grand cru ("great growth") is the epitome of greatness in Burgundy. The designation is reserved for specific vineyards that, based on their location and long-term track record, produce the best wines. The labels will bear only the name of the vineyard—not the name of any village.

Traveling from north to south through the heart of France, you pass through the subregions of Burgundy in sequence:

- **Chablis**—known for its dry white wines
- **Côte de Nuits**—home of the most noteworthy reds

- **Côte de Beaune**—producer of both reds and whites, but known especially for great whites
- **Côte Chalonnaise**—regarded as a lesser region but still home to good reds and whites
- **Mâcon**—known for whites that offer excellent values
- **Beaujolais**—home to the red Gamay grape

Role of Négociants

Négociant is French for "merchant" or "dealer." Traditionally, négociants bought wines, blended and bottled them, and shipped them. They could take wines from small producers and market them on a more commercially viable scale. More recently, their roles have expanded to buying grapes and making wine. They represent wines of all quality levels—including grand cru.

Large négociant houses blend wines to produce their own house styles. Some of these well-known houses include Louis Jadot, Joseph Drouhin, Georges Duboeuf, and Louis Latour.

Rhone

Continuing south from Burgundy, you enter the Rhone Valley—home to red and white wines vastly different from those in Bordeaux and Burgundy. The northern and southern regions of the Rhone are distinctly different in terms of their wines. Northern reds are Syrah-based and worthy of aging. You'll run into names like Côte Rôtie, Hermitage, Crozes-Hermitage, Cornas, and St. Joseph. White wines bearing these names are made from Viognier (like Condrieu) or a blend of Marsanne and Roussane (like Hermitage).

Most Rhone wines come from the south—in the form of Côtes du Rhone. The primary grape variety is Grenache. The Southern Rhone is also famous for its Châteauneuf-du-Pape, which can be made with as many as thirteen grape varieties—both red and white (although Grenache, Mourvèdre, and Syrah predominate).

Vino Veritas

Châteuneuf-du-Pape means "new home of the pope." It dates back to the fourteenth century when the papal court was relocated to nearby Avignon and a summer palace was built in a village just north of the city (now known as Châteauneuf-du-Pape).

Southwest of Châteauneuf-du-Pape is Tavel, home to France's best-known and most distinguished rosés. They're dry and full-bodied and have an international reputation.

Loire

The Loire Valley stretches across northwest France, following the Loire River. The area has a reputation for its non-Chardonnay white wines. The most important ones are:

- **Muscadet**—a light, dry wine uniquely named not after its region of origin but after its grape variety
- **Vouvray**—made from the Chenin Blanc grape into wines that can range from bone dry to off-dry to sparkling
- **Pouilly-Fumé**—straight Sauvignon Blanc made in a rich style
- **Sancerre**—unblended Sauvignon Blanc in a lighter, drier, more lively style than the Pouilly-Fumé

It's easy to confuse the names Pouilly-Fumé and Pouilly-Fuissé, but they're two different wines from two entirely different areas in France. Pouilly-Fuissé is a Chardonnay from the Mâcon region of Burgundy and is a much more full-bodied wine.

Alsace

Historically, Alsace (the area across the Rhine River from Germany) has either been part of France or part of Germany. Since World War I, it's belonged to France. Because of its background, Alsace has much in common with Germany, including the grapes grown within its borders. The packaging of Alsatian wines is unique from the rest of France in that the grape variety may be displayed on the label. You'll never see Cabernet Sauvignon or Merlot listed prominently on bottles of Bordeaux wine, but things are different in Alsace. Regulations in Alsace require that a wine carrying a varietal name contain 100 percent of that grape. The most important varietals are:

- Riesling
- Muscat
- Gewürztraminer
- Sylvaner
- Pinot Gris

A small amount of Pinot Noir (the only grape permitted for red wine) is grown in Alsace and is often used for rosé wines.

Italy

Italy produces—and drinks—more wine than any other country. The entire country is practically a vineyard. In 2008 Italy bested France for the title of world's biggest producer for the first time in a decade, at nearly 1.6 billion gallons. Italians consume almost sixteen gallons of wine per capita, an astonishing number when compared to the paltry two gallons per capita consumed by Americans per year.

Savvy Sipping

Italy makes more than 2,000 kinds of wine within its borders. Everywhere you go in Italy, you see grapevines growing, and the grapes are overwhelmingly indigenous to Italy, including Nebbiolo, Sangiovese, Barbera, and Dolcetto.

In 1963 Italy developed a system—modeled after the French one—to control the quality of their wines and classify them. The regulations, enforced by the Italian Ministry of Agriculture, govern yields, grapes that can be used for specific wines, viticultural practices, and alcohol levels. From top to bottom, the categories are as follows:

- **Denominazione di Origine Controllata e Garantita (DOCG)**—As of January 2010, only forty-four regions in Italy have been given this status, and producers in these areas wanting to print DOCG on their bottle labels must abide by the strictest standards. Wines are even subject to chemical analysis and taste tests to qualify for this designation. French AOC wines are not even subject to this scrutiny.
- **Denominazione di Origine Controllata (DOC)**—This category is the Italian equivalent of the French AOC, and there are 321 DOC regions in the books.
- **Vino da tavola**—Historically, this category was attached to wines made in areas without much pedigree. The wines were simple

and good for quaffing. Wines with this status have few restrictions attached to them. This category is the Italian equivalent of the French vin de table.

These three categories do not tell the whole story of Italian wine. In the 1970s a group of winemakers in Chianti, a sub-region of Tuscany, ran afoul of the DOC regulations by blending prohibited grape varieties such as Cabernet Sauvignon and Merlot with native Sangiovese grapes. The wines turned out to be terrific and their prices soared, but they were labeled "vino da tavola." They became known as "Super Tuscans," an unofficial category. To qualify for the Chianti DOC designation, the wines were required to be 100 percent Sangiovese. (Chianti is now a DOCG, but red wines must still be 100 percent Sangiovese.)

Since then, a new official quality category, called IGT (Indicazione Geografica Tipica), has been created whose rules are less strict than those of the DOC. Some of the esteemed Super Tuscans were thus upgraded to IGT status.

Italy's Wine Regions

Italy has twenty wine regions that are geographically identical to its political regions. The wine regions in the north are the most recognized, but wine regions in southern Italy, namely Campania, Umbria, Basilicata, and the islands of Sicily and Sardinia, are making huge inroads in producing wines of quality and marketability. Unique indigenous grape varieties—like the whites Fiano di Avellino from Campania and Vermentino from Sardinia—have surged in popularity.

In the north, the regions of Piedmont, Tuscany, and Veneto are the most familiar. Piedmont (meaning "foot of the mountain") in the northwest lies at the base of the Alps. Nebbiolo reigns, producing the famous powerful reds Barolo and Barbaresco. They're very similar to each other, but Barolo is fuller-bodied and needs more aging. (Barolo is sometimes referred to as the "king" of Italian wines.) Other popular reds include Barbera, Dolcetto, and Bonardo. Among the whites are the Muscat-based Asti Spumante and Moscato d'Asti and the dry white Gavi from the Cortese grape.

Tuscany, with its enchanted landscapes and historic castles, is responsible for the world-famous Chianti—whose production goes back centuries.

Much more recent is Brunello di Montalcino, made in an area south of Chianti from a Sangiovese clone. It is big, tannic, and powerful and has one of the longest aging requirements (four years) in Italy.

Message in a Bottle

In 2008 scandal erupted in Tuscany when several producers were accused of adding prohibited grapes to their 2003 Brunello di Montalcino wines. 2003 was not the best year in Tuscany, which may explain the transgression. Some producers accepted a downgrade to IGT from DOCG.

Another Tuscan favorite is Vino Nobile di Montepulciano from 70 percent to 100 percent Sangiovese. Tuscany's most important white grape is Trebbiano.

Veneto in the northeast is the third largest region in terms of production and serves up some of the more familiar Italian exports: Soave, the sparkling Prosecco, and Valpolicella. While Valpolicella is rather light and fruity, another version—Amarone della Valpolicella—is rich, high in alcohol (14 to 16 percent), and long-lived. Known simply as Amarone, the wine is made from grapes that have been dried on mats for several months before fermentation, concentrating the sugars and flavors.

Let's not forget Pinot Grigio, the number one imported table wine in the United States. Probably the best ones come from the two northeastern most regions of Alto Adige (which borders Austria) and Fruili (bordering Slovenia).

Germany

A common misperception among American wine drinkers is that all German wines are sweet. This, of course, is not true, but because German wine labels are so difficult to understand, this misperception is understandable. The only thing more confounding than the German wine label is the fact that grapes can grow there at all. The northernmost German wine regions are situated north of Champagne. Needless to say, it's cold there, but some grapes, including the great Riesling, have flourished.

In the German quality rating system, the highest quality wines are labeled QmP (Qualitätswein mit Prädikat), meaning "quality wine with distinction." QmP wines (the ones primarily exported) are categorized by the ripeness of the grapes at harvest. Because Germany's vineyards are so far north, It's often difficult to grow ripe grapes. Hence, grape sugars are highly prized. The riper the grape, the higher the sugar content, and the higher the wine's potential alcohol. From the least ripe to the ripest are:

- Kabinett
- Spätlese
- Auslese
- Beerenauslese
- Trockenbeerenauslese
- Eiswein

The quality of a Kabinett wine is not higher than that of an Auslese wine. These terms simply have to do with the grapes' ripeness level at harvest. If the bottle has the QmP designation, or Qualitätswein mit Prädikat, you know it is a quality wine.

At the Kabinett, Spatlese, and Auslese levels, the grapes can be fermented to produce a completely dry wine. So, a rule of thumb for choosing a dry German wine is to look for Kabinett on the label. Other terms to look for are "Trocken" (German for dry), "Classic," or "Selection." At the highest ripeness levels, the grapes have so much sugar at harvest that the wines almost can't help but be sweet.

Vino Veritas

Why do German wines come in different colored bottles?
The color of the tall, slender bottles tells you what region the wine comes from. Brown bottles come from the Rhine region. Green bottles come from the Mosel area or from Alsace. The shape is used elsewhere around the world for wines made from grape varieties associated with Germany—like Riesling and Gewürztraminer.

Despite the prevalence of dry German wines, Germany's sweet wines have achieved the most international acclaim. The most notable are Trockenbeerenauslese wines made from grapes affected by the noble rot, Botrytis cinerea; the late harvest Beerenauslese wines which may or may not have been affected by Bortrytis; and the thick, intensely sweet ice wines, made from frozen grapes.

Germany's Wine Regions

With the exception of a couple of regions in the east, most of Germany's wine regions are concentrated in the south and southwestern part of the country. Germany's most famous winemaking areas are the Mosel-Saar-Ruwer region (along the Mosel River and its two tributaries) and the three contiguous regions along the Rhine River—Rheingau, Rheinhessen, and Pfalz.

With Germany's climate, 85 percent of the country's wines are white and relatively low in alcohol. Riesling is Germany's signature grape. Another popular grape is Müller-Thurgau, a cross between Riesling and Sylvaner, which ripens more reliably. However, wines made from Müller-Thurgau have failed to reach the otherworldly greatness of Riesling.

Recently, German producers have found success with Pinot Noir in the Baden region, which also happens to be Germany's largest in terms of physical size. Pinot Noir wines are known as Spätburgunders in Germany.

Spain

There are more vineyards in Spain than in any other country on earth. However, Spain is only the third largest producer of wine after France and Italy, because many of those vineyards are located in areas so arid that the vines barely produce. Spanish wine remained relatively undistinguished until the late nineteenth century, when winemakers forced out of France due to phylloxera moved to Spain and set up shop. These winemakers even brought with them a variation of their Appellation d'Origine Controllee quality hierarchy, which today is administered by the Instituto Nacional de Denominaciones de Origen (INDO).

Spain's rating system from highest quality to lowest is as follows:

- **Denominación de Origen Calificada (DOCa)**—Spain has only two of these, Rioja and Priorat. These areas have centuries-old reputations for quality wine, and wines from these areas labeled DOCa must be the product of clearly defined vineyard and winemaking practices.

- **Denominación de Origen (DO)**—Meaning "designation of origin," DOs account for more than half of Spanish vineyards. For a DO region to be promoted to DOCa status, it must have been a DO for at least ten years.
- **Vino de Mesa**—This is a table wine category with only local standards to uphold.

Within the Vino de Mesa category there is a slightly higher sub-category called Vino de la Tierra. These wines must be produced from a specific area within Spain and have a minimum alcohol content.

Spain also awards Vino de Pago status to high-quality wines made from single vineyards in any part of the country. For example, a producer making exceptional wines from high-quality vineyards in an otherwise nondescript Vino de Mesa region can qualify for Vino de Pago status.

Rioja

Rioja, Spain's oldest and most famous wine region, became the first DO when the system was set up in 1926. When the system was refined in 1991, Rioja became the first region to be promoted to DOCa status. Tempranillo is king in Rioja. Other grapes—Garnacha, Graciano, and Mazuelo—are used for blending, but Tempranillo takes center stage.

The wines range from delicate to big and alcoholic. The traditional method of production includes significant aging in oak barrels. Reds aged for one year in barrel and some time in bottle may be labeled crianza. After one year in oak and at least one full year in bottle, they may become a reserva. A gran reserva is made only in the finest years, and it must be aged for a minimum of two years in oak and three years in bottle before release.

Vino Veritas

After the phylloxera epidemic in the late nineteenth century, France imported wines from Spain to make up the local shortfall. The wines were not exactly up to French standards—so French winemakers went to Spain and introduced their winemaking practices, which included aging in oak barrels. Instead of French oak barrels, Spanish winemakers chose American oak, which impart a stronger flavor to the wine.

Other Spanish Winemaking Regions

Rioja used to be the only game in town. In 1999 it was joined by another DOCa, Priorat, located not far from Barcelona. The red wines of Priorat are largely made from Grenache and Carignan grapes. Wine lovers should also be on the lookout for these regions:

- Penedés is home to most of the Cava (sparkling wine) producers. Whereas Champagne is made from Pinot Noir, Chardonnay, and Pinot Meunier, Cava is made from the white grapes Xarello, Macabeo, and Parellada.
- Navarra is best known for its rosés but has recently complemented them with red wines made from Tempranillo, Cabernet Sauvignon, and Merlot.
- Rías Baixas is producing the much-acclaimed Albariño—the rich and complex white with high levels of acidity and alcohol.

Portugal

Vineyards have flourished in Portugal since Roman times. The country may be better known for its stunning Ports and Madeiras, but its dry table wines are growing in esteem with each passing year. When Portugal joined the European Union in 1986, its wine laws were aligned with those of other Old World countries, namely the French Appellation d'Origine Controllee system:

- Denominacao de Origem Controlada (French AOC)
- Indicacao de Proveniencia Regulamentada (French VDQS)
- Vinho regional (French vin de pays)
- Vinho de mesa (French vin de table)

The Wines and the Regions

Arguably the most famous Portuguese wine besides port and Madeira is Vinho Verde, which is exported to the United States. Vinho Verde, which is also the name of the DOC, means "green wine," because it is intended for immediate consumption. The wine is red or white and often has a slight effervescence. The better versions are made from the Alvarinho grape—the same one that makes Spain's Albariño wine.

The great Spanish grape Tempranillo has a home in Portugal, where it is called Tinta Roriz. Portugal's most famous indigenous grape is Touriga Nacional, which, along with Tinta Roriz, is used for port. Touriga Nacional also is used in the great dry non-fortified red wines of the Dao and Douro Valley.

Austria

Austria has perhaps the most stringent wine production and labeling regulations anywhere—the result of a scandal in 1985. Because sweet, late harvest wines are so prized and expensive, a small group of unscrupulous producers adulterated ordinary wines with diethylene glycol (a substance related to antifreeze) to sweeten them. They labeled them late harvest and tried to pass them off as the real thing. The affair caused Austrian wine exports to plummet within the year to less than one-fifth of what they had been sending to other countries. The government stepped in, and new regulations were implemented to keep anything similar from happening again. Today, Austria is successfully exporting more of its wines than ever, both dry and sweet.

Austria and its neighbor, Germany, have much in common. Riesling has a home in Austria, though most of it is dry. Austria also ranks its wines according to grape ripeness levels at harvest, but Kabinett-level wines are placed in a lower quality category. The highest quality category, called Prädikatswein, contains these tiers (lowest to highest):

- Spatlese
- Auslese
- Beerenauslese
- Ausbruch
- Trockenbeerenauslese

Austria's most famous grape is the white Grüner Veltliner—a longtime favorite with Austrians and now making a big splash around the world. It produces wines that are typically dry, medium-bodied, and spicy. Red wines don't have as much success in Austria, but Blauer Zweigelt is the most popular, with Pinot Noir not far behind.

CHAPTER 7

Wine Regions of the "New World"

"New World" was at one time a less than flattering term for the upstart winemakers outside of Europe. Since then, many of the philosophical borders between the Old World and the New World have eroded as Old World countries adapt to technological innovation and New World winemakers increasingly adopt traditional techniques. In winemaking, though, the effect of the land on the final product is paramount, and geography will always separate the two worlds.

Australia

For a country once known for its beer drinking, Australia has made a name for itself in the wine world. In fact, Australia has become the biggest wine exporter after Italy, France, and Spain. What makes it such an awesome feat is that 70 percent of Australia's land can't support agriculture of any kind. There are no native vines in Australia, and the wine industry there would not have taken shape were it not for European immigration.

The New Settlers

Beginning in 1788 England shipped off its felons to Australia—to exile them and to provide labor to create an infrastructure there. The "relocation" stopped in the middle of the nineteenth century when there were enough people to do the work.

The state of South Australia was the only "free" state, meaning that it was the only area not settled by British convicts. In 1836 the land was awarded to George Fife Angus, founder of the South Australian Company. He needed settlers to help develop the land, and he began to recruit them. It was ideal timing for European Lutherans who were fleeing the Continent because of religious persecution. They could buy land in South Australia for very little money in return for farming the land.

Many of the new immigrants came from Germany and left their imprint in town names, traditional foods, and wines. The area is still renowned for its Rieslings. By the 1890s the Barossa, Hunter, and Yarra Valleys were all producing wine.

Aussie Wines

Prior to the 1950s wine production focused on fortified wines. They were the most affordable wines during the worldwide Depression, and the added alcohol made them better for longer storage. The 1960s and 1970s saw a shift toward table wines—first the sweeter versions and, ultimately, dry styles.

While there is amazing diversity in Australian wines, they could be described as fun, bold, and affordable. Winemakers have been creative in their blends of Chardonnay-Sémillon and Shiraz-Cabernet Sauvignon. Probably the country's best reds are blends of Shiraz—recently with Viogner and other Rhone varieties as well as with Cabernet. Shiraz, the Aussie name for Syrah, is Australia's utility grape. Classic Australian Shiraz is big and ripe with touches of American oak, perfect for a well-aged steak. Australia has been so successful in marketing their Shiraz wines that other countries have recently chosen to label their Syrah "Shiraz."

Vino Veritas

Australia was responsible in the 1970s for creating a phenomenon that's generating renewed interest today: wine in a box. Aussies have been drinking wine from a box nonstop since the 1970s. Now it's catching on elsewhere as wine producers seek ways to package their wines to keep them away from corks and oxygen.

You can find some true treasures in Australia's dessert wines—nicknamed "stickies." Also of local interest is sparkling Shiraz—dark, dry, and slightly fizzy.

Australia's Wine Regions

Like the United States, Australia has a number of outstanding wine regions—fifty regions and subregions spread throughout the country. Many of them are clustered in southeastern Australia—particularly in the states of South Australia, Victoria, and New South Wales—and the more isolated maritime area of Western Australia.

- The Barossa Valley in South Australia is home to some of Australia's most famous wineries, including Penfolds, which produces Grange, the country's most celebrated Shiraz. Grenache and Cabernet Sauvignon also dominate the region.
- Coonawara in South Australia is noteworthy for its reddish "terra rossa" soil. Cabernet Sauvignon is especially popular, but Shiraz does well here too.
- The Yarra Valley in Victoria is a cooler region known for its Pinot Noir, Chardonnay, and Riesling.
- Hunter Valley in New South Wales produces Sémillon and Shiraz, among many others.
- The island state of Tasmania is famous in that it produces more Pinot Noir than any other region in Australia.

New Zealand

For most of the twentieth century, the New Zealand wine industry was a tiny blip on the world radar screen. Grapevines had first been planted there in 1819, but its wine-producing neighbor to the northwest, Australia, garnered most of the accolades and acclaim for that part of the world. Then in 1985 a winery called Cloudy Bay in the Marlborough region of New Zealand's south island released a Sauvignon Blanc so racy and fresh that wine drinkers immediately took notice. The rest is history. While Sauvignon Blanc has become something of the country's goodwill ambassador to the rest of the world, New Zealand's other wines have as much to offer.

A Land of Distinction

New Zealand has the distinction of having the most easterly vineyards—being closest to the International Date Line—and the world's most southerly vineyards. The country's winemaking regions are located on the two large islands that comprise most of New Zealand. The North Island is warmer overall than the South Island, but both benefit from the cool ocean breezes. No location in New Zealand is more than seventy-five miles away from the ocean.

The emphasis, then, is on growing grapes that suit cool growing conditions—mostly Chardonnay, Sauvignon Blanc, and Pinot Noir. These varieties make up 70 percent of the country's total vineyard area. Some regions of the North Island, such as Northland, achieve ripeness in Merlot and Cabernet Sauvignon.

Savvy Sipping

With land so suitable for cool weather grapes such as Chardonnay and Pinot Noir, the backbones of Champagne, New Zealand does turn out a fair share of sparkling wine. The famous Cloudy Bay winery has a sparkler in its portfolio.

Regions and their Wines

The cultivated areas of New Zealand span 720 miles from north to south, and, except for the most southerly region, they all are on the eastern coastline. The development of vineyard land has roughly corresponded to population growth, which, in the twentieth century, started in the area around Auckland.

North Island

Auckland has a third of the country's population. While it produces its own wines, it's also a center of wine commerce where wines from other regions are vinified and blended. Gisborne produces over a third of the country's wine, and most of it is bulk wine, but it also has a reputation for fine wines and has been called the Chardonnay capital of New Zealand.

Hawke's Bay is one of New Zealand's older and best wine regions and often records the most sunshine hours. Chardonnay and Cabernet Sauvignon have been the most important varietals. Wellington is known for outstanding Pinot Noirs.

South Island

Marlborough's first vineyards were first planted in 1973. And by 1990, the region had become the largest vine-growing area with 40 percent of the country's total vineyards. Sauvignon Blanc is the most popular varietal, with Chardonnay second. Riesling is grown too—and, increasingly, Pinot Noir. Central Otago is the most southerly region where the vineyards are planted in hillside locations to minimize the danger of frost. The area is particularly known for its Pinot Noir and Riesling.

South Africa

Most of South Africa's vineyards are clustered in the southwest in an area near the Cape of Good Hope. The region has a Mediterranean climate—warm, dry summers and rainfall during the mild winter months—and grapes love it. The scenery in South Africa's wine regions is among the world's most breathtaking, making it a popular stop for tourists.

In the eighteenth century, the Cape established itself on the world wine stage with its Muscat-based dessert wine called Constantia. It was much in demand at all the royal courts of Europe. Napoleon, it is rumored, even ordered it from his exile on St. Helena. In spite of the wild success of Constantia, the wine industry went into a 200-year decline thanks to the arrival of phylloxera and overproduction. In 1918 a large farmers' cooperative (the

KWV) was formed to control production and the market. It established prices for all wine and limited the number of vines per producer, hardly a system to encourage innovation. Apartheid didn't help the industry either as the international community imposed punishing sanctions.

Message in a Bottle

Winemaking goes back to the early Dutch settlers. In fact, it was Dutch governor Jan van Riebeeck who, in 1655, planted the first vines. Four years later the grapes were pressed into wine. But it was really the French Huguenots—fleeing religious persecution back home—who brought a serious tradition of winemaking to South Africa.

Democracy Turns the Tide

With apartheid abolished in 1991 and sanctions lifted, the South African wine industry could turn its attention to improving its wines to compete in the world market. It imported better vine cuttings, expanded oak aging to commercial wines, and upgraded vineyard management, among other things.

Today, South Africa has only 1.5 percent of the world's vineyards, relegating it to seventeenth globally in area planted to grapes. In terms of wine production, however, South Africa is easily in the top ten.

White varieties account for about two-thirds of South Africa's grapes, with Chenin Blanc leading the charge. Called Steen in South Africa, it can be found in dry, sparkling, and late harvest styles. Sauvignon Blanc and Chardonnay are quickly increasing in popularity, but most new plantings in South Africa these days are red varieties. Cabernet Sauvignon is the most planted red variety, followed by Pinotage and Shiraz.

South Africa's most famous wine regions are:

- **Stellenbosch**—Just east of Cape Town, Stellenbosch is home to South Africa's only viticulture and enology department, based at the University of Stellenbosch. Its fame is largely due to its red wines.
- **Paarl**—Northwest of Cape Town, Paarl is home to the KWV and a large number of well-known estates.
- **Constantia**—The closest wine region to Cape Town, Constantia is where the first South African vines were planted. Its fame stems from

its eponymous dessert wine, but Sauvignon Blanc and several red varieties are bringing more recognition.

- **Walker Bay**—A cool area with a maritime climate, Walker Bay is South Africa's Burgundy. Chardonnay and Pinot Noir are the most exciting grape varieties here.

Vino Veritas

Pinotage is South Africa's contribution to grape breeding. In 1925 a professor from Stellenbosch University crossed Pinot Noir with Cinsault (called Hermitage in South Africa, hence, the name). The first international critiques of Pinotage wines were unkind. But, over time, the wines have earned respect.

Chile

Missionaries traveling with the conquistadors in the mid-1500s brought vine cuttings to Chile from their native Spain to produce wine for sacramental purposes. The wines were mostly rustic renditions of Spanish varietals—Pais and Moscatel. The grapes did so well that by the 1800s, Chilean wines were giving Spanish imports a run for their money. That was a problem, at least to the Spanish Crown. The Spanish government levied heavy taxes and imposed severe restrictions on winemaking—all of which took its toll on Chilean vineyards.

Following the wars of independence in the nineteenth century, the newly prosperous upper class of Chileans traveled to Europe, where they developed a fondness for French wines. Cuttings from the great Bordeaux varieties were imported, and the modern era of winemaking in Chile was underway.

Isolation Has Its Advantages

In the second half of the nineteenth century, the phylloxera epidemic wiped out the vineyards of Europe and North America. Chile was isolated by natural conditions. It has the Andes to the east, the Pacific to the west, and barren deserts to the north. Chile remained free of the insect while the rest of the wine world was decimated. To this day, Chile remains the only country unaffected by phylloxera. Its *Vitis vinifera* vines are the only ones in the world still growing on their own rootstocks.

Carmenère: The Great Masquerade

Carmenère used to be an important grape in Bordeaux. When Chile imported vine cuttings from France in the mid-1800s, Carmenère was high on the list. However, when Bordeaux was replanted after phylloxera, Carmenère was conspicuously left out in favor of Merlot. Carmenère is especially susceptible to a condition called coulure, in which grapes fail to set properly on the vine. Cloudy, cold, and wet weather contribute to coulure, making Bordeaux ground zero for this condition. Merlot is less difficult to deal with, and it ripens earlier with higher yields, so Carmenère was out; Merlot was in.

The climate in Chile, however, is perfect for Carmenère, so it grew happily for years alongside Merlot. Given Merlot's international reputation and its striking resemblance to Carmenère, soon all Camenère vines came to be called Merlot.

As Chilean wines gained popularity in recent years, more of it made its way into the world market. It didn't go unnoticed that Chilean Merlot tasted somewhat stronger and spicier than Merlots from elsewhere. Then in 1994, it was discovered through DNA testing that the Merlot was actually Carmenère!

Politics and Investment

The Chilean wine industry has had its ups and downs, in spite of nearly perfect conditions for growing grapes. In the 1940s Chilean wines grew in popularity—only to lose ground when the government nationalized many of the wineries and restricted production. Even when government regimes changed, civil war brought further instability to the wine industry. By 1980 almost half the country's vineyards were out of production.

Message in a Bottle

In 1996, under the new appellation system, Chile established the 75 percent rule. Seventy-five percent of the contents of a bottle of wine must come from the exact location, variety, and vintage specified on the label. Twenty-five percent is allowed for blending purposes. "Reserva" wines aren't as tightly controlled, and are required only to indicate a place of origin on the label.

With stability restored in the 1980s, Chile was able to attract significant investment from companies in France, the United States, Australia, Spain, and Japan. Modern technology and replanted vineyards brought new life to Chilean wines. They became known, almost overnight, as excellent, value-priced varietals, but fine wines were on the way.

Varietals

While Pais and Moscatel are still being turned into wine for the domestic market, the wine industry has invested heavily in high-quality reds for export. Cabernet Sauvignon, Merlot, Pinot Noir, Syrah—and, of course, Carmenère—are the focus. White varietals include Chardonnay, Sauvignon Blanc, Riesling, and Sémillon.

Argentina

Argentina's wines and wine history have always been tied to the country's economic and political circumstances. Spanish settlers first brought "work horse" vines to Argentina as early as the mid-1500s. Criolla (related to Chile's Pais grape) and Cereza were plentiful but didn't make wines of much character. The wines were made with an eye toward ensuring they were able to survive the harrowing shipping conditions to other South American countries.

Two waves of European immigration were responsible for introducing new varieties. In the 1820s after Argentina's independence from Spain and again at the turn of the century, settlers from France, Spain, and Italy brought vine cuttings to make the wines they had enjoyed in Europe. More than 50 percent of the Argentine population is of Italian descent. The French brought with them their Malbec, Cabernet Sauvignon, Merlot, and Chenin Blanc. The Spanish added Torrontés and Tempranillo, while the Italians planted Sangiovese, Nebbiolo, Dolcetto, and Barbera.

Quantity versus Quality

By the 1920s Argentina had become the eighth richest nation in the world. The Depression set it back, but, under Juan Perón, the country seemed to be recovering. In the mid-1950s Perón was deposed and a succession of military governments plunged the country into economic and political decline.

With a population that, frankly, drank a lot of wine (twenty-one gallons per capita per year), Argentina's winemakers focused on quantity rather than quality. Oceans of rustic table wine were produced to satisfy domestic demand. When runaway inflation hit in the late '80s and early '90s, price controls were put on wine, forcing some growers to shift to crops other than grapes. For those who continued to grow grapes, a tax policy was established that rewarded the destruction of older vineyards of traditional grape varieties in favor or planting inferior, but high-volume, varieties.

Wine Exports

Argentina, one of the largest producers of wine, always had such an enormous domestic market for its product that it didn't worry too much about exports. However, thanks to competition from beer and soft drinks in the late twentieth century, the country's per capita consumption dropped to around eight gallons a year, making exporting more attractive. While Argentines still consume 95 percent of the wine, exports are on the rise. Foreign and domestic investment has helped the wine industry to improve its product.

Message in a Bottle

Mendoza is Argentina's largest and best wine-producing region. It makes the country's top wines. When Spanish settlers brought *Vitis vinifera* vines to Argentina via Chile and Peru, they discovered that the best place to grow the grapes was at the foot of the Andes. They established the city of Mendoza there in 1561, and it remains the center of Argentina's winemaking industry today.

Malbec has emerged as the country's premier grape. It is to Argentina what Carmenère is to Chile, although Malbec can still be found in Bordeaux and France's southwest. Argentine Malbec has taken the wine world by storm. With its inky black color, enormous concentration of dark fruit aromas and flavors, and subtle notes of violet and spice, it is no surprise that Argentine Malbecs have become the darlings of wine lovers everywhere.

Canada

Canada and sweet wine do not always go together. Winemaking in Canada goes back to the 1800s when European settlers tried to grow *Vitis vinifera* grapes in Ontario province. Like their neighbors to the south, the settlers were unsuccessful in their attempts, but the region's native grapes flourished. So, for the next hundred years, Canadian winemakers used *Vitis labrusca* and *Vitis riparia* and hybrids such as Niagara, Concord, and Catawba. By all reports, the table wines made from these grapes were unsuccessful. When they were used to make fortified wines, however, they found favor in England.

Message in a Bottle

Canada has an appellation system, Vintners Quality Alliance (VQA), similar to France's AOC system. It ensures minimum quality standards through panel tastings and by regulating winemaking techniques and grape ripeness. The VQA recognizes three designated Viticultural Areas in Ontario (Niagara Peninsula, Pelee Island, and Lake Erie North Shore) and four in British Columbia (Okanagan Valley, Similkameen Valley, Fraser Valley, and Vancouver Island).

The Turn of the Century

By 1900 winemaking was introduced to the western province of British Columbia, and growers had more success with the *Vitis vinifera* vines. Sadly, in 1916, something else was introduced—a temperance movement that culminated in Canada's Prohibition. Unlike Prohibition in the United States, wine wasn't banned and wineries stayed in business. Once Canadian Prohibition ended in 1927, the individual provinces took over control of production, distribution, and sale of alcoholic beverages.

Dozens of wineries were in operation when Prohibition came to an end, but a period of consolidation began such that by 1974, there were only six wineries in the whole country.

A New Era

In 1974 the first winery license since Prohibition was awarded to partners Donald Ziraldo and Karl Kaiser who named their boutique winery

Inniskillin. Their vision was to produce only the finest wines from traditional *Vitis vinifera* grapes. They were a model for other winemakers and brought Canada into a new era of winemaking.

At the 1991 VinExpo in Bordeaux, Inniskillin won the prestigious Prix d'Honneur for its 1989 Icewine. It was the first of many awards to come for Canadian producers.

Weather Prevails

Canada winters are freezing, and this has allowed the country to produce some of the world's most coveted ice wines. In fact, Canada is the world's largest producer of ice wines, far more than Germany (where ice wine originated) and Austria. Canadian ice wines are made from the tough French hybrid grape Vidal, although Riesling is often used as well.

Ice wine does not tell the whole story of Canadian wine. The Okanagan Valley in British Columbia is warm enough in the summer to produce grapes you would associate with Napa Valley. Chardonnay and Pinot Gris, are the major white varieties, while among the reds Merlot, Pinot Noir, Cabernet Sauvignon, and Cabernet Franc have found success.

CHAPTER 8

New Frontiers in the Wine World

When you think of fine wine regions, the first places that come to mind are probably Napa, Bordeaux, and Chianti. While these places deserve their international reputation, other wine regions are beginning to emerge on the world stage, some of which have been producing wine for thousands of years. Thanks to more sophisticated marketing efforts and improved winemaking and vineyard practices in these burgeoning areas, you soon might find yourself saying to your dining companion, "Care for some more Mavrodaphne?"

Greece

For more than 2,000 years, the Greeks have been producing wine. Ancient Greek poets and artists present wine as an essential part of life. This wine culture persists, although frequent invasions and internal strife have frustrated attempts to bring Greek wine to a global audience. In the 1960s, when Greece decided to begin preparations to enter the European Union, the government began to address the issues preventing the country from developing a world-class wine industry. Greece now has more than 400 wineries, and many of their wines are finding their way to the United States.

Greek Grapes

Greece has a Mediterranean climate, perfect for growing high-quality grapes. Most Greek wines are still made from indigenous grapes varieties, many of which are not known outside of the country. This is changing, however, as growers are finding that international varieties such as Syrah, Cabernet Sauvignon, Merlot, Chardonnay, and Sauvignon Blanc do well in certain areas. Of the 350 grapes varieties grown in Greece, six account for 90 percent of Greece's dry wine production:

WHITE GRAPES:
- Assyrtiko—native to Santorini and other Aegean islands
- Roditis—mainly grown in Peloponnese in the south
- Savatiano—largely found around Athens

The Savatiano grape deserves special recognition, because it is the staple grape of most retsina, Greece's most famous style of wine. To make retsina, vintners add small amounts of resin from the Aleppo pine tree to Savatiano grape juice during fermentation, giving the wine its characteristic "piney" flavor. Retsina is adored especially in rural areas of Greece but has failed to win the hearts of international wine lovers.

RED GRAPES:
- Agiorgitiko—grown largely in southern Greece
- Xynomavro—present in Macedonia, northern Greece)
- Mandelari—tannic grape found in Crete and the Aegean islands.

Not to be forgotten is the Mavrodaphne grape, which is used to make a decadent fortified dessert wine of the same name. The wine is akin to port. This grape is most widely planted in Peloponnese.

Greek Wine Laws

As many European nations had done before them, Greece eventually adopted the Appellation d'Origine Controlée (AOC) laws of France as a way of setting quality standards in its wine industry. Sweet wines produced in defined areas according to approved techniques get the Controlled Appellation of Origin designation, while dry wines get the label Appellation of Origin of Superior Quality. Wines that fall outside this system can be labeled *topikos oenos* (regional wines) or *epitrapezios oenos* (table wines). The latter are mainly bulk wines consumed locally, whereas the former have more international appeal since they are often blends of indigenous Greek grapes and varieties such as Cabernet Sauvignon and Merlot.

Hungary

Quite simply, the scourge of Communism is the main reason why Hungarian wines are not adored and treasured in the Western world. When Hungary was freed from Communist control in 1989, the country's indigenous wine culture, which has been traced to Roman times, immediately reasserted itself. Today the most famous wines of Hungary are sweet, but demand is rising for the country's dry table wines.

The Land and the Grapes

Hungary possesses a continental climate with hot summers and cold winters. Without hot summers, grapes fail to ripen properly. The best growing regions in Hungary, such as the area around the town of Eger, northeast of Budapest, have well-draining volcanic soils which help concentrate grape flavor.

Hungarian winemakers have experience growing and producing wine from international grape varieties such as Cabernet Sauvignon and Chardonnay, but many take pride in working with native varieties such as Harslevelu (white), Kadarka (red) and Kekoporto (red). The most famous

Hungarian grape variety by far is Furmint (white), which has the acidity to make solid dry table wines but also the country's most prized sweet wines.

Message in a Bottle

> One of Hungary's best known red wines is playfully called Bull's Blood. In the mid-1500s, outnumbered defenders of the town of Eger drank copious amounts of red wine as they fought invading Turks, so that their beards became stained. When the Turks saw this, they fled in fear, thinking their opponents' ferocity came from drinking the blood of bulls!

The Romance of Tokay Aszu

Tokay is the English spelling of Tokaji, a region about one-third the size of Napa Valley located about 120 miles northeast of Budapest. Aszu is the word for shriveled grapes, which may not sound terribly appetizing when it comes to wine. Tokay Aszu is the name of a lusciously sweet wine made largely from Furmint grapes which have shriveled on the vine thanks to *Botrytis cinerea,* a fungus which dehydrates the grapes and leaves an incredibly concentrated, sugar-laden juice behind. Thanks to the high sugar content, fermentation of this juice proceeds very slowly, but the wines are worth the wait. Were it not for the Furmint grape's naturally high acidity, drinking Tokay would be like drinking grape syrup, but instead the wine is well balanced and not cloying.

Vino Veritas

> **How was Tokay Aszu discovered?**
> According to legend, in the mid-1600s a priest named Mate Szepsi Laczko was experimenting with letting grapes raisinate on the vine. Then the Turks suddenly invaded, and everyone fled. When they returned, the grapes were rotten, but they were picked anyway. The sweet juice was added to other wine, and voila!

Tokay wines are among the world's most hedonistic, and some sell for stratospherically high prices. In fact, in the late 1600s Czar Peter the Great of Russia began stationing troops in Tokay to make sure that plenty of the precious nectar made it to the royal court.

Uruguay

Uruguay is a small country on the Atlantic coast of South America, but it produces the most wine in South America after Argentina, Chile, and Brazil. Winemaking did not really begin in the country until the 1870s when Italian settlers along with Spanish and French Basques brought the grape with them from Europe. Today more than 20,000 acres of grapes are being cultivated by approximately 1,800 wine producers.

The Success of Tannat

The Tannat grape has come to define Uruguayan wine. Tannat is indigenous to southwest France, and it now represents approximately 40 percent of Uruguay's wine production. It is also known as Harriague, the surname of the French Basque who first brought Tannat to the country. Merlot and Cabernet Sauvignon also have a foothold in Uruguay, the climate of which has been compared to Bordeaux, which makes some of the most highly coveted Merlot and Cabernet Sauvignon-based wines in the world.

Tannat is a hardy grape, producing quite possibly the world's darkest red wines. Due to Tannat's firm tannins, which can make the wines somewhat astringent in their youth, wine producers often blend Merlot or Pinot Noir into the mix, tempering the tannins with softer fruit. This firm backbone of tannins, however, can make Uruguayan Tannats fine candidates for cellaring.

Israel

In the Western world, there is a strong link between wine and religion. This link is intense in Israel, where wine has been produced since biblical times. Wine plays a prominent role in the Jewish Passover Seder meal. The wine consumed at such events is kosher, and kosher wines historically have not been made to garner scores in the '90s from wine critics such as Robert Parker. This stigma surrounding kosher wines has unfortunately tainted the reputation of Israeli wines as a whole, but this is rapidly changing.

Roots of the Modern Israeli Wine Industry

Archaeologists have dated cisterns for wine production and storage located in what is now Israel to 3000 BC. In 1848 Rabbi Shore in Jerusalem built the first winery for commercial kosher wine production. The most famous name to grace the early Israeli kosher wine industry was Baron Edmond de Rothschild, owner of the legendary Chateau Lafite in Bordeaux, who brought French expertise to the winemaking. His initial project exists today as the Carmel Winery.

By the 1980s, wines with international appeal began to complement kosher wines. Stainless steel fermentation tanks along with French and American aging barrels became commonplace at wineries. Today, while three wineries produce 80 percent of Israeli wine (Carmel, Barkan Wine Cellars and Golan Heights Winery), the boutique-winery phenomenon, which most connoisseurs associate with the Napa Valley, has taken hold. There are now no fewer than one hundred such wineries, producing anywhere from a few thousand to 20,000 bottles annually. Famous boutique wineries include Domaine du Castel, Margalit and Yatir.

Savvy Sipping

The red 2003 Yatir Forest label from a subsidiary of Carmel Winery received a score of 93 points from American wine critic Robert Parker.

The Land and the Grapes

It is true that Israel has desert areas inhospitable to grapes, but most of Israel has a Mediterranean climate, perfect for local and international grape varieties. The area with the best reputation for high-quality wines is Galilee in the north, but modern irrigation techniques are helping turn previously barren areas into lush vineyards.

While Cabernet Sauvignon, Merlot, Chardonnay, and Sauvignon Blanc are finding homes in Israeli wine regions, arguably the most popular grape is Emerald Riesling. This grape is not true Riesling; it is a cross between Muscadelle and true Riesling developed by a researcher at the University of California at Davis. Emerald Riesling produces table wines with an acidity that makes them a good food match, and wines such as this are rare in hot growing regions.

China

China might seem an odd mention in a chapter on emerging wine regions, but China is worth noting for two main reasons: Chinese wine consumption is exploding on an unprecedented scale, and internationally recognized wine companies are beginning to invest millions to plant vineyards in areas only locals know about. These companies are banking that wine connoisseurs around the world will soon think of Napa and Penglai in the same thought.

No Stranger to Fermented Beverage

Archeologists have discovered texts dating back to approximately 1122 BC that state that the Chinese upper classes drank alcoholic beverages. Were any of these beverages made from actual grapes? Your guess is as good as mine. Almost two thousand years passed before scholars learned about Mare's Nipple. In AD 694 Emperor Tai-Tsung received a grape variety from people living in what is now Turkey, which the Chinese called Mare's Nipple. This grape still has a home in China, and producers continue to ferment its juice. Most fermented beverages in ancient China, however, were made from rice and wheat.

By 1892 European white grape variety Welschriesling (not true Riesling) had found its way to China thanks to government officer Zhang Bishi, who also founded a winery called Chang Yu in Yantai, north of Shanghai.

One hundred years later, European companies such as Remy Martin and Pernod-Ricard had established brands in China. By the late 1990s wineries such as Grace Vineyards in Shanxi province, complete with a replica of a French chateau, had been established. Today China has no fewer than five hundred wineries.

Savvy Sipping

Perhaps the most internationally recognized Chinese wine today is Dragon Seal, which has won medals in France and England for its Chardonnays, Merlots, and Cabernet Sauvignons. The vineyards are located about ninety-five miles north of Beijing, and the winemaker, Jérôme Sabaté, is French!

Does China Have Any Napa Valleys?

Vineyards occupy approximately 1.1 million acres in China. Virtually all are located north of the Yangtze River, with the greatest concentration of wineries in the extreme northwest part of the country. The most significant wine regions here, which roughly lie on the same latitude as California, are Hebei, Shangdong, Henan and Tianjin. The major headache to winemakers in these regions is the threat of monsoons, which can quickly strip vines of grapes or rot any grapes left behind.

No wine region has yet achieved the glamour and prestige of California's Napa Valley, but a historic development in March 2009 bodes well for a peninsula 500 miles north of Shanghai called Penglai. The great Chateau Lafite agreed to develop approximately 60 acres of vines in an area already home to China's most prominent producers of Cabernet Sauvignon, Cabernet Franc, and Merlot.

Message in a Bottle

Western wine companies are also taking an interest in China because of the population's increasing purchasing power. At the 2008 Napa Valley Wine Auction, Shanghai Internet entrepreneur David Li dropped $500,000 for six magnums of 1992 Screaming Eagle, one of California's most coveted Cabernet Sauvignons.

Wine Consumption in China

The Chinese are consuming wine at a rate that would cause any Western wine company to salivate. According to the Hong Kong Trade Development Council, mainland China and Hong Kong together drink 60 percent of all wine consumed in Asia. According to the International Wine and Spirit Record in London, the Chinese are expected to be drinking more than 1.1 billion bottles of wine a year by 2011, double the number in 2007.

As mainland producers refine their winemaking techniques and as Western producers hone their marketing outreach, the future of wine in China is nothing but bright.

India

The consumption of fermented beverages in India has a somewhat uneven history due to a convergence of religious traditions—Islam, Buddhism, Hinduism—that have generally frowned upon such consumption. During the British occupation, wine drinking expanded, and vineyards were established in Kashmir, Baramati, Surat, and Goalkonda. Any possibility of establishing a modern industry was thwarted by phylloxera, which wiped just about everything out in the 1890s. When India declared independence from Great Britain in 1947, the industry grew very slowly, but more than sixty years later, Indian vineyards and wine consumption are expanding at breakneck speed.

Obstacles and Opportunities

One of the greatest obstacles standing in the way of the development of a modern Indian wine industry is the fact that India is the world's biggest whiskey market, and many locals look at wine as just another form of alcohol, not a beverage belonging at the dinner table. Another obstacle is that grape growers must often contend with a climate so humid that rot is a fact of life. Couple this with the threat of monsoons and many prospective vineyard owners abandon the idea altogether.

Message in a Bottle

India does have indigenous grape varieties such as Arkavati, Arkashyam, and Anabeshahi, but these are mainly grown as table grapes, not wine grapes. The most commonly grown grape in India is Thompson Seedless, which is also found in most American grocery stores.

This is not to say that the situation is impossible. India has more than 1 billion people, and change tends to happen more slowly here. Changes in social mores are favoring wine consumption, especially among the young. In the last thirty years, three producers have come to exert the most influence in the burgeoning Indian wine industry. Grover Vineyards opened in 1988 near Bangalore and counts among its winemaking consultants Michel Rolland of Bordeaux. The vineyards are home to Cabernet Sauvignon,

Shiraz, Viognier, and Sauvignon Blanc and are largely protected from monsoons. At about the same time, Chateau Indage began releasing sparkling wines made with French equipment. Stanford-educated Ranjeev Samant launched Sula Wines in 2000 and quickly developed the reputation as India's finest white-wine producer, most notably of Chenin Blanc and Sauvignon Blanc.

The Future of Indian Wine and Wine in India

At the time of this writing, the Indian wine industry produces about 1.2 million cases a year, with more imported from Europe, Australia, and the United States. Yet another famous French winemaker, Stephane Derenoncourt, has decided to consult for Alpine Winery, recently founded in the southern state of Karnakata. Derenoncourt has consulted for the likes of Francis Ford Coppola in Napa Valley. In addition, on April 1, 2010, India joined the Paris-based International Organization of Vine and Wine, an agency that helps uphold the most innovative winemaking and grape growing practices around the world.

As India grows more and more prosperous economically, wine consumption is forecast to rise 20 to 30 percent a year. Not bad for one of the youngest modern wine industries in the world.

Switzerland

Switzerland is surrounded by four of Europe's preeminent wine-producing countries—France, Italy, Germany, and Austria—yet most wine connoisseurs think that Switzerland is too cold and mountainous to support any type of grapevine. Quite the opposite is true. So little Swiss wine makes it to the United States, that when Americans think of Switzerland they think of chocolate and cheese, and Swiss wine is barely an afterthought.

It's Not Too Cold or Too High

Switzerland is more diverse than you might think, and climate is just the beginning. Switzerland has three distinct cultural regions divided by language, and, to some extent, by the grapes that thrive there. Each of these cultural regions is divided further into cantons, and each canton is permitted to regulate its wine industry on its own terms. This lack of central control allows for a huge diversity in wine styles, making Switzerland a wine connoisseur's playground.

Vino Veritas

> **Isn't Switzerland too mountainous for vineyards?**
> It is true that the country has forty-eight mountains over 13,000 feet high, but this reality hasn't stopped vineyards! Many Swiss vineyards are grown on tablars (terraces) literally cut into mountainsides. All vineyard work must be done by hand.

French Switzerland

Located in western Switzerland, French Switzerland makes the most wine and has the most rigorous *appellation controllee*-based system. The most planted Swiss grape variety, Chasselas, is largely planted here. Sylvaner and Pinot Gris are other popular white grapes, with Gamay and Pinot Noir comprising most of the red grapes.

Valais is the largest and most important canton in wine-producing French Switzerland. Some call it the most important canton in *all* of wine-producing Switzerland, as 40 percent of Swiss wine comes from Valais. It is sandwiched between France to the west and Italy to the east and is fascinating for its indigenous grape varieties, which include Amigne, Petite Arvine, Humagne Blanche, and Cornalin du Valais.

German Switzerland

German Switzerland is the largest of the three Swiss cultural areas, and red wine production dominates. Pinot Noir, called Blauburgunder here, is the leading red grape.

Italian Switzerland

Ticino is the main canton in Italian Switzerland, and Merlot accounts for a whopping 85 percent of its wine production. At higher elevations Pinot Noir and white grapes find a home, but Merlot is king. Ticino locals also routinely quaff a white Merlot (Merlot bianco), which is made by separating the red Merlot grape skins from the juice prior to fermentation.

CHAPTER 9

Wine Regions of the United States

From the East Coast to the West Coast, the United States grows grapes and makes wine. Each of the fifty states, even Alaska and Hawaii, has commercial wineries. For a country whose citizens drink so little wine per capita (about two gallons per person a year)—compared to places like Italy or France (fourteen gallons)—wine is becoming an inseparable component of American culture.

Declaration of Wine Independence

Americans have always had their own ways of doing things. They've never been shy about declaring their independence, even in terms of winemaking. American winemakers produced entirely different styles of wines with the same grapes the Europeans used, and then, instead of naming the wines after the place they were produced as had been the tradition, they named their wines after the grape.

Until 1979 the United States had no coordinated system to designate or control geographical winemaking areas. France had made its AOC system into law in the 1930s, and it had become a model for other countries. It strictly regulates varieties that can be grown, yields, alcohol levels, and vineyard practices. American wine producers had no predilection for such regulation; they wanted to retain the independence to make their wines using whatever grapes and methods they chose.

The federal government set up the American Viticultural Area (AVA) system as part of the Treasury Department—first under the auspices of the Bureau of Alcohol, Tobacco, and Firearms and more recently under the supervision of the Alcohol and Tobacco Tax and Trade Bureau. Unlike in the French and other European systems, the only requirement to use an AVA on the label is that 85 percent of the grapes used in making the wine come from the named region.

Smaller AVAs can exist within larger AVAs. For example, if a winery on Howell Mountain in the Napa Valley produces a Cabernet Sauvignon with 90 percent Howell Mountain fruit, Howell Mountain may legally appear on the bottle label. If 75 percent of the fruit is from Howell Mountain and 25 percent is from St. Helena, then Napa Valley alone can appear on the label.

Vino Veritas

An AVA can be enormous or very small. The largest is the 26,000-square-mile, 16.5 million-acre Ohio River Valley AVA. It includes portions of several states: Indiana, Kentucky, Ohio, and West Virginia. The smallest is the Cole Ranch in California's Mendocino County which covers a mere 189 acres.

By February 2010, 193 AVAs had been approved. If you see the name of a geographical region on a bottle of American wine, such as California, Santa Barbara, or Carneros, that is the AVA. Applicants wanting to establish a new AVA must provide proof of their region's geographic and climatic significance, historical precedent for wine production, and boundary suggestion and mapping. As opposed to systems in other countries, AVAs don't assure quality. They only differentiate the growing areas.

California

California is, hands down, the wine capital of the United States. It accounts for more than 90 percent of all the wines made in the country and 75 percent of all the wines consumed within its borders. The climate has a lot to do with California's preeminence. Not only is it ideal for growing grapes, it is so reliable that there is little variation in the wine from year to year. Getting enough sun every year to ripen the grapes is never a problem in California. The challenge is to find areas cool enough to allow the grapes to ripen slowly, thus allowing full flavor development.

Wineries have popped up all over the state, from the far reaches of the north to the Mexican border in the south. The following areas are most notable for winegrowing:

- The North Coast includes Napa, Sonoma, Mendocino, and Lake Counties.
- The Central Coast stretches from San Francisco to Los Angeles. It includes Monterey, Santa Cruz, and Livermore in the northern part and San Luis Obispo and Santa Barbara in the south.
- The Sierra Foothills are on the western edge of the Sierra Nevada Mountains.
- The massive Central Valley extends from Sacramento in the north to the San Joaquin Valley in the south.

Napa and Sonoma

The Napa Valley has almost become synonymous with the term "wine country." It is famous for its expensive wines, rich history, and breathtaking landscapes. Inside its thirty-five-mile stretch, you can eat at world-class restaurants and taste wine from 400 different producers as hot air balloons pass overhead.

The Napa Valley AVA has fifteen distinct sub-AVAs, each with diverse microclimates. In the south, Carneros benefits from cool breezes where it meets the bay, perfect for Pinot Noir. As you move north and temperatures warm, Cabernet Sauvignon begins showing up in Oakville and St. Helena. Napa Valley even has higher-altitude vineyards on Mount Veeder, Spring Mountain, and Howell Mountain, where climate, soil, and exposure differ from what vineyards on the Valley floor enjoy. Cabernet Sauvignon is king in Napa Valley, and among its "subjects" are Chardonnay, Sauvignon Blanc, Merlot, and Zinfandel. Some of the Napa sub-AVAs that you'll probably recognize from wine labels are:

- Rutherford
- Howell Mountain
- Atlas Peak
- Mount Veeder
- Oakville
- Spring Mountain
- Stags' Leap District

Often lost in Napa Valley's shadow is its neighbor to the west, Sonoma, which was planted to wine grapes before Napa. Sonoma has a more relaxed personality and more of the character of "Old California."

Sonoma is twice as big as Napa, and due to its proximity to the Pacific coast, it has a more diverse climate. Sonoma's most distinctive AVAs include the following:

- Alexander Valley—famous for its Cabs and Chardonnays
- Russian River Valley—produces Pinot Noir (thanks to its cooler climate); also known for Chardonnay and sparkling wine
- Dry Creek Valley—known for Zinfandel
- Sonoma Valley and Sonoma Mountain—produce Cabernet, Pinot Noir, and Chardonnay

The Carneros AVA is particularly interesting. It straddles Sonoma and Napa to the south, right next to San Pablo Bay, the northern area of San Francisco Bay. It has a cool climate, making it an ideal area for growing

Chardonnay and Pinot Noir. These grapes are perfect for both dry and sparkling wine. Because of its climate, Carneros attracted a number of sparkling wine producers from Europe.

Mendocino and Lake County

Northern California has had a reputation for attracting residents who liked to "do their own thing." Mendocino and Lake County are California's northernmost wine-producing areas, and the winemakers there are open-minded and experimental about what grapes to grow. Growers have also been especially sensitive regarding their farming methods, such that Mendocino is credited with being at the forefront of sustainable agriculture and organic farming.

Mendocino and Lake County are cool, making Pinot Noir and Chardonnay obvious planting choices, although Gewürztraminer, Riesling, and Pinot Blanc are rapidly gaining respect. Notable producers are Navarro, Guenoc, and Roederer.

Sierra Foothills and Livermore Valley

The Sierra Foothills are the site of the historic California Gold Rush of the nineteenth century. The AVA is mountainous and cool. The most cultivated grapes are Syrah, Zinfandel, and Petite Sirah, but you'll also find Barbera, Sangiovese, and Mourvèdre.

About an hour outside of San Francisco to the southeast lies the Livermore Valley, a historic wine-producing area with a warm and windy climate. It's situated between the cool, marine air of the San Francisco Bay and the hot, dry air of the Central Valley. Sauvignon Blanc and Sémillon were first planted there by the French immigrants in the 1870s and 1880s. They remain and thrive. Other varieties include Chardonnay, Cabernet Sauvignon, Petite Sirah, and Zinfandel.

The Central Coast

The areas within the Central Coast AVA are numerous and disparate. Each one has its own distinctive qualities. Of course, the one with the most celebrity is the Santa Ynez Valley, north of the town of Santa Barbara.

When a movie filmed in your backyard gets an Academy Award nomination—like *Sideways* did in 2005—fame is soon to follow. As great as the wines of Santa Ynez Valley are, there is much more to the Central Coast. From the blazingly hot Paso Robles area to the cooler Edna Valley, the Central Coast is home to grape varieties as varied as Syrah and Viognier.

Central Valley

No fine wine producer brags that its grapes come from the Central Valley. This huge expanse of inland vineyards produces the majority of California's bulk wine, accounting for three-quarters of the state's wine production. (The region also grows table grapes and raisins.) However, new facilities and technology are bringing much-deserved respect to the Central Valley AVAs of Lodi and Clarksburg.

California Is Trendsetting

In the 1980s some progressive winemakers got tired of producing only Chardonnay and Cabernet Sauvignon. They wanted to express more of their creativity. In the vein of "everything old becomes new again," they looked to the Old World for inspiration. One group, dubbed the "Rhone Rangers," took their inspiration from southern France and concentrated on making wines from traditional Rhone varieties such Syrah, Grenache, and Mourvedre. The idea caught on, and plantings of those grapes were expanded.

Meanwhile, another group of Francophile winemakers wanted to express their creativity in blending, rather than producing strictly varietal wines. They looked to Bordeaux and its tradition of blending as many as six "noble" grapes together to produce a single wine: Cabernet Sauvignon, Merlot, Petit Verdot, Malbec, Cabernet Franc, and Carmenère (all but extinct in Bordeaux). The result of their collaboration was Meritage wines and the Meritage Association.

Vino Veritas

Meritage wines have to blend at least two of the Bordeaux varieties, and no single variety can make up more than 90 percent of the blend. Producers must be members of the Meritage Alliance to employ the Meritage name.

What's next? Because winemaking practices and the popular enjoyment of wine are cyclical, you can probably look to history for the answer. One trend seems to be the shift away from heavily oaked California wines. For twenty-five years California winemakers were fascinated with oak and used a lot of it. On another continent, the wine-producing regions of France— like the Loire Valley and Rhone—have always relied on the true taste of the fermented grape and have met with popular approval. Today, California winemakers are making the move to create softer, more fruit-driven wine— with a more judicial use of oak.

New York

New York is the third largest wine-producing state in the United States after California and Washington, but it often gets overlooked in the mind of the public. Until 1960, New York wines came from native American varieties such as Concord, Catawba, Niagara, and Delaware and hybrid grapes such as Seyval Blanc and Baco Noir. The hybrids, in particular, are still produced, but the more popular *Vitis vinifera* wines have usurped their position.

The Finger Lakes

For years it was accepted that New York winters were too cold for *Vitis vinifera* vines to survive. Then a Russian immigrant, Dr. Konstantin Frank, who had taught viticulture in his native Ukraine, got a job at the New York State Agricultural Experiment Station in 1951. He observed the lack of *Vitis vinifera* vines in the Finger Lakes area, and when he asked why, he was given the expected answer. Frank was unperturbed, and after having grown *vinifera* grapes successfully in the much colder Ukraine, he decided to plant Riesling in Hammondsport, New York, in 1953. His winery is still open for business fifty years later.

Message in a Bottle

Given New York's rank among wine-producing states, the state is perhaps better known for its grape juice. Welch's grape juice is made from the Concord grape, which flourishes in New York. In fact, about 50 percent of New York's grapes become grape juice.

Today, the Finger Lakes region is an officially recognized AVA, whose Rieslings compare favorably with their European counterparts. The area encompasses 4,000 square miles and has 15,000 acres of vines. The area has more than one hundred wineries and is home to Constellation Brands (formerly Canandaigua), one of the world's largest wine suppliers. Finger Lakes producers do particularly well with Riesling, Chardonnay, Pinot Noir, sparkling wines, and ice wines.

Hudson River Valley

North of New York City along the majestic Hudson River is the historic Hudson Valley. It was a pioneering region for French-American hybrids such as Seyval Blanc and Baco Noir. These days it also grows Chardonnay and Cabernet Franc. The area has at least thirty wineries including the oldest continuously running winery in the country. Brotherhood Winery produced the first commercial vintage in 1839. It was able to keep its doors open through Prohibition by making sacramental wine.

Long Island

The Finger Lakes and Hudson Valley may have a rich past, but New York's Long Island has a bright future. It's the new kid on the block and quite a success story so far. In 1973 when Alex and Louisa Hargrave were looking for a suitable place to plant some grapevines, they heard that Long Island had a maritime microclimate similar to that of Bordeaux.

After researching and soil testing—but mostly because of intuition—the Hargraves put down roots on seventeen acres of the island's North Fork. Two years later they bottled their first wines and released them in 1977. Today, more than thirty wineries are producing wines from grapes on 3,000 acres of land.

Long Island has been compared to the Napa of twenty-five years ago, and in some ways it's true. There's the proximity to a world-class city—Manhattan is to the North Fork as San Francisco is to Napa—and then there are all those celebrities buying up wine properties. Long Island's most important connection to Napa is its relentless pursuit of quality. If its current Merlot, Cab, Cabernet Franc, and Chardonnay wines are any indication, it is off to a good start.

Oregon

Although wines were made in Oregon in the nineteenth century, Prohibition effectively wiped out the wine industry. Oregon's wine pioneers arrived in the 1960s. At that time no *Vitis vinifera* vines were planted. Those first pioneers brought enthusiasm, new ideas, and, in some cases, degrees from UC Davis.

Oregon's climate is marked by cool growing seasons and plenty of rain. It presents more challenges than its neighbor California, but rather than give up, Oregon's new winemakers were simply more discerning about where and how they planted their vineyards. Unlike in California where sprawling vineyard tracts were the norm, Oregon vineyards were planted in small pockets to take advantage of the best weather conditions. There are enough of these small pockets to make Oregon the fourth largest producer of wine in the United States.

Pinot Noir Takes Root

Oregon's location along the 45th parallel, in addition to its maritime weather, makes the growing climate very similar to that of Burgundy, France. One of Oregon's pioneers, David Lett of Eyrie Vineyard, was convinced that the traditional grapes of Burgundy could grow well in Oregon, and certainly grow better than they did in California. He planted the first Pinot Noir vines in 1965. A decade or so later, his Pinot Noir wines would bring serious recognition to Oregon among wine connoisseurs.

Message in a Bottle

In a 1979 Paris tasting with entries from 330 countries, the 1975 Eyrie Pinot Noir placed in the top ten. In a follow-up match in early 1980, it came in second to—and less than a point behind—the 1959 Drouhin Chambolle-Musigny. It was an international achievement! Since then Pinot Noir has become Oregon's flagship wine.

Oregon's Other Pinot

Pinot Noir's companion grape in Burgundy is Chardonnay, and it's no stranger to Oregon. Chardonnay, however, has not seen the success of Pinot

Gris, one of the great white grapes of Alsace, France. Again, thanks to David Lett, Pinot Gris was introduced to the region in 1965 and has since been adopted by winemakers across the state.

The style of Oregon's Pinot Gris has been compared to that made in Alsace, but subtle variations exist. In general, Oregon's Pinot Gris is medium-bodied, yellow to copper pink in color, crisp, with full fruit flavors. The wines from Alsace are medium- to full-bodied, slightly floral, and less fruity. Pinot Gris is the same grape as Pinot Grigio, but Pinot Grigio wines have a markedly different style. They are typically light-bodied, light in color, and neutral in flavor.

Growing Regions

Oregon has more than ten officially recognized AVAs, three of which are shared with neighboring Washington State. The following four have the most clout:

- The **Willamette Valley** is the largest and most important region. This fertile river valley is located directly south of Portland in the northwest end of the state. It produces primarily Pinot Noir, Pinot Gris, Chardonnay, and Riesling.
- The **Umpqua Valley** is the site of Oregon's first winery, Hillcrest Vineyard. South of Willamette Valley, it has a warm climate and produces Chardonnay, Pinot Noir, Cabernet Sauvignon, Riesling, and Sauvignon Blanc.
- The **Rogue Valley** is further south of the Umpqua Valley and has a dry, warm climate. Varietals include Pinot Gris, Riesling, Chardonnay, and Gewürztraminer.
- The **Applegate Valley** AVA falls within the Rogue Valley AVA. It produces Cabernet Franc, Sémillon, Cabernet Sauvignon, and Merlot.

Washington

Like Oregon, Washington was late getting into the wine business. Washington's two largest wineries—Columbia Winery and Château Ste. Michelle—planted the first commercial-scale vineyards in the 1960s, but it wasn't until the 1980s that growth really exploded. Today Washington has close to 600 wineries, second only to California. It also has the second highest grape crop and the second highest level of wine production.

Washington shares the Cascade Mountains with Oregon, and this range divides the state into two very different climatic regions. West of the mountain range, the climate is cool with plenty of rain and vegetation. To the east of the mountains, the land is practically a desert, with hot, dry summers and cold winters. Ninety-eight percent of the state's grapes grow east of the Cascades.

Washington beats California in terms of summer sun: It enjoys two more hours of summer sunlight each day than in California regions, without the accompanying heat. Grapes just love it. The cool autumn temperatures help the grapes maintain desirable acid levels as they reach maturity.

Wine Regions

Washington's five most elite AVAs are in the arid east, where irrigation has made commercial vine growing possible. Washington has a total of eleven AVAs.

- The **Yakima Valley** is Washington's very first AVA, and it now has more than forty wineries. The most widely planted grapes are Chardonnay, followed by Merlot and Cabernet and significant acreage of Riesling and Syrah.
- The **Columbia Valley** is one of the largest AVAs in the United States. It represents a full third of Washington's landmass. Merlot dominates, followed by Cabernet, Chardonnay, Riesling, and Syrah.
- The **Walla Walla Valley** AVA is shared with Oregon. The region has more than fifty-five wineries and produces Cabernet Sauvignon, Merlot, Chardonnay, Syrah, Gewürztraminer, and Cabernet Franc.
- The **Red Mountain** AVA is at the east end of the Yakima Valley. It's known for its red varietals: Cabernet, Merlot, Cabernet Franc, Syrah, and Sangiovese.
- The **Columbia Gorge** AVA was established in 2004 and is also shared with Oregon. It produces Chardonnay, Gewürztraminer, Riesling, and Pinot Gris.

- The **Puget Sound** AVA is near Seattle. It has eighty vineyard acres of *Vitis vinifera* grapes and about forty-five wineries. Because of its proximity to the ocean, frost is not as big a threat as it is in other AVAs. Many of the larger wineries are located in this area, but obtain almost all their grapes from the Columbia and Yakima Valleys.

Message in a Bottle

Most of Washington's wineries are quite small, and their wines difficult to find. Ste. Michelle Wine Estates produces about half of all Washington's wines. The company's labels include Columbia Crest, Snoqualmie, Northstar, Eroica, and Col Solare—a joint venture with Italy's Antinori.

The "Other" 46

California, New York, Oregon, and Washington may be the big wine players in the United States, but every state has its own unique wine story to tell. Missouri, for example, made more wine in the 1860s than California and New York combined. The influx of German immigrants to the town of Hermann, on the banks of the Missouri River west of St. Louis, dubbed the area as the Rhineland of Missouri. Sadly, the great German grape Riesling did not thrive, but cellar-worthy reds appeared from the indigenous Norton and Cynthiana grapes. Important white grapes included Vignoles, Seyval Blanc, and Vidal Blanc.

Vino Veritas

Archaeologists discovered a brick-lined wine cellar and intact wine bottles in Jamestown, Virginia—the first permanent English colony in America. The cellar, which dates back to the late 1600s, is one of the earliest wine cellars known in the United States. It's believed the cellar was part of a private home.

Deep in the Heart of Texas

The Lone Star State comes in at number five in wine production, right after California, New York, Washington, and Oregon. Texas developed a close association with France during the phylloxera epidemic of the late 1800s. A French scientist from Cognac, Pierre Viala, was sent to Texas to try to find a way to stop this devastating insect. He traveled to Denison, Texas, because the soil composition there was similar to that of Cognac. Viala was introduced to T. V. Munson, a Texas scientist who knew Texas rootstocks were resistant to phylloxera. At Munson's suggestion Viala shipped the Texas rootstocks back to France where they were grafted to French vines. For his contribution to France, Munson was given the highest honor awarded to a foreign civilian, the Chevalier du Mérite Agricole.

New Mexico Stands Proud

New Mexico has forty-one wineries, which is impressive given that so much of the state is an arid desert. No winery shines as brightly as Gruet, which released its first wines in 1987. Its founder, Gilbert Gruet, had made Champagne in France, and on a trip to the American Southwest discovered that sparkling wine grapes could flourish in certain areas. The Gruet family now produces seven different sparkling wines, and their vineyards are located at 4,300 feet, an altitude that spares grapes from being roasted by the desert heat. *Wine Spectator*, the *Wall Street Journal,* and British wine expert Jancis Robinson have all taken notice of Gruet brand.

CHAPTER 10

Tasting Wine Like a Pro

You walk into a wine shop, and the clerk asks if he can help you select a wine. You pause in thought, then turn in embarrassment and walk out the door. You know what kind of wine you like when you taste it, but you just don't know how to communicate that to the salesperson. Determining why you enjoy one wine over another and expressing yourself articulately are just a matter of practice and a few well-chosen words.

The Physiology of Taste

Taste is arguably subjective when art, fashion, or music is the subject of conversation. When wine is the subject, you will find that everyone may have different "tastes" in wine, but tasting wine has an objective component. For one thing, tasting wine (or anything!) involves not just taste, but sight, smell, and touch. These fours senses send objective information to your brain, and this helps you evaluate, not merely appreciate, that glass in front of you. Whether you like what your brain is telling you, that is where subjectivity enters the picture. What you like is very much tied to your upbringing and cultural influences.

Whether you are evaluating wine or appreciating wine, setting is enormously important. That incredible bottle of Chianti you shared over a romantic dinner didn't measure up when you drank it alone in front of the TV, did it? Your taste is affected by your mood, by your health, and by your environment. Try to enjoy a floral Viognier when you have a cold or when you're in a smoke-filled room. It will be quite a challenge.

Vino Veritas

Individuals have genetic differences that determine their ability to taste. People can be divided into categories of supertasters, nontasters, and normal tasters. Supertasters are especially sensitive to sweetness, bitterness, and the creamy sensation of fat. Apparently, they have more taste buds than everyone else—as many as a hundred times more than nontasters. About 25 percent of the population are supertasters, and two-thirds of all supertasters are women.

Sight

A wine's appearance influences your judgment. Color and clarity are the key things to look for. Is the color what you expected, or is it somehow off? Is clarity lacking because of any cloudiness that would indicate the wine is unfined? Are there any perfectly harmless tartrate crystals in that glass of white wine? In blind wine tastings, participants are sometimes given black, opaque glasses so they're not prejudiced by what the wine looks like, even by the color.

Color can tell you something about the age of wine. As white wines get older, they get darker. As red wines age, they lose color.

Smell

Your sense of smell is your most acute sense and is many times more sensitive than your sense of taste. You sense aromas either directly by inhaling through your nose or, indirectly, through the nasal passage at the back of your mouth. Taste and smell are so linked that when you experience the generous dark fruit of a Cabernet Sauvignon, you are actually tasting aromas of that dark fruit. Speaking of fruit, don't be surprised if you think of blackberries as you smell your Cab. Wine is made up of hundreds of chemical compounds, many of which are similar—or identical—to those in fruits, vegetables, flowers, herbs, and spices. The winemaker did not add essence of blackberry to that wine; your brain is simply picking up one of those compounds.

Taste

In contrast to the multitude of aromas the nose can identify, the tongue recognizes only four basic tastes: sweetness, saltiness, acidity, and bitterness, and some might say umami. Saltiness doesn't come into play when tasting wine, but the others are critical. The tongue does not register these four or five tastes at distinct sites as was previously thought. It has been proven that taste occurs everywhere on the tongue.

Message in a Bottle

When tasting wine, never judge a wine on the first sip. Your mouth must first adjust to the alcohol and acidity before it can more accurately convey that wine's other attributes. It's also better to taste before lunch or dinner, not after. Your senses heighten as you get hungry.

Sweetness and acidity are the yin and yang of the winetasting world. They balance each other. Think of lemonade. Lemon juice on its own is a mouth-puckering experience. The more sugar you add to the juice, the less you notice the acidity.

Bitterness plays a role in winetasting as well. Red wine tannin, while having more of a tactile nature than a taste, can give you the impression of bitterness.

Touch

Wines have texture that you can feel in your mouth. A wine can be thin—like water. Or it can be full—like cream. That's what a wine's "body" is all about. "Full-bodied" and "light-bodied" are not subjective judgments; they are descriptions.

Your mouth distinguishes other sensations as well. Tannins, the elements responsible for a wine's ability to age, have an astringent, mouth-drying effect very much like the impression you get when you drink oversteeped tea. The alcohol in the wine will give you a hot feeling at the back of your throat and on the roof of your mouth.

Your perception of a wine's body—its texture and fullness—is due mostly to the amount of alcohol in the wine. The more potent a wine is, the more full-bodied it will seem. For example, a big Zinfandel with 16 percent alcohol content will have more body than a Riesling with 9 percent.

Right and Wrong Ways to Taste

There's nothing wrong with simply picking up your glass of wine and taking a swig. If you really want to understand the wine while you're enjoying it, you might to employ techniques used by wine-industry professionals.

Swirling

After examining the color and clarity, give the wine a swirl. If you are afraid of ruining your brand new polo shirt, set the glass on a smooth surface, grasp the stem near the base, and move the glass in circles. As the wine rotates, aromas intensify and tannins soften ever so slightly. Before the aromas escape and are lost, stick your nose right into the glass. Don't just sniff; rather, inhale deeply.

Once is rarely enough. Swirl the wine again and inhale. You can't possibly take in all the aroma nuances at once. Close your eyes. What scents are you detecting? You may smell something new each time.

Swishing and Slurping

After experiencing the wine's aromas, it's time to taste. Wine pros savor the moment. Take a generous sip and give it time to linger in your mouth. Better yet, swish the wine around in your mouth. Touch every surface of your tongue with wine. Hit every taste receptor. Quickly swallowing a small sip barely does the wine justice. If you are tasting a tart, herbal Sauvignon Blanc, that quick sip will probably just leave the impression of tartness and little else.

Once you've mastered swishing, try slurping. Purse your lips and draw in some air across the wine on your tongue. It's called slurping because that's the sound this technique makes. Slurping intensely aerates the wine, making it easier for aroma compounds to waft up your rear nasal passage and reach the olfactory bulb that allows your brain to make sense of those aromas.

Depending on the number of wines you plan to sample, you may want to spit out the wine you just evaluated. Alcohol dulls the senses over time, so if learning is your goal, it's perfectly fine to spit.

Mastering the Lingo

When wine lovers get excited about a new wine find, they want to share the experience. The only trouble is that words are often so inadequate. Talking about wine has become intimidating, since many terms seem mysterious and pretentious. A place to start is to compare your glass of Merlot to things that are familiar to you, such as your aunt's famous cherry pie. For those wine lovers who may not have sampled your aunt's pie, here some public terms that every wine lover should be familiar with.

- **Dry**—It's the opposite of sweet. When all the sugar in the grape juice has been converted to alcohol and carbon dioxide, the wine is said to be bone dry. There is a continuum, however, between really sweet and really dry. If enough residual sugar remains to give the wine a slight sweetness, the wine is off-dry.
- **Balance**—None of the wine's components is out of whack. The acid, alcohol, fruit, and tannins all work together so that one doesn't stand apart from the rest.

- **Finish**—A wine's aftertaste, or the flavor or aroma that lingers after you've swallowed the wine, is referred to as its finish. If it has one, it's considered a good thing and the longer the better. A "long finish" is a real compliment.
- **Complex**—Layers and nuances of flavor make a wine complex. A complex wine will continue to reveal itself as you sip it. This multi-dimensional quality is often achieved with aging. A complex wine is also said to have depth.
- **Crisp**—A wine with good acidity and no excessive sweetness is crisp. Think of an apple. The wine is relatively high in acidity, but the acidity doesn't overwhelm the other components.

In general some of the aromas you'll be able to discern from white wines are melon, apple, pineapple, pear, citrus, vanilla, caramel, flowers, herbs, grass, minerals, olives, and butterscotch. Some flavors and aromas from red wines are berries, cedar, currants, plums, cherries, blackberries, flowers, earth, wood, smoke, chocolate, tobacco, leather, and coffee.

Message in a Bottle

Many people confuse sweetness and fruitiness. They can't be blamed. Very often, wine labels describe sweet wine as fruity. If you have some doubt about what you're tasting, take a sip of the wine while holding your nose. If the wine is sweet, you'll taste its sweetness on your tongue—instead of sensing the aroma of the fruit.

Recognizing "Flaws"

Wine flaws are not necessarily the result of bad winemaking. Wines can be defective if they have been improperly handled or stored. That said, the presence of a wine flaw or defect does not automatically make the wine bad and worthy of cooking. The key is knowing how much is too much. Certain characteristics that make a wine flawed can actually, in small amounts, be considered by some people to be a plus. It's similar to adding garlic to food: A little bit enhances the dish, but too much ruins it. Here are common culprits behind most wine faults.

Corks

Your wine smells of damp cardboard or musty basement. Whether the odor is pronounced or just slightly dank, it came from a cork tainted with a chemical compound called TCA. When the wine is damaged in this way, it's said to be corked. By industry estimates, 3 to 5 percent of all wines are corked. Cork processing improvements have been made to eliminate TCA, but many wineries are so fed up they are resorting to closures such as screw tops as permanent remedies. Very rarely does cork taint enhance a wine, even in small doses.

Oxygen

The wine tastes dull, cooked, or a little sherry-like. A white wine has an off color—brownish or very dark yellow. These are all indications that the wine has been exposed to excessive oxygen.

It could have happened while the wine was being made or when it was being stored. If wines are stored upright for long periods instead of on their sides, the cork can dry out and let air into the bottle.

Perhaps your wine smells like vinegar or nail polish remover. This is an extreme case traceable to a bacterium called acetobacter and oxygen. Acetobacter is everywhere—on grape skins, winery walls, barrels. By itself, it has no aroma or flavor, but when it meets oxygen in winemaking, it first produces the compound ethyl acetate (nail polish remover) before completely reducing the wine to acetic acid (the vinegar aroma). The term "volatile acidity" (VA) accounts for these two conditions, although once a wine reaches the level of acetic acid, it's considered oxidized. Many wine connoisseurs enjoy low levels of ethyl acetate.

Vino Veritas

Many people assume that when a wine gets too old, it turns to vinegar. More likely, it will become dull and take on a nutty taste. Thanks to Louis Pasteur and his groundbreaking work on fermentation, winemakers learned to keep wines out of contact with air and bacteria during the production process. Unless something goes terribly wrong with the cork, oxidation is rarely the winemaker's fault.

Yeast

Your wine smells like a barnyard. It may be the result of a yeast called brettanomyces—brett, for short. Brett grows on grapes and in wineries and is difficult to eradicate. Winemakers use special filters to help reduce its growth. Some wine drinkers enjoy a low level of brett, maintaining that it adds complexity to the wine's aroma, but too much completely spoils the wine.

Sulfur Dioxide

Your wine smells like a struck match. Winemakers add sulfur dioxide to preserve the wine, but in excess it ruins the wine. Cheap white wines are most likely to have sulfur problems.

Heat

The wine is brown, and it smells like it's been cooked. In Madeira, this is a plus and part of the wine's essential character. Elsewhere, it's a flaw, and the term "maderized" will be used. The wine has likely experienced severe fluctuations of temperature in a short period of time or been stored in extreme heat. If the cork is protruding slightly from an unopened bottle, the wine could be maderized.

Style Preferences

Personal preferences don't reflect a failure in the winemaking process, but if you don't like oak in wine, you will probably consider that rich California Chardonnay to be flawed. Other wine drinkers cannot tolerate acidity, meaning that such a person will push an otherwise flawless dry Riesling away from his plate.

Do Critics Know Best?

Wine critics are like movie critics. There is no guarantee that you will like what they like, but they can still help you make informed decisions about how to spend your precious entertainment (or drinking) dollars. For example, Roger Ebert may give a four-star review to the latest Clint Eastwood western, but if you hate westerns and love romantic comedies, you will more than likely see the latter, even if the latest one received only two stars. By extension, just because a wine critic has anointed a bottle of California Cabernet with a perfect score of 100 doesn't mean that it will win an Academy Award at your house over dinner.

However, in a week when twelve movies are released, hundreds of wines could be released from producers all over the world. Wine novices trying to build up personal catalog of taste preferences can be so overwhelmed by the sheer number of bottles confronting them that they turn to a wine critic. Like movie critics, some wine critics have much more star power than others.

The Experts

Without question, the wine world's most influential critic is Robert Parker. In 1978 he published a monthly newsletter called *The Wine Advocate* while working as a lawyer in Maryland. No such wine-focused publication existed in the United States in those days. Today *The Wine Advocate* has more than 50,000 subscribers around the world, and Mr. Parker no longer works as a lawyer. Parker is most famous for introducing the 100-point scale for rating wines, a scale several other wine critics have imitated.

Vino Veritas

What does it mean when an expert talks about a wine's legs?
When you swirl a glass of wine, little streams of wine fall back down the sides of the glass. These are the legs. They have nothing to do with quality. Wines with better legs generally have higher alcohol contents.

Parker's influence is measurable. When he gives a wine a high score, the price goes up and availability goes down. Some producers in Bordeaux wait for Parker's scores before they set the release prices of their wines. His ratings have also been instrumental in creating Napa's famous cult wines. If a new producer gets a Parker score of 99 on a 3,000-case Cabernet Sauvignon, that wine explodes in price and becomes a cult Cab, given its scant quantity.

Over time, wine writers have tracked the styles of wine receiving high scores from Parker and have created a profile of what he prefers. Some writers strongly dislike this Parker wine style, which underscores the importance of knowing a reviewer's taste preferences before following his or her advice. Not all reviewers are created equal, but collectively they've raised the public's consciousness about wine and its enjoyment.

Rating Systems

Robert Parker's ratings are based on single-blind, peer-group tastings, which means that he might focus only on California Cabernet Sauvignons at a tasting session. He does not taste red and white wines together, in other words, and he has no knowledge of the wines' producers during the tasting.

Each wine automatically gets 50 points—maybe just for the effort that went into making it. Color and appearance can earn up to 5 points. Aroma can get 15 points. Flavor and finish merit up to 20 points. Overall quality and aging potential can earn up to 10.

Other critics who use the 100-point scale are James Laube (*Wine Spectator*) and Steve Heimoff (*Wine Enthusiast*). Critics writing for the British wine magazine *Decanter* employ a 1-to-5 star rating. English wine writer Clive Coates uses a 20-point system.

Savvy Sipping

Another rating system—Quality/Price Ratio (QPR)—is becoming popular. It measures the correlation between what a wine sells for and its relative quality. A score of 100 percent means the price matches the quality. A score under 100 percent means you're getting a good deal for your money. A score over 100 percent means you're paying too much.

Rating the Vintages

Vintages, or the harvest years in wine regions around world, get rated in addition to the individual wines coming from them. Wine-growing regions vary according to their weather conditions every year—some with dramatic fluctuations—and these can affect wine quality. *Wine Spectator* is famous for publishing a vintage chart every year, which directs you to the best years for each region or subregion.

Vintage charts vary in their level of detail, but each should contain regional scores (as is done with individual wines) mapped on a grid to indicate the potential of that area's wine for that year. More comprehensive charts will tell you whether to hold the wine for aging or drink it now—or whether it's past its peak.

Even in the best years, a mediocre wine can show up. During average years, a talented winemaker can produce a very good wine. While vintage charts are useful and informative, nothing substitutes focusing on the track record of a winery over a period of years.

Buy These, If You Can

Here are some highly recommended wines from recognized wine critics:

- 2004 Standish Shiraz / Viognier The Relic, Australia
  (99 points, Robert Parker)
- 2006 Cardinale Napa Valley Cabernet Sauvignon
  (100 points, Steve Heimoff, *Wine Enthusiast*)
- 2007 Louis Jadot, Premier Cru Clos-St.-Jacques, Burgundy
  (19/20, *Decanter* magazine, UK)
- 2005 Alban Syrah Edna Valley Lorraine, California
  (96 points, James Laube, *Wine Spectator*)
- 2009 Corriente del Bio Pinot Noir, Bio Bio Valley, Chile
  (89 points, Jamie Goode, *www.wineanorak.com*)

When it comes to enjoying wine—no matter what the vintage year, no matter what the critics say—it's ultimately up to you. Your personal preferences will guide you to make the right selections. This is part of the fun!

CHAPTER 11

Wine and Food

A century ago, everyone just drank their local wine and didn't fret about the "perfect match" for a meal. Then, as diners began demanding more from their gastronomical experiences, a set of "rules" developed governing the pairing of food and wine. The classic is red wine with meat and white wine with fish, but as chefs became more inventive, the number of rules grew. The truth is food and wine pairing is somewhat subjective, but there are certain principles that can guide you.

The Dynamics of Food and Wine

Food and wine are like a pair of ballroom dancers. Each one affects the performance of the partner. Sometimes they're slightly out of step, but sometimes their footwork meshes seamlessly. On occasion, they move as one and transform a simple dance into a moment of magic. Even on those rare occasions when both partners seem to have two left feet, the experience was still probably worth it.

Food and wine, whatever their individual personalities, influence the way each other tastes. A particular food can exaggerate or diminish the flavor of a wine. A certain wine can overwhelm a certain dish.

Wine as a Condiment

Cooks who are passionate about wine often choose the wine first and match the food to it. The general practice, however, is to start with the food and add the wine later. When the time comes to pick the wine, it helps to think of the wine as a condiment. The most basic step in matching wine and food is to assess their common flavors and textures.

Fine dining restaurants exert a great deal of effort in this department. Many menus will suggest wines for each course, and these recommendations are not made at the whim of the chef. Before anything gets into print, the chef, the sommelier, and sometimes the wait staff all taste-test various combinations. They might taste Hermitage and Bordeaux with the rosemary-crusted rack of lamb or Sancerre and Chablis with the seared scallops tossed in butter and ginger.

They compare and discuss, and often disagree, but they save time by knowing that some food textures (creamy, oily, crunchy) simply will not complement certain wine textures (crisp, astringent, viscous).

Too Many Variables

It used to be you could order a steak and French fries and a glass of Cabernet. Things became more complicated with the advent of fusion food, with dozens of ingredients in one preparation.

Ingredients are not the only things influencing the flavors of a dish; cooking processes do as well. You can have your food baked, boiled, broiled, grilled, poached, sautéed, fried, marinated, pasteurized, tenderized, and liquefied. You would not suggest the same wine with baked chicken as you would for barbecued chicken.

Wine can be even more complicated, with thousands of grapes, endless blending combinations, a dry-to-sweet continuum, oak-aging variables, and numerous alcohol ranges, to name a few. It's enough to make you want to throw your hands up in defeat and just order a beer. Rest assured that only a handful of food and wine pairings with actually ruin your meal. What follows is simply to help you get the most out of your dining experience, whether at home or at a restaurant.

Matching Likes to Likes

The following principles won't tell you exactly what to order on your next night out, but they'll help you understand why some foods and some wines make compatible partners. The principles are based on the four tastes that the tongue can discern—sweet, sour, salty, and bitter—and the idea is to match similar tastes in both the food and the wine.

A Sour Taste in Your Mouth

Foods that have a sour component are good matches for wines that are high in acid. A salad with a vinaigrette dressing and a fish fillet squirted with lemon both cry out for a high-acid wine. Acid is the bridge connecting the wine and the food. Compare the sensation of squeezing some lemon juice onto your tongue with that of sipping a Sauvignon Blanc. Your mouth will pucker. That's the acidity. (Notice here that you're not matching the wine to the fish fillet itself or to the lettuce in the salad. You're taking into consideration the preparation.) Tomatoes, onions, green peppers, and green apples are examples of other high-acid foods.

Savvy Sipping

Acidity is much more important in the taste and structure of white wines than red wines. Red wines do have acidity, although in many of them the bitterness of tannins influences your perception of that acidity. White wines have minimal tannins, so acidity plays a greater role.

Potential high-acid wine partners include Sauvignon Blanc and the northern French whites of Sancerre, Pouilly-Fumé, Vouvray, and Chablis. The wines of Alsace and Germany generally have high acidity. The acids in reds are often masked by the tannins, but safe bets are Italian reds. (Why do you think Italian wines go so perfectly with tomato-based pasta sauces?) The following whites are listed from low acid levels to high acid levels:

- Gewürztraminer (low)
- California Chardonnay (low to medium)
- Pinot Gris/Pinot Grigio (medium)
- Champagne (medium to high)
- Chablis (high)
- Chenin Blanc (high)
- Sancerre/Sauvignon Blanc (high)
- German Riesling (high)

Sweet Thing

The sweeter the food, the less sweet and more dull a wine will taste. If you pair a slice of roast pork with a glass of off-dry Chenin Blanc, the sweetness of the wine will be obvious. Top your pork with a heaping spoonful of pineapple glaze and your glass of wine will taste positively dry. When you get to dessert, the rule of thumb is to drink a wine that's sweeter than your food. Even a moderately sweet wine can taste thin, unpleasantly dry, and even sour when you pair it with a sugar blockbuster. Some suggested pairings:

- Pear tart and Sauternes
- New York cheesecake and Muscat
- Bread pudding and late harvest Riesling
- Tiramisu and Port
- Dark chocolate mousse and Banyuls

Vino Veritas

Is there a way to tell how sweet or dry a wine is before you buy it? Look at the size of the bottle. Most dry wines are packaged in 750 ml bottles. Historically, dessert wines come in 375 ml half-bottles.

Don't Be Bitter

Bitterness in wine is caused by tannins, compounds that enter the wine from the skins of the grape submerged in the fermentation tank with the grape juice. Oak barrels also impart tannins, but skins are the main source. Tannins only apply to red wines. When you eat food with a hint of bitterness (olives, bok choy, or sauerkraut) and drink a wine with some bitterness, the bitterness and accompanying astringency is magnified. So be careful pairing Cabernet Sauvignon with German food! The following red wines are listed from low to high tannin levels:

- Beaujolais (low)
- Pinot Noir (low)
- Sangiovese (medium)
- Merlot (medium)
- Zinfandel (medium to high)
- Syrah/Shiraz (high)
- Cabernet Sauvignon (high)

Salt of the Earth

There are no salty wines, but there are plenty of salty foods: ham, smoked salmon, oysters, and teriyaki beef. The best way to cut salt is with high-acid wines. The salt in the food can also minimize the tartness of the wine and amplify the fruit.

More Than Taste

Once you understand how the taste of food and the taste of wine influence each other, the next piece to consider is how weight or body affects food and wine match. Wine, like food, has power. Compare a Champagne Brut with a Napa Valley Cabernet Sauvignon. The latter has more muscle. The Champagne would never hold up to a fiery French pepper steak the way the Cabernet would.

Alcohol is one of the contributors to a wine's sense of body and weight. The higher the alcohol, the greater the body or heavier the weight. So, even before tasting the wine, you can gauge its body by its alcohol content. A fuller-bodied wine will generally have more than 13 percent alcohol. Lighter-bodied wines typically are under 13 percent alcohol.

Cutting the Fat

A common impression is that tannic wines will "cut the fat." This is true, but not in the sense that it cuts the fat content of your ten-ounce filet mignon. Tannins are attracted to fatty proteins. As you chew your steak, your mouth is left with a coating of those fatty proteins. When you sip your glass of Cabernet, the tannin molecules attach themselves to the protein molecules—taking them along for the ride when you swallow. Not only is the Cabernet well matched in terms of weight, the ability of the steak to rob the wine of its tannins really brings out the rich, dark fruit of the wine.

Spice Up Your Life!

When you walk on the fiery side with dishes from Thailand, Mexico or India, choosing a wine can be tough. Your usual dry favorites somehow make the exciting heat of the food downright painful. Tannins and alcohol are to blame. However, this does not mean you have to put wine aside altogether and reach for a glass of milk.

A sweeter, lower-alcohol wine is a much more soothing match for spicy foods. Try an off-dry Riesling or Gewürztraminer. If you only like red wine, Pinot Noir and Beaujolais are definite candidates, with their lower alcohol and tannin levels.

Message in a Bottle

It's not foolproof, but one way to estimate a wine's tannin level is by its color. The lighter it is, the less tannin the wine is likely to have. It stands to reason: The longer the skins stay in contact with the clear grape juice during fermentation, the more color and tannins they impart.

Wine and Cheese: The Classic Match

Wine and cheese both date back to ancient times—although cheese is the newer kid on the block by about 4,000 years. Wine and cheese both reflect their place of origin and continue to mature as they age. With so much in common, their matchup is a natural.

An old wine merchant's saying goes, "Buy on an apple and sell on cheese." It means that wine sipped with a sweet, acidic fruit will taste thin and metallic. The same wine drunk with cheese will seem fuller and softer. While not all wines pair well with all cheeses, certain pairings are classics:

- Goat cheese and Sancerre
- Brie and unoaked Chardonnay or Pinot Noir
- Mozzarella and Chianti
- Parmigiano-Reggiano and Barolo
- Gouda and Riesling
- Chèvre and Gewürztraminer
- Sharp Cheddar and Cabernet Sauvignon
- Stilton and Port
- Roquefort and Sauternes

Wine and Cheese Pairing Guidelines

With the almost infinite number of wines and cheeses available, experimentation is a fun way to learn. These guidelines help narrow your options:

- The **softer** the cheese, the more it coats your mouth, requiring higher acidity in the wine.
- The **sweeter** the cheese, the sweeter the wine should be. Some mild cheeses, especially, have a sweetness that requires an off-dry wine. Dry wines may be perceived as acidic.
- **Strong, pungent** cheeses need strong wines. Extreme flavors in cheese can be matched by big red wines, sweet wines, and fortified wines.
- The **harder** the cheese, the higher level of tannins a wine can have.

Warning: Bad Matches Ahead

Some foods are difficult to match with wine—not impossible, but problematic. Here are a few of the less than ideal candidates for wine partnerships:

- Artichokes
- Olives
- Asparagus
- Spinach
- Chocolate

When "difficult" foods are part of the menu, there's a way to get around the food-wine clash (assuming the difficult partner isn't the only food on the plate): Take a bite of something neutral, such as rice or bread, between bites and sips. Some difficult foods can be made less difficult with the addition of salt or a squirt of lemon, but they might still impart a metallic taste or blast of bitterness when you bring them together with your favorite red wine.

Enemies of Food

On occasion, the wine is the difficult partner. There are some elements in wine that, when in full force, just don't taste good with food. Alcohol is one of them. It's a defining part of wine, but highly alcoholic wines are better drunk by themselves. More often than not, lower alcohol wines are more flexible with foods.

Oak can be another problem. The toasty or vanilla flavor it adds is pleasant and popular, but is hardly a friend of food. These wines might be best enjoyed during the cocktail hour before you sit down to dinner.

Fail-Safe Measures

If you ever find yourself frantically trying to put together a last-minute dinner for your wine-savvy son and his new girlfriend whom you haven't yet met, there is no time to consult your list of food and wine pairing rules. When situations such as these occur, here are some fast and easy ways to make your food and wine experience more enjoyable.

Back to the Home Country

If your meal has German, Italian, French, or Spanish connections, the simple wine solution comes from the home country. Europeans have rarely made a big deal about matching food and wine. They just cooked the way they wanted and made wines that went well with their foods. Globalization of wine notwithstanding, Europeans still produce wines that taste good with their traditional fare.

If paella is on the menu, a red Rioja will be the best choice. Schnitzel and spaetzle? German Riesling. Osso buco screams for Barolo, and a Côtes du Rhone would nicely complement your pot-au-feu.

Instantly Food-Friendly Wines

Of course, the system breaks down when the ethnic region of choice has no long history of winemaking. Chinese, Thai, Cuban, and Indian cuisines come to mind immediately. There is still hope, however. Some wines are just naturally friendly. They make ideal dining partners no matter what you eat. You can choose one of them in any situation with the confidence that it will make a good match:

1. Champagne or sparkling wine
2. Riesling, if you're in the mood for white
3. Pinot Noir, if you feel like a red

Savvy Sipping

If the dish you're serving is overly salty and you can't repair the food somehow, the wine can come to the rescue. Serve a wine on the sweeter side—perhaps an off-dry Riesling or Muscat. It will make the food taste less salty.

Cooking with Wine

"I cook with wine; sometimes I even add it to the food." It's a funny line from W. C. Fields, but the underlying idea illuminates one of the surest ways to successfully match wine with a meal: Cook with the same wine you serve.

Wine Quality for Cooking

The best chefs and home cooks wouldn't be caught dead shaking powdered Parmesan from a can onto their spaghetti. Their meals are magnificent because they use the finest and freshest natural ingredients, and they also know not to skimp on the wine as an ingredient.

You've undoubtedly run across bottles of "cooking wine" during your last trip to the supermarket. They are right above the vinegars, which should tell you something. They're tempting to purchase because they cost so much less than a real bottle of wine, but if you wouldn't drink it, don't add it to your marinade! For one thing, the wines they started out with weren't so hot. (Their undrinkability makes them exempt from alcoholic beverages taxes—another reason they're so cheap.) On top of that, they contain salt as a preservative and food coloring to make them look better than they really are. There are plenty of wines available for $10 or less that make perfect candidates for cooking, and for sipping while you cook. Trader Joe's is a perfect place to find such wines.

Other great candidates for cooking are fortified wines, such as port, Madeira, Marsala, and Sherry. Each has a massive concentration of flavor, and they have the ability to stay fresh for quite a while after opening, thanks to their high alcohol content.

Rules for Cooking with Wine

Wine has certain cooking properties that you should be aware of. Some "rules" are hard and fast because they're based on chemistry. Others are based on common sense.

- When using wine in dishes with milk, cream, eggs, or butter, add the wine first to prevent curdling.
- Add table wines at the beginning of cooking to allow the alcohol to evaporate and produce a subtle taste.
- Add fortified wines at the end of cooking to retain their full-bodied taste.
- To intensify a wine's flavor, reduce it. One cup of wine will reduce to ¼ cup when you cook it uncovered for about ten minutes.
- Using wine in a marinade will tenderize in addition to adding flavor.
- If you use wine in a recipe that doesn't call for wine, use it as part of the recipe's total liquid—not in addition.
- Unless the recipe specifies otherwise, use medium-dry to dry wine.
- Use white wine for light-colored and mildly flavored dishes and reds for darker-colored and more highly flavored dishes.

CHAPTER 12

The Cost of Wine: What Goes into the Bottle

You're standing in front of a shelf of Cabernet Sauvignons wondering whether to buy the $10 bottle or the $50 bottle. Your wallet says go for the cheaper one; your palate wonders if the more expensive bottle is five times better. A bottle of wine acquires costs at every stage of its life from the vineyard to the table. Knowing all the costs won't make the $50 bottle any cheaper or the $10 bottle any better. But it will guide you toward realistic expectations and, ultimately, a reasonable decision.

Costs of Wine Production

The fact that one bottle sells for $10 and another for $50 isn't a matter of chance. Winemakers can choose whether they want to make their wines cheaply or expensively. There are lots of variables that go into pricing wine—but it all begins with the grapes.

Growing grapes takes land. Like any real estate, the watchwords for vineyard land are "location, location, location." Some properties are ideal for growing grapes: good soil, proper drainage, good breezes, and the right sun exposure. Of course, not all vineyard land is created equal. Some properties, because of the cachet they acquire, command top dollar. The Napa Valley is a perfect example. In 1960 you could have bought an acre of vineyard land there for $2,000. Today, the average price per acre is $200,000. Not all vineyard land is that exorbitant. Elsewhere in the United States and certainly in areas like South America, you'll find affordable land for growing grapes. The cost of the vineyard land goes into your bottle of wine.

Vino Veritas

Winemakers who produce high-end wines like to brag about the low yields of their vineyards. It's not uncommon to hear about yields of less than a ton of grapes per acre. Contrast this to the grapes headed for the lower-priced wines. The yields can be from six tons per acre up to ten tons per acre.

How the grapes are grown affects price. It stands to reason that the more grapes you grow on an acre of land, the more wine you can make. On the other hand, it's generally agreed that lower yields produce better quality grapes and more concentrated flavors in the juice. So producers of high-quality wines seek to lower yields even though it will result in less juice. A winemaker who grows grapes in high-yielding vineyards will harvest the grapes by machine with minimum labor cost. To achieve lower yields, another winemaker will thin the vines—meaning she'll remove whole clusters of grapes—by hand. The cost of the bottle goes up again.

Buying Grapes

Winemakers who don't grow their own grapes buy them from other growers. The price they pay depends on the grape variety, the location of the vineyard and, of course, supply and demand. In 2009 the average ton of Cabernet Sauvignon grapes from Napa Valley sold for about $4,700, whereas in some parts of California's Central Valley, Cabernet Sauvignon sold for as little as $350 per ton.

Grape variety makes a difference. A less in-demand grape will cost less. In the same year that Cabernet grapes from Napa Valley sold for $4,700 a ton, other grape varieties from the same region had lower price tags. The average cost for a ton of Chardonnay or Pinot Noir grapes was about half the Cabernet price. That too is reflected in your bottle.

Turning Grapes into Wine

Pressing, fermenting, and aging all contribute to price. One winemaker might squeeze as much juice as possible out of the grapes and then ferment it in huge tanks—filtering and bottling after only a few weeks. Another producer might use minimal pressing, using only the free-run juice, and ferment and age the wine in oak barrels.

Oak is a major cost. American oak barrels sell for about $700 each, while French oak barrels can top $1,000 each. Barrels hold about three hundred bottles of wine. The sad part is that these barrels have a short life span. With each successive use, they have a smaller effect on the wine's flavor and eventually have to be replaced. Blue chip producers might use them three or four times before buying new ones. Some producers buy new barrels every year for their most exclusive wines.

More Winemaker Decisions

Once the winemaker has her expensive French oak barrels and begins aging her Cabernet Sauvignon in them, she will probably have to wait a good two years before that bottle hits the marketplace. Some winemakers will age their Cabernets in bottle for an additional year before release. The reality of the business is that winemakers do not make any money in the short term to cover production costs. At least they have time to consider all the other costs looming before them.

Packaging to Sell

When wines are ready for bottling, distinctive packaging is a must. The bottle itself can start at fifty cents and go up to $2 for a thicker, higher-quality version. Corks can cost anywhere from ten cents to $1.

The wine needs a label. First, someone has to design it. Then, the labels have to be printed—at twenty to thirty cents apiece. And before the wine goes out the door, it goes into a cardboard case, which can cost up to $7.

Establishing a Price

The winery has measurable production costs that it has to cover if it's going to stay in business. But, in setting a price for the wine, there are other matters to consider. One is the winery's profit. How does the producer allocate that on a per bottle basis? It will depend on the number of bottles produced. The fewer bottles the winery has to sell, the more it has to charge per bottle. Larger volumes will make up for a smaller per bottle margin.

Another consideration is the perceived value of the wine. The winery wants to position its wine at a price that is in line with other wines of the same caliber and stature. If the producer prices it too high, consumers will buy other wines instead. If the producer prices it too low, not only will the company lose money, but it will hurt the reputation of the wine as well. The winery's goal is to price it high enough to attract serious wine drinkers, but low enough to make sure it all gets sold.

Marketing Costs

Wine producers do advertise, but the money they spend on such outreach pales to what big brands such as Coca-Cola and McDonald's spend. Wine marketing dollars mainly pay for tasting rooms, a sales force, and promotions. In addition, given that wines are sold through distributors in each state means that most of a winery's marketing efforts are directed toward building relationships with those entities, rather than with individual consumers.

The Distribution System

After Prohibition ended, state and federal laws went into effect that separated the activities of the producers of wine (and all alcoholic beverages) and the activities of the sellers, namely the retailers. Enter the distributor or wholesaler—the middleman. This arrangement for conducting business is known as the three-tier system.

How It's Supposed to Work

Say a California winery (tier one) wants to sell its wine in Tennessee. It shops around for a wholesaler (tier two), chooses the one that provides the best deal, and starts shipping wine. The wholesaler sells the wine to retailers and restaurants (tier three) and pays the state the appropriate excise taxes. The retailer then sells the wine to the consumer.

In the process, the wholesaler:

- Ships the wine to its warehouse from the winery.
- Stores the wine in its warehouse.
- Sells the wine to stores and restaurants.
- Delivers the wine to purchasers.

A wholesale operation requires people, buildings, and equipment. While markups will vary, a wholesaler will add about 30 to 40 percent to the cost of your wine.

State-by-State Variations

Every state has a different way of implementing the three-tier system. Some states have state-controlled liquor boards that act as wholesalers. States such as Pennsylvania also assume the retailer role with their state-run stores. State laws may mandate price posting and specify markups, or prohibit quantity discounts and deliveries to retailers' distribution centers.

Some state laws regulate in-state and out-of-state wineries differently. Many states allow in-state wineries to sell directly to consumers but won't allow out-of-state wineries to do the same. Some states allow their own wineries to sell directly to retailers but, again, prohibit out-of-staters from taking part in the same activity.

These practices have been the basis in the last several years of litigation to open up free trade for wine between the states. A coalition of smaller, family owned wineries has argued that the system prevents them from engaging in interstate commerce.

Savvy Sipping

States impose taxes on wine, and they go into the price you pay. The average state excise tax is sixty-seven cents a gallon—the highest being Alaska at $2.50 a gallon and the lowest being Louisiana at eleven cents a gallon. State and local sales taxes also apply. With state budget deficits, many states are considering increasing taxes and fees on alcohol to supplement their income.

The Changing Landscape of Wine Distribution

A couple from Utah goes on vacation to California and visits wine country. While there, they find some wines they'd like to send home to enjoy when they get back. That's when they find out about shipping bans between the states. Utah is one of thirteen states that completely prohibit direct shipment of wine to consumers.

Wineries have always objected to the direct shipping prohibition, but until the advent of the Internet, it was not much more than an irritant to wine drinkers. The power of the Internet to get online merchandise delivered to homes overnight has revolutionized the way people think about free trade and getting the best products at the best prices. These days, with thousands of websites selling wines that aren't available anywhere else, interstate shipping of wine has become a national obsession.

Vino Veritas

There are tens of thousands of different wines available for sale to consumers in the United States, but only a fraction of them have access to the crowded distribution system and are sold through traditional stores. Online retail sales, which include wine, have grown at ten times the rate of store sales.

The Supreme Court Acts

In December 2004 a groundbreaking case, *Granholm v. Heald*, went before the Supreme Court. At issue was the clash between the Twenty-first Amendment, which gives the states the right to regulate their own alcohol sales, and the Commerce Clause of the Constitution, which prohibits states from discriminating against out-of-state competitors. One of the reasons the Supreme Court will hear a case is to settle conflicting decisions by lower courts. In the domain of interstate wine shipping, two court decisions—one in Michigan and one in New York—came to opposite conclusions. Both states discriminated against out-of-state wineries in preference of in-state producers. The Michigan court ruled that Michigan's ban on direct shipping was permitted under the Twenty-first Amendment. The New York Court ruled that the shipping ban was unconstitutional.

Six months later the Court ruled that it's unconstitutional to grant preference to in-state wine shippers, opening the way for interstate shipment of wine. U.S. states must now allow shipment of wine from other states if they permit in-state wine shipments, but states that do not permit shipping wine at all may still continue to ban it.

Big Retailers Flex Their Muscles

Giant retailers such as Wal-Mart and Costco have been able to offer their customers low prices in part because they negotiate large volume buys directly from suppliers. Under the three-tier system in many states, the retailers can't buy from the producers and can't negotiate for lower prices.

Vino Veritas

Of the 6,500 wineries in the United States, only several hundred have an output of more than 10,000 cases per year. The wines from large producers are the ones you see most often in the stores because they're the ones that the wholesalers buy. Small wineries without distributor representation rely more heavily on direct sales to consumers.

Increasingly, the big-box retailers are looking to state courts for remedies, contending that state liquor regulations violate fair trade laws. Those retailers have a big stake in the outcome. While the court cases may take years to resolve, the decisions will affect what consumers ultimately pay for their wine.

From Wholesaler to the Table

The tier-one folks (the producers) and the tier-two people (the wholesalers) have made the wine, packaged it, and delivered it to its selling destination—with their attendant markups. Now, it's on to tier three, the retail store and restaurant.

Places that sell wine come in various forms. Depending on where you live, you can buy wine from a corner market, an exclusive wine shop, a supermarket, or a supersized discount warehouse. The similarity among the venues is an average markup of 50 percent over what the wholesaler charged them.

At a restaurant, three times the wholesale price is the standard markup when you buy a bottle to accompany your meal. The markups can vary among restaurants. A "white tablecloth" restaurant probably charges more than a neighborhood joint for the same bottle.

Message in a Bottle

Charles Shaw wines, better known as "Two-Buck Chuck," introduced a new category of American wines—Super Value Wines—that sell in the $2 range. The winery took advantage of the California grape glut of 2000 and made an exclusive deal with Trader Joe stores to carry its varietals. It made wine cheaper than bottled water, and gave consumers a good reason to buy.

Markup variations occur also within a restaurant's own wine list. The least expensive bottles and the most expensive bottles may have higher markups than bottles in the midrange. Wines sold by the glass, a real convenience to many wine lovers, are unfortunately marked up the most.

Demand for Wine

Scarcity in supply determines wine prices. Consider the so-called "cult" wines of Napa Valley, such as Screaming Eagle, Harlan, and Bond. These critically acclaimed Cabernet Sauvignons are made in such miniscule quantities that wine collectors are willing to pay incredible sums for them. It's a universal economic rule at work. When you have a small supply of a product, you can charge a higher price.

Look at single vineyard wines. The quantity of wine that can be produced in a single vineyard in a single year is finite. When it's gone, it's gone. A winemaker can't go buy more grapes elsewhere. As a result, the price of a winery's single vineyard wine tends to be more expensive than its others.

A Good Review Doesn't Hurt

Like a good movie review, a good wine review can drive demand. When the latest issue of *Wine Spectator* arrives in the mailbox, many wine lovers flock to their local retailers to see if they carry that 95-point Pinot Noir or 98-point Barolo. High-profile experts such as Robert Parker (*Wine Advocate*) and Jim Laube (*Wine Spectator*) have enormous power in spurring sales of wines they endorse.

For other wine lovers, the guy next door has even more influence. Word of mouth is powerful, particularly when the mouth belongs to someone whose opinion you respect. Unlike the movies where the price at the ticket window stays the same regardless of a movie's ratings, a wine's popularity has an eventual effect on price.

Price Influences Demand

Certainly, demand affects price, but it also works the other way around. Consider this revealing, perhaps apocryphal, story about Ernest Gallo, the founder of the giant American wine company. During his early years selling wine, he visited a New York buyer. He offered the buyer two samples of the same red wine. The buyer tasted the first one and asked about the price. Gallo told him it was five cents a bottle. The buyer tried the second wine and asked the price. This time Gallo said the wine cost ten cents a bottle.

The buyer chose the ten-cent bottle. Sometimes, the more expensive the wine is, the more desirable it becomes. The reverse, however, can also be true.

Message in a Bottle

In 2008 the California Institute of Technology released a study indicating that subjects given a flight of wines of increasing price will prefer the more expensive wines. The subjects knew the prices before tasting, and even when the $90 wine was put in a glass marked $10, they preferred the glass marked $90.

A Price-Influences-Demand Case History

In the late 1990s the United States experienced a domestic grape shortage. In order to maximize their revenue, American producers concentrated on making wines that sold for over $14 a bottle. That left a giant opportunity in the low-priced wine market. An Australian company was poised to take advantage of that opportunity.

Back in 1957 Filippo and Maria Casella arrived in Australia from Sicily. After several years of cutting sugarcane and picking grapes, Filippo bought a forty-acre farm. In 1969 he started producing wine. For the next quarter of a century, the Casellas made wine and lived in the small, one story house nestled in their vineyards.

In 1994 Filippo turned the business over to his son John, who expanded the capacity of the winery. By the late 1990s the Casella winery was producing a low priced, well respected wine that, in its first year and a half, sold 19,000 cases.

In January 2001 John took samples of his wine to a New York importer. The importer liked the easy drinking, fruity taste and the $7 retail price, although he had reservations about the kangaroo on the label. Well, they immediately introduced the wine into the American market, and in the first seven months, the Yellow Tail brand sold 200,000 cases. The American wine-drinking public jumped on the bandwagon. Three years after its introduction, sales of Yellow Tail reached 7 million cases.

"Hot" Wines Priced to Sell

The early years of the twenty-first century brought with them an over-supply of grapes to the wine business. Overplanting of vineyards in Northern and Central California led to a glut, and prices took a nosedive. It meant that producers could get inexpensive grapes and upgrade the quality of their wines at the same time. Similar to Yellow Tail's strategy, the domestic producers identified a price they would sell their wines for and tailored their production and marketing plans to make the price possible.

A number of these "market driven" wines were introduced that combined above average quality and prices in the $10 range.

- Rex-Goliath Cabernet, Merlot, Pinot Noir, and Chardonnay: $8
- Castle Rock Winery Cabernet, Merlot, Pinot Noir, Syrah, Zinfandel, Chardonnay, and Sauvignon Blanc: $7 to $12
- Three Thieves Zinfandel, Cabernet, Bianco in one-liter jugs: $7 to $10
- McManis Family Vineyards Cabernet, Merlot, Syrah, Chardonnay, and Pinot Grigio: $9 to $10

CHAPTER 13

The Power of Packaging

Making a great wine is one thing, but presenting it to the consumer in such a way that the consumer will want to buy it is something else entirely. From the label to the cork, the bottle to the box, packaging is a key concern for wineries. In a marketplace where there are literally thousands of wines competing for your attention, a winery will often spend as much time perfecting its labels as it does perfecting its wine.

The Bottle

Where would wine be without the bottle? Actually, in the history of wine, selling wine by the bottle is a fairly recent innovation. Thousands of years ago in Greece, wine was transported in and served from large, often cumbersome jars called amphorae. Although there is evidence the Romans knew how to blow glass bottles, it was not until the seventeenth century that glass bottles became the primary vessel for transporting wine.

Bottle Sizes

Today, the standard bottle size is 750 milliliters. Legend has it that in the early days of glass blowing, one lungful of air blown into a mass of molten glass produced a bottle with a capacity of 750 milliliters. The rest is history.

Larger and smaller deviations from the standard bottle size are easy to find. The most common smaller size is the half bottle (375ml), while the magnum (1.5L, 2 bottles) is the most common larger size. You can also find dry wines in three liter sized double magnums and six liter sized imperials, but these are mainly prized by wine collectors, as larger bottles favor longer, slower aging of the wine inside.

Bottle Shapes

The most common wine bottle shapes in the marketplace are the Bordeaux and Burgundy styles. The next time you buy a bottle of Cabernet Sauvignon, you're looking at the Bordeaux style, with its broader, higher shoulders. Buy a Pinot Noir for your duck confit and you have before you the Burgundy bottle style, with its more slender, graceful shape. Bordeaux and Burgundy are, of course, regions in France, the former known for Merlot and Cabernet Sauvignon grapes, the latter for Pinot Noir and Chardonnay grapes. As these grapes made their way to newer wine regions such as New Zealand and California, the traditional bottle shapes went along with them.

Champagne or sparkling wine bottles will appear in the Burgundy shape, but these bottles will be much thicker and heavier than their counterparts. Champagne bottles must be able to withstand the six atmospheres of pressure pressing against the glass from the inside.

The unique shape of the German wine bottle is loved by consumers but often despised by retailers. The bottles are 750ml in size, but they have much longer necks. Consumers love their graceful appearance, whereas many retailers grumble that their added height makes them more difficult to display. Nevertheless, this bottle shape is a badge of honor for many producers. One German wine region with a bottle shape all its own is Franken, the easternmost of German wine regions. The bottle is called a Bocksbeutel, and it is squat, flask-like, and green in color. In marketing terms, this is a great way to get your bottle noticed.

Bottle Color

Much like the shapes of wine bottles, their colors owe much to tradition and to marketing. Practically, however, darker glass is preferable, as it protects the wine from the damaging effects of light. Wines packaged in clear bottles are meant for immediate consumption, and these often include rosés and crisp, fresh whites such as Sauvignon Blanc.

The Ripe Stuff

Why is there an indentation, or punt, on wine bottles?
Punts make stacking Champagne bottles easier for riddling, while for still wines it provides stability and a convenient place for your thumb as you serve.

To Cork or Not to Cork

Perhaps the most controversial issue in packaging wine is whether to use a cork to seal the bottle. Proponents of cork often say that a wine cannot evolve and improve without it, whereas proponents of screwcaps argue that using corks increases the likelihood that a bottle will be flawed. As the marketing battle rages, this doesn't change the fact that the cork trade is a fascinating one.

Cork Production

Corks come from trees. The cork tree is actually an oak of the *Quercus suber* variety, and it prefers hot, dry Mediterranean climates. Portugal has more cork trees than any other country, some 1.6 million acres of them. Spain is not far behind.

The techniques used to produce wine corks have changed little over the years. Workers remove the outer layer of bark from the tree and leave it outside for about six months to season. This process allows the wood to dry out. The wood is then boiled to remove contaminants and to increase its flexibility. Next, the wood is cut into strips and the individual corks are punched out of them. The corks are then sanitized, usually with a hydrogen peroxide solution, before being assessed for quality and stored. Only the best cork is used for wine closures; most of it is used for floors and bulletin boards.

Why Use Cork?

Cork has been used commercially to close bottles of wine since bottles became widely used for wine transport in the seventeenth century. Cork is flexible, making it easy to insert into the bottle and relatively easy to remove with the proper equipment. Cork also provides a reliable seal against air, too much of which turns a wine into vinegar.

Many supporters of the cork argue that while too much air damages wine, just a little helps a wine evolve over time and develop its refinement and complex array of flavors and aromas. These supporters claim that the cork either allows a microscopic amount of air into the bottle over time for this evolution to take place, or that the cork itself releases air into the wine from the millions of tiny air pockets contained in it. Either way, without the cork, the wine would not change for the better.

Reasons to Ditch the Cork

The main criticism levied against the cork is its susceptibility to flaws, namely TCA contamination. TCA is shorthand for 2,4,6-trichloroanisole, a nasty compound, which, though harmless, can ruin a bottle of wine.

Savvy Sipping

The wine industry estimates that as many as 5 percent of all wines sold worldwide with a cork have been contaminated by TCA.

TCA is also a headache because it can form under a variety of conditions, but its three main catalysts seem to be mold, moisture, and organic phenols. Even if the cork is sanitized properly before it leaves Portugal, a damp California warehouse built with phenol-laced wood siding may cause TCA to form in corks stored there. If such a cork ends up in your wine bottle, the wine will smell like soggy old cardboard.

Cork can also dry out in the bottle if the bottle is not stored on its side. When cork dries out, it shrinks, and that allows copious amounts of air inside the bottle, leading to vinegar.

A Death Knell for the Cork?

For many wine drinkers, a bottle of wine simply must have a cork. Anything else is sacrilegious. Many enjoy the pageantry of hearing the cork pop out of the beautifully labeled bottle before the fragrant liquid flows into the polished glass. The sound of a tin cap being unscrewed can be enough to swiftly kill the evening's elegance.

However, with tainted corks ruining so many wines—disappointing consumers and costing winemakers millions in the process—many in the wine business scrambled to find alternative closures. To ease the transition away from the natural cork, synthetic corks were devised, but screwcaps were not far behind.

Synthetic Corks

Synthetic, or plastic, corks did little to appease cork traditionalists in the early days. Yes, wine lovers still heard the pop, but the early synthetics were difficult to remove and reinsert, and they permitted too much air to enter the bottle. They did have more aesthetic appeal, coming in red, purple, yellow, and black colors.

Vino Veritas

Get out your "church-key" for these drink-me-now sparklers. Unlike other sparkling wines that keep the bubbles locked up with corks, Il Prosecco and Il Moscato from Mionetto Wines are topped with a crown cap. They're lightly sparking—frizzante, in Italian—and low in alcohol. And they're meant to be drunk right away.

Today, the best synthetic corks do not have the flaws of their older siblings. Many are encased in a plastic sleeve that eases their removal from a bottle. This is all well and good, but several synthetic cork producers uses phrases such as "oxygen management" in marketing their wares, a sign that you should not consider long-term aging of bottles with synthetic closures.

Anatomy of a Screwcap

Screwcaps have been a tough sell in the United States, because many of the low quality jug wines emerging from California after Prohibition had screwcaps on them. Countries such as Australia and New Zealand lacked this cultural baggage, and given their malcontent with wine flaws stemming from the cork they were quicker to embrace this closure. Screwcaps are often referred to as the Stelvin closure, a shortened version of Stelcap-vin, the name used by a French company who began releasing them for use in 1959.

Message in a Bottle

Outside the United States, buying boxed wine is not a big deal. In Sweden, 65 percent of wines sold are in the box format, In Australia, the figure is 52 percent. And in Norway, boxed wines make up 40 percent of all wines sold.

Not all screwcaps are created equal, which is good news for those believing that a bottle needs to breathe for the wine inside it to evolve. Screwcap manufacturers have the option of including a polyethylene liner underneath the aluminum alloy cap, and this liner drastically slows, if not stops, the amount of air seeping into the bottle. Many screwcapped white wines have this feature, which preserves freshness. Absent the liner, the screwcap is little different than the natural cork, except that TCA contamination is not possible. Screwcaps also cost less than the highest quality natural corks.

Boxed Wines Come Out of the Closet

Perhaps even more horrifying to wine connoisseurs than a screwcap on a wine bottle is the lack of a bottle in the first place. Indeed, wine packaged in boxes is not intended for long-term aging, but this does not mean that boxed wine cannot be enjoyable. Given the benefits of packaging wine in boxes, it's amazing that more wineries have not made the transition from bottles to boxes. The perception that all boxed wines are cheap swill is the chief factor, but here are the advantages:

- Wines packaged in boxes are in vacuum-sealed bags, which minimize oxidation. When you release some wine from the box, the bag collapses around the remaining wine, keeping the air out. If you buy a Syrah in a 750ml bottle, once you pull the cork and drink a glass or two, the remaining wine will only remain fresh for a few days, thanks to the oxygen that flowed into the bottle. If you buy a box, the wine will remain fresh for up to four weeks.
- Glass bottles are more expensive to produce, so when you buy a three liter box of wine, for example, you get four 750ml bottles for the price of three.
- Boxes consume far less energy to manufacture and transport, generating less than 50 percent of the carbon footprint of bottled wines.
- Boxes don't break, and you don't need a corkscrew to open them. This way you can enjoy that glass of Merlot just about anywhere.

A few of the new wines available in a box are:

- Black Box Chardonnay, Merlot, Cabernet Sauvignon, Shiraz
- Delicato Shiraz, Merlot, Chardonnay, Cabernet Sauvignon
- Jean-Marc Brocard Chablis Jurassique
- Banrock Station Chardonnay, Merlot, Cabernet Sauvignon, Shiraz
- Hardys Chardonnay, Merlot, Cabernet Sauvignon, Shiraz

Vino Veritas

If boxes are so popular, will cans be far behind?
They're here! Sofia Blanc de Blanc, a sparkling wine in a bold, pink, single serving can, is sold in a four-pack—straws included. It's named after Sofia Coppola, daughter of film director Francis Ford Coppola, who just happens to own the winery. It has become the drink of choice at many nightclubs.

The All-Powerful Label

The label on the wine bottle (or box) is undoubtedly the most powerful marketing tool available to a winery. Unless you are familiar with that winery's unique story or reputation, the label is one of the fastest ways to connect you to that bottle begging to be purchased. Wineries do have some control over how the label looks, but governments control the information that must appear on the label. If you understand this information, you can make more informed buying decisions.

Wine labels and the regulations governing them vary from country to country. The specific information on the label has to conform to the rules where the wine is eventually sold—not where it's produced. If a wine is sold in the same country where it's produced, it will have one label. If the wine is also destined for export, it may well have another version of the label—and both labels have to be approved by government agencies in the countries where the wine will be sold. The single thing that all wine labels have in common is that if you see a year printed on the label, that is the year the grapes used to make that wine were harvested.

The United States

The Alcohol and Tobacco Tax and Trade Bureau (TTB) requires that seven items be included on wine labels in the United States:

- **Brand name**—The name of the wine's producer will likely be displayed most prominently on the label. This is the brand name.
- **Class or type of wine**—U.S. wine law recognizes five classes or types of wines: 1) fruit wine (non-grape); 2) rice wine; 3) honey wine; 4) sparkling grape wine; 5) still grape wine. The still grape wine category includes varietal wines, or those bottles that say "Cabernet Sauvignon," "Chardonnay," and "Pinot Noir." Such bottles must contain at least 75 percent of the grape variety listed. In addition, a winery choosing to label a bottle with the grape variety must also include the appellation of origin, or where the grapes came from. If a legally defined area is mentioned, such as Napa Valley, then 85 percent of that bottle must contain grapes grown in Napa Valley. If a specific

vineyard is mentioned on the label, then 95 percent of that bottle must originate from the stated vineyard.

- **Name and address of bottler or importer**—Most of the time, the bottler and the producer are the same. In this case, the words "estate bottled" will appear on the label. If the producer crushed 75 percent or less of the grapes used to make the wine, then other terms may appear.
- **Alcohol content of the wine**—This percentage will appear on all U.S. wine labels. If a wine is less than 14 percent alcohol, the TTB allows a variation of plus or minus 1.5 percent between the alcohol content printed on the label and the actual content of the wine. For wines with an alcohol content greater than 14 percent, the TTB is less generous, allowing a variation of plus or minus 1 percent.
- **Sulfite statement**—Since 1987 wines containing more than ten parts per million of sulfur dioxide must include "Contains Sulfites" on the label.
- **Health warning**—Since 1989 U.S. wine labels must include a statement regarding the potential health risks of alcohol consumption.
- **Net content of the bottle**—The volume of the wine bottle, usually 750 ml, must be included on the label.

France

In order to understand the degrees of specificity of French wine labeling, think of an archery target. The outer circle is all of France. The next-largest circle is a region of France, such as Bordeaux. The next circle in is a district—Médoc, for example. Within that circle is the commune—say, Pauillac. Finally, the bull's-eye: the individual producer—a château or domaine. The better—and usually more expensive—the wine, the more specific is the indicated source of the wine.

Vino Veritas

Beginning with the 1946 vintage, the immortal Chateau Mouton-Rothschild in Bordeaux has commissioned a famous artist to design the label for each successive vintage. Artists have included Salvador Dali and Jean Cocteau.

Therefore, when you buy a bottle of French wine, the producer, or chateau, will appear in the largest type on the label. As the origin of the wine becomes less specific, the type becomes smaller. Even if it is in small print, French law requires that the Appellation of Origin appear on the label if that wine has satisfied the requirements of that prestigious category. Famous Appellations of Origin include Pauillac and Saint-Julien. Wines qualifying for the other French quality levels will have those designations on their labels—VDQS (Vin délimité de qualité supérieure), vin de pays, or vin de table. Very few of these end up on American store shelves.

Bordeaux chateaux lucky enough to be included in the famous 1855 Classification will have "Grand Cru Classe en 1855" on the label, and only the five first growths can put "Premier Grand Cru Classé" on their labels.

The name of the company responsible for that wine, bottle volume, alcohol content, and vintage year must also be included on the bottles.

To an American, one of the glaring omissions on a French bottle of wine is the grape! This seeming omission is the product of centuries of tradition and the French preoccupation with place. The lone exception is Alsace, which does include grape varieties on its wine labels. Here are some guidelines:

- Red Bordeaux wines are largely made from blends of Cabernet Sauvignon and Merlot, with some Petit Verdot and Cabernet Franc added for good measure. White Bordeaux wines are made from Sauvignon Blanc.
- Red Burgundy wines are made from Pinot Noir. White Burgundy wines are made from Chardonnay.
- White wines from the Loire Valley consist of either Chenin Blanc (Vouvray) or Sauvignon Blanc (Sancerre). The red wines are mainly Cabernet Franc.
- Red wines from the Rhone consist of Syrah, Grenache, and Mourvèdre. Whites consist of Marsanne and Roussanne.
- Champagnes are usually blends of Chardonnay, Pinot Noir, and Pinot Meunier.

Italy

Italians also take seriously the French tradition of emphasizing place when it comes to wine labeling. On Italian labels, the producer tends to dominate the label, followed by the region, vintage, and quality designation (DOCG, DOC, IGT, or vino di tavola). In Italy, however, there are always exceptions.

Some regions are named after the grape variety largely grown within its borders, such as Barbera d'Asti and Dolcetto d'Alba, and this can make choosing an Italian wine easier. Other bottles list only the regions, such as Barolo (Nebbiolo grape) and Chianti (Sangiovese). Often the name of the wine itself, which in Italy usually corresponds to the single vineyard of origin, dominates the label. The following terms may also pop up here and there:

- **Bianco:** white
- **Classico:** usually given to wines which epitomize the characteristics of a given region, such as Chianti Classico
- **Dolce:** sweet
- **Frizzante:** lightly sparkling
- **Rosato:** rosé
- **Rosso:** red
- **Secco:** dry
- **Spumante:** sparkling

Germany

German wine labels are among the most notoriously difficult to understand, but given the European paradigm of emphasizing place, this should make things easier. In addition, German labels also squeeze the grape variety onto the bottle. Perhaps the most difficult language to penetrate is "Qualitatswein mit Pradikat" (QmP) and "Qualitatswein bestimmer Anbaugebiete" (QbA). The former signifies Germany's highest quality wines, and while the latter can still be quite good and bargains to match, but they do not have the same cache.

A major difference between QmP and QbA wines is that the latter do not carry ripeness levels—Kabinett, Auslese, Spatlese, Beerenauslese, and Trockenbeerenauslese. This is because QbA wines may be chapatilized, or have sugar added to prop up alcohol levels. Chapatilization is forbidden for QmP wines.

Here's another clue for understanding German wine labels: In the German language, adding "er" at the end of a noun makes it possessive. On wine labels, "er" is added to the name of the town or village where the wine was made. The name of the town in the possessive form is followed by the name of the specific vineyard. So, a label that reads "Niersteiner Oelberg Riesling Spätlese" tells you that the name of the town is Nierstein, the vineyard (in the town of Nierstein) is Oelberg, the varietal is Riesling, and the ripeness level is Spätlese.

Another interesting feature of the German wine label is the ten to twelve digit Amtliche Prufungsnummer, or AP number, which appears on every bottle of QmP or QbA wine. A wine with this number on the label has passed the official German testing procedure, and encoded in the number is the village in which the wine was tasted, the village where the estate is located, the grower identification number, the order in which the estate presented its wine to the tasting panel, and the year the wine was presented for approval.

Spain

In the spirit of their French and Italian counterparts, Spanish wines emphasize region on their labels, not the grape varieties used to make them. Quality levels appear—DOCa, DO, and vino de mesa—as do vintage years, alcohol levels, and bottle volumes.

Other terms often show up, such as Crianza, Reserva, and Gran Reserva, but these have to do with the amount of time the wine has spent aging in barrel and bottle, not the ripeness level of the grapes when harvested. The Spanish have an easier time ripening their grapes than the Germans. Gran Reservas are only made in years of exceptional quality.

Australia and New Zealand

Australia and New Zealand are New World wine regions, and one of the hallmarks of such regions is that labeling laws are much less strict. The shorter list of Australian labeling laws is managed by the Wine and Brandy Corporation. Here are the highlights:

- If a grape variety appears on the label, 85 percent of the wine must consist of the named grape.
- If a growing region appears on the label, 85 percent of the fruit must come from that area.

- If two wines are blended together to form a single wine, and neither one accounts for 85 percent of the bottle, they must be listed in descending order of percentage. For example, a Merlot-Cabernet Sauvignon has more Merlot than Cabernet.

Australia's neighbor, New Zealand, shares the same laws, except the percentages drop to 75 percent.

Argentina and Chile

Argentina and Chile are South America's premier growing regions, and they are firmly ensconced in New World traditions. Chilean wine law is the product of conversations between wineries, the Ministerio de Agricultura, and the Servicio Agricola Ganadero. Seventy-five percent is the minimum proportion for varietal, vintage, and place of origin.

Argentina's wine laws could not be more removed from the traditions of Europe. The major standard in the wine industry, as required by the Instituto Nacionale de Vitivinicultura, is that if a grape variety appears on the bottle label, 80 percent of the wine must be composed of that grape.

CHAPTER 14

Strategies for Buying Wine

The world of wine changes every day. New vintages hit store shelves, new boutique wineries pop up all over the world, and wine lovers rediscover old grape varieties. The wine marketplace is no different. American wine consumers, depending on the alcohol laws of their states, have never had more choices or ways to acquire stunning bottles of wine. From the Internet to the auction house, it is now possible to drink better than ever before.

Wine Stores

Depending on where you live, your wine shopping options can be abundant—or severely restricted. With each state able to set rules for wine sales, consumers have unequal opportunities to buy wine. At one extreme are the states that control all aspects of wine sales—from choosing the wines to put on the shelves, to posting store hours, to employing the clerks who bag your purchases. At the other end of the spectrum are states that freely allow sales in locations such as supermarkets, discount warehouses, convenience stores, drugstores, and gas stations, in addition to traditional wine shops.

Anatomy of a Wine Store

Wine specialty stores vary in size, selection, price points, and employee expertise, but they are the best place for the novice wine drinker to start. You have a good chance of finding someone knowledgeable about wine in general, or at least knowledgeable about the store's inventory.

In a store that's run by an owner or that has good staff training, the person behind the counter has likely tasted most of the wines the store carries. She can direct you to the types of wines you're looking for in your price category, suggest alternatives you might enjoy, or help you select a special occasion or food-matched wine.

When you want to explore the wine shelves on your own, it's helpful to know a few things common to most stores:

Organization

Wines are often organized by country of origin. For classic regions like France, wines may be organized into smaller regions such as Bordeaux, Burgundy, and the Rhone. Red wines and whites may be in separate sections. Many stores will organize their wines by varietal. Sparkling wines will likely be in a separate section altogether. Rare and expensive wines are often located in a specially designated, climate controlled room.

"Sale" Wines

At some point every store has to make room for new inventory and will put wines on sale. You'll often find them in special bins or boxes with case cards—large cardboard signs—describing the wines.

Cold Wines

If you are on your way to a friend's house for dinner and need a chilled bottle to take with you, most wine stores have a refrigerator full of wines just for you. You'll generally find bestselling whites along with (sometimes pricey) sparkling wines. If you're picking up a bottle to take to a tailgate bash, you may or may not be able to buy a corkscrew at the same time. Some states prohibit wine stores from selling wine accessories.

It is extremely important to take note of a retailer's storage conditions. Wines parked in the sunlight or in the heat are not being treated well. If a wine shop seems a bit cool to you, that is a good sign. Good wine retailers will also have their wines (except, perhaps, mass market wines that move quickly) lying in a horizontal position.

Shelf Talkers

You've undoubtedly noticed little cards taped to the store shelves that describe individual wines and tell you how well the wine "pairs beautifully with chicken." These are the "shelf talkers," and they are usually written by wholesalers or the wineries that produced the wine. Still other shelf talkers give you numerical scores. These scores come from wine critics deemed professionals in the area of assessing a wine's implicit value. A score of 90 or above will likely attract your attention. These scores typically reflect the preferences of the critic, so use them as guides, not as objective assessments.

Vino Veritas

Supermarkets account for 30 percent of U.S. wine sales. A combination of convenience and attractive pricing is pushing that number upward. Wine selection at supermarkets reflects the personality of the chain: mass market and highly advertised wines at mass retailers and more esoteric bottles at upscale markets.

In-Store Tastings

Some states allow retailers to host wine tastings. These are worth attending because you get to sample a variety of wines before buying anything. The tasting portion will be small, and you may be sampling a wine the store or wholesaler wants to push, but it is still better than buying blind. In areas where in-store tastings are prohibited, retailers often co-sponsor wine tastings with restaurants. Such events are inexpensive ways to sample a variety of wines, and, of course, you know where to buy the wines afterward.

The Miracle of Trader Joe's

If learning about the wines of the world on a budget is your goal, there is no better place to shop than Trader Joe's. One reason why their food and wine is so reasonably priced is because the chain buys direct from suppliers whenever possible. They also buy in volume and contract early to get the best prices. Trader Joe's, unlike many of the larger grocery store chains, refuses to charge their suppliers fees for putting an item on the shelf, and this practice keeps prices low.

In the wine world Trader Joe's is famous for being the exclusive retailer of Charles Shaw wines (also referred to as Two or Three Buck Chuck). These wines are certainly not for long-term aging, as are most of the wines sold at Trader Joe's. This is hardly a criticism; Trader Joe's extends to the American wine consumer an enormous service by offering accessible wines for great prices that also happen to complement many of the food items also for sale.

What Are You Looking For?

The more wines you taste, the more you hone your skills for identifying a good deal. Whether you're a beginner trying to develop your tastes or a wine enthusiast searching for the "ultimate" bottle, the best advice is to get to know your local wine retailer. He can give you more than recommendations. Once he knows your preferences, he can let you know about special arrivals and give you advanced notification of promotions and sales.

Knowing What You Want

With the thousands of bottles confronting you when you walk into a store, it is difficult to know where to start. The best advice is to start small. First, become familiar with a certain grape. If you particularly like Sauvignon Blanc, try Sauvignon Blanc wines from California, New Zealand,

South Africa, Chile, and the Loire Valley of France. An even better strategy is to try them side by side. The differences—and similarities—become obvious.

Another strategy is to become familiar with a particular wine region. If the Cabernet Sauvignon you like is from Alexander Valley, California, try a different Cabernet from that same region. Look for similar tastes that might be due to the climate and soil (terroir).

You can also focus on a producer and try all the wines in its portfolio. If you like the Chardonnay from Napa Valley's Château Montelena, take a chance and buy a bottle of its Cabernet Sauvignon, Zinfandel, and Riesling. The wines are different, but the winemaker and the philosophy of winemaking are the same.

The key is not to be afraid to try new things. There is nothing wrong with purchasing a wine you enjoy over and over again, but if your goal is truly to learn about wine, you must take risks. There are plenty of inexpensive wines available that give you an experience of regional varietals and the philosophies of the winemakers behind them.

Look for Lesser-Known Varietals

Wine and clothing have something in common. Each has styles that go in and out of fashion. One wine varietal can be hot for a time before receding into the background as another takes its place.

Message in a Bottle

When a varietal achieves a certain level of popularity, everyone starts to produce it to cash in on the craze. The inevitable result is an influx of mediocre wines. Merlot is a perfect example. There will always be quality Merlots, but the true fad-chasers will drop what used to be hot and embrace something else, like Malbec.

Popularity is one factor among many determining the price of a bottle of wine. Cabernet Sauvignon and Chardonnay are still among the big sellers, and the best producers will have higher price tags.

For better deals, look here:

FOR REDS, TRY:
- Malbec
- Mourvèdre
- Tempranillo
- Grenache

FOR WHITES, CHECK OUT:
- Chenin Blanc
- Pinot Gris
- Gewürztraminer
- Viognier
- Pinot Blanc

Buy Wines from Less Prestigious Regions

Another great way to save money and still enjoy good wine is to avoid most labels saying Napa Valley, Bordeaux, Burgundy, and Tuscany. Other wine-producing regions around the world with less expensive real estate offer good wine value. If France is your objective, get a bottle from Provence, the Loire Valley, or the Languedoc-Roussillon. If you're in the mood for Italian, look for wines from Campania, Calabria, Puglia, or Sicily. The best Spanish Rioja can be expensive, but thankfully you can still find bargains from regions such as Galicia, Rueda, Navarra, and Priorat. South American wines are also amazing deals, with Chile and Argentina leading the way.

Seek Second Labels

Wineries with world-class reputations are extremely selective about the wines bottled under their primary—and most prestigious—labels. Wines which do not make the final cut are typically bottled under "second" labels. Château Lafite reportedly started this practice in the eighteenth century, and other Bordeaux châteaux have followed suit. Second labels are not bad wines; if they were, why would the winery have bottled them in the first place? In great vintage years, the gap between a winery's primary label and its second label is narrow, making second labels bargains compared to their first label counterparts. Here are second labels from famous Bordeaux châteaux:

- Carruades de Lafite from Château Lafite Rothschild
- Pavillon Rouge from Château Margaux
- Haut-Bages-Averous from Château Lynch-Bages
- Les Pagodes de Cos from Château Cos d'Estournel

The second label phenomenon is not as prevalent among United States wineries. Arguably the two most famous U.S. second labels are Decoy from Duckhorn and Overture from Opus One, both from Napa Valley.

Unknown Producers in Great Years

If Bordeaux has an extraordinary vintage, such as 2000, 2005, or 2009, wine prices from the most famous chateaux will skyrocket. However, a better than average winemaker from a smaller, less prestigious chateau a few miles down the road from Chateau Lafite also benefits from the vintage and can produce great wines at a fraction of the price. Thus, any bottle that has "2000" and "Bordeaux" on the label will likely be more than passable.

In regions such as the Napa Valley, where the climate is more consistent from year to year, smaller, unknown producers will likely charge higher prices for their debut wines, as they have the cachet of the region behind them, in addition to higher business costs.

Check Out the Bin End Sales

When a store is making room for new inventory and puts the old bottles on sale, you could run into some treasures. Larger stores might discount whole cases. This is a bargain hunter's paradise. Because you may not be able to tell at a glance which bottles are treasures and which ones are better for cooking, it is prudent to buy just one and try it out first before investing in more.

Buy by the Case

Most retailers offer case discounts and will let you fill the twelve bottle slots with the wines of your choice. The usual case discount is 10 percent, although some wine merchants offer higher discounts if you buy a case of the same wine. You don't need to have an elaborate wine cellar to take advantage of case savings. It just makes sense if you buy wine on a regular basis.

Buying Wine Online

If you use the Internet regularly, you probably cannot imagine how you lived without Amazon.com. At the click of a mouse, books, music, sporting goods, and more will arrive at your doorstep. Ever wanted to try real Spanish saffron but can't afford the plane ticket to Madrid? Visit *www.tienda.com* and have some shipped to you. If only wine were so easy to buy online. Because wine is a highly regulated product, many obstacles stand in the way of prospective online wine retailers. If you've already tried making an online wine purchase, you've noticed that one of the first questions you're asked is where you live. Your state of residence determines whether wine can be shipped to you.

Savvy Sipping

In September 2008 Amazon.com announced its plans to begin selling wine online. By October 2009, the company abandoned the enterprise, citing the myriad of laws regulating the shipment of alcohol from state to state.

Wine-searcher.com and Snooth.com

If you live in Indiana and wish to purchase a bottle of Loire Chenin Blanc from a California online wine merchant, you will be denied due to shipping laws. However, this does not mean that Indiana residents should abandon the Internet entirely for their wine shopping needs. Perhaps that bottle of Loire Chenin Blanc is available at a wine shop down the street. You could just call the shop and ask if they have it, but why not learn more about the Loire and Chenin Blanc and compare prices on other Chenin Blancs at the same time? Enter wine-searcher.com and snooth.com.

Wine-searcher.com was founded in New Zealand in 1999. On the homepage, you begin by entering any information about a wine—vintage, producer, region—followed by your country and/or state of residence. You can even enter your zip code. At the click of a mouse, you learn which wine retailers nearby carry that wine and what they charge for it.

Snooth.com takes the wine-searcher.com theme to a whole new level. Not only does it connect you to local retailers, it also connects you to other lovers of Loire Chenin Blanc, for example. You can learn which ones are worth buying while downloading a recipe to complement the one you eventually decide to buy!

Buying Direct from Wineries

All fifty states have wineries, and many of these have online wine shops. Again, where you live determines whether a winery can ship directly to you, but it is worth the effort to explore the shipping options available.

For example, Napa Valley sparkling wine producer Domaine Carneros can ship to Indiana residents! Indiana is one of three "Nondirect Three Tier" states, which means that Domaine Carneros must first send a shipment to a local distributor, then to a local retailer, and then, finally, to the consumer's home. That consumer will pay more for the shipment, thanks to taxes collected at each stage, and it could take weeks for the shipment to arrive, but at least shipping is possible.

There are many states to which even Domaine Carneros cannot ship. Besides the winery itself, a good resource for learning about your state's alcohol shipping regulations is the Wine Institute (*www.wineinstitute.org*).

Online Wine Clearing Houses

Recessions are a nightmare for wineries, but they can pose great opportunities for wine lovers. During recessions, expensive wines just sit in warehouses, but wineries need to move them to make room for the new vintage that just rolled off the bottling line.

This reality has given rise to websites such as *http://cinderellawine.com* and *http://thewinespies.com*, which offer buyers exclusive one day only specials on exclusive wines at drastically reduced prices. Buyers can sign up for email alerts that announce deals as soon as they become available. Deals usually expire at midnight or earlier if the wine sells out quickly.

Rare Finds at Auctions

If you are a serious wine collector, you need to be aware of what happens at wine auctions. Not only will you get a sense of what your bottles are worth, you may be able to pick up cases of less-famous bottles you particularly like without taking out a second mortgage on your house. Buying older wines from auction houses is always the best course, as these institutions have experts who have verified that the wines up for auction are authentic and were stored properly. The most reputable wine auction authorities in the United States are Hart Davis Hart of Chicago and Sotheby's and Christie's of London, each with major operations in New York City.

Vino Veritas

Some of the wines you read about in newspapers that are sold for astronomical sums at auction aren't even drinkable. The 1787 Château Lafite that sold at Christie's for $160,000 was acquired for collecting—not consuming. It had at one time belonged to the famous enophile, Thomas Jefferson.

If you attend a wine auction, expect to pay a buyer's premium of 10 to 15 percent of your bid. One way to avoid spending yourself into a hole when the bidding gets fierce is to obtain the catalog ahead of time, identify the wines you want, and set bidding limits for yourself. Of course, this is easier said than done, especially if the auction is benefiting a worthwhile organization that will put your money to good use.

Keeping Track of What You Like

Whether you are a casual or serious wine connoisseur, you will inevitably taste wines you either love or loathe. Given the vast array of wines available in the marketplace, it is practically impossible to remember exactly what you tasted at what event, unless you find a way to write at least one sentence about each wine you try. Writing something down is critical to remembering, and regarding wine, you will capture your preferences and avoid unnecessary disappointments down the road.

If all varietals were created equal, remembering what you enjoyed wouldn't be so difficult, but not all Chardonnays are the same, and no two Merlots taste alike. It is not uncommon for someone to taste a certain type of wine—maybe an Australian Shiraz—and become an instant devotee. That same person may, over time, come to realize that she really only likes one Shiraz out of every three or four she tastes. Without record keeping, it may take a while to track down the producer of the one she liked most.

A Wine Journal

You can easily purchase an "official" wine journal at certain retail locations, with pages designed to help you remember all the information you need to record about a wine. If you only have a generic pad of paper, here's some of the information you need to jot down:

- Name of the wine
- Name of the producer
- Country and region
- Vintage year (if it has one)
- Price
- Where and when you tasted it (and with whom)
- Food you ate with it
- Color
- Aroma
- Taste
- Any other comments that may help you remember the wine later

One of the most helpful visual elements in remembering a wine is the label. Removing it can be frustrating, but there are products on the market that can simplify the task. One popular label removal system is a large adhesive strip that you lay over the label and then pull away from the bottle. It splits the wine label and removes only the printed surface, which you can adhere to the page of your journal.

Getting the label off without such aids can be a snap—or it can be problematic, depending on the adhesive the bottler uses. To test, use a razor to take up the corner of the back label. If the back of the label is sticky, fill the empty bottle with the hot water and let it stand for a few minutes. Test the back label again by sliding the razor under the label. It should peel right off.

If the back of the label isn't sticky, you've got more work to do. After you've filled the bottle with hot water, submerge the whole bottle into more hot water and let it soak. It could take minutes or hours. Then try removing the label, starting the process with the razor. A last resort is to add soap or ammonia to the soaking water. The process might be more fun if you drink wine along the way.

CHAPTER 15

Enjoying Wine at Home

Wine is an amazingly versatile beverage. It can complement a weekday meal at home, add elegance to a formal dinner party, or even be the focal point of a casual gathering of friends. Just like you would never present yourself at a formal dinner party wearing jeans, how you prepare, present, and serve wine can greatly help you and your guests get the most enjoyment out of that bottle.

Proper Storage Conditions for Wine

Wine changes over time, often for the better, and one way to ensure that your bottles survive until that special dinner or event takes place is to store them properly. It is true that some wines do get better with age, but you must still handle them carefully to enjoy them at their best.

Temperature

If you plan to store a reputable Napa Valley Cabernet Sauvignon or Italian Chianti for a decade to enjoy at your twenty-fifth wedding anniversary, temperature should be your number one consideration. The ideal temperature is 55°F. If this is impossible, at least make sure the temperature in your storage area is lower than 70°F. Cool temperatures slow the aging process; higher temperatures cause wines to develop prematurely.

Short-term exposure to high temperatures can also be destructive. Leaving that case of Syrah in the trunk of your car for a few hours on a hot August day should be fine, but taking a three day detour through the desert will literally bake the wine. That $60 bottle of Syrah will now taste like stewed prunes.

When storing wine, it's better to err on the side of too cold than too hot. However, drastic temperature swings, such as repeatedly taking the bottle out of the refrigerator and putting it back in, can adversely affect your wine. Temperature fluctuations change the pressure inside the bottle, such that the cork begins to push out ever so slightly. This can increase the amount of air entering the bottle, and you will quickly have a bottle of vinegar.

Light

Cool temperatures will do little good if ultraviolet light strikes the bottle. Sunlight is the biggest culprit. Just as free radicals from sunlight cause the skin to wrinkle, they also promote oxidation of wine. White wines in clear bottles are the most vulnerable to such damage, but over time, ultraviolet light will also affect your Bordeaux in the dark green bottle.

Bottle Orientation

Bottles with real corks should be stored on their sides to maintain contact between the cork and the wine. Without this contact, the cork may dry out, shrink, and let in air. This obviously does not apply to bottles with screw caps and synthetic corks, but make sure such bottles are still stored in cool, dark places.

Wine Refrigerators

For amateur and serious wine collectors alike, a wine refrigerator will address many of your storage concerns. With a modest investment of a $100 or so and access to a standard wall electrical outlet, you can pamper your wines with ideal temperature, humidity, and positioning. Compact units may only hold six to twenty bottles, but the more you spend, the more options you have. For a few thousand dollars, your wine refrigerator can have a 700 bottle capacity, mahogany racking, digital cooling system, and French doors.

Wines Worth Cellaring

Not all wines age gracefully. Some are the drink-me-now kind of wines that will only decline over time. This is not to say that you won't want to include young drinking wines in your collection. Just put them in an obvious location so you'll remember to drink them before it's too late.

For advice about aging specific wines, ask the salesperson at the time of your purchase, or go to the winery's website, which may contain cellaring information. Aging wine is not predictable with any precision. However, consider some general tips on aging for these popular varietals and categories.

Cabernet Sauvignon

Cabs are meant for aging. Just how long depends on the quality of the wine. Cabs from Napa and Bordeaux can improve over decades. Check out the best vintages, because frankly, a mediocre wine at the time of release isn't going to develop into a better wine no matter how long you keep it. The softer, more easy drinking Cabs will cellar nicely for a couple of years. The sky's the limit for serious, collectible Cabs.

Merlot

Not all Merlots are soft, fruity, and simple. Remember, this is one of the "noble" grape varieties. It has the potential to be every bit as big, powerful, and robust as the noble Cab—if in a more velvety style. Drink inexpensive Merlots soon after you bring them home. A high quality Merlot can age for five to twenty-five years, maybe longer.

Nebbiolo

Nebbiolo-based wines—particularly Northern Italy's Barolo and Barbaresco—hold up well for long-term cellaring. Age releases their complexity. Barolos will age for fifteen to forty years. Barbaresco will age for somewhat less.

Pinot Noir

Pinot shows its finicky personality all through its growing and production stages. Predicting its ageworthiness with any precision is no picnic either. Fine Burgundies have been known to evolve into real beauties over several decades. But Pinots from California, Oregon, and New Zealand, for example, are probably at their peak at seven to ten years.

Syrah/Shiraz

Syrah/Shiraz, as a varietal on its own or in blends, has maturing potential. In wines of the Rhone, Syrah is the principal grape. Côte Rôtie can easily age for ten years or more, and Hermitage, intense and tannic in its youth, can age fifteen to forty years.

Riesling

Of all white wines, Riesling is the longest-lived. The best German Rieslings have a history of tasting delicious after decades of aging. In fact, the young ones can be austere and benefit from cellaring. The aging potential of Rieslings from other parts of the world varies, but a general guideline is from two to ten years.

Chardonnay

Chardonnays are all over the map in terms of longevity, although great Chardonnays outlast most other whites. With Chardonnays, you can pretty much determine cellaring potential by price. Drink less expensive ones soon after purchase. Higher priced ones will improve for at most a decade.

Dessert Wines

Dessert wines, particularly fortified wines, having huge cellaring potential. Vintage Ports—with their high alcohol, good acidity, and plentiful tannins—have been known to outlive their owners. It's not unusual to hear about Port lasting 100 years. Wines with a lot of sweetness, such as Sauternes, ice wines, and late harvest Rieslings, can age gracefully for many years.

Message in a Bottle

Only after tasting a wine do you really know if it needs further aging. So what are you supposed to do if you have only one bottle? A quick and easy (although not foolproof) method of deciding what bottles to age is by price. If you paid more than $30 for the bottle, it might be worth saving. If you paid less, drink up!

"Balanced" Choices

The wines you choose for cellaring—just like the ones you choose for immediate consumption—should be balanced. It's especially important for aging considerations because whatever is out of whack with a wine will become more pronounced over time. A few things to consider:

- **Alcohol**—If a wine tastes of too much alcohol now, it will only taste more so later.
- **Acid**—Acidity is critical for long-term aging, but if it overpowers the wine's other components in the short term, it will become even more pronounced in the long term as the fruit fades.
- **Oak**—Oak doesn't mellow. It can overpower the other elements after long aging.
- **Tannin**—Tannin is definitely tamed with age, but if the tannin is overbearing to start, it might outlast its fruit partner.

The Power of the Glass

Once you bring out your perfectly stored bottle of 1961 Chateau Petrus and your friends gasp in disbelief, it's time to serve that wine in a fitting container. A stemless plastic cup will not totally mask the wine's delicate bouquet, but better choices are available. If you want the wine to sing, use the proper glass, which, unlike plastic, is inert and doesn't affect the taste of the wine. However, if your glass does not meet the following criteria, it will detract from your enjoyment of that wine.

- **Clean**—You might think that goes without saying, but there are all sorts of lingering "contaminants" that can make a wine taste off. Even if you've done your best in washing the glass but haven't rinsed it well, it will have detergent residue. If you've dried it with a dirty dishtowel, it'll have the telltale odor. Even dust will affect the wine's taste.
- **Clear**—Most wine enthusiasts will tell you it's important to see the wine—to check its clarity, to determine its age, or to just admire the color. A colored glass will not let you do any of those.
- **Thin**—In case a wine is served too cold, a thin glass will warm it more quickly.
- **Stemmed**—The stem is the handle of the wine glass. Holding the glass by the bowl more quickly warms the wine past its proper temperature.
- **Tulip-shaped**—The bowl should narrow at the rim. This will keep you from spilling when you swirl. It will also capture the aromas and not let them evaporate before you get your nose to the glass to sniff.

Message in a Bottle

Once you move beyond the basics of stemware, other details might be important to you. Crystal, with an inherently rougher surface than glass, will create more turbulence when you swirl your wine—adding to the aromas. If you want different glasses for reds and whites, the one for reds should have a rounder bowl than the one for whites because reds are generally more aromatic.

Buying Wineglasses

Do you need a different wineglass for each kind of wine? No. Do you *want* a different glass for each wine? Only you can answer that. It certainly depends on your interest, your budget, and your storage space. If you're just starting a glassware collection, it's helpful to know which ones to buy first, second, and third. This is a logical approach to purchasing stemware:

1. Start out with a twelve-ounce glass. You might think that sounds pretty big considering that a typical serving of wine is four to five ounces. But you want to leave plenty of room for swirling. You can use this as an all-purpose glass for either red or white wine.

2. A Champagne flute should be next on the list. Champagnes are the only wines that shouldn't be served from an all-purpose glass. The flute is tulip-shaped to keep the effervescence contained. The sherbet-style glasses let the bubbles dissipate too quickly.

3. Now it's time for another all-purpose glass—either larger or smaller. It depends on whether you want to use it for red wines (which traditionally are served in the larger glass) or for white wines. This decision will depend on your personal preference. If you want to choose whatever is in fashion, opt for the larger one.

4. If you especially enjoy dessert wines and fortified wines, your next purchase should be a copita. It looks like a miniature version of the Champagne flute. The average serving size of a dessert wine is two to three ounces—so a smaller glass is called for.

Opening the Bottle

Even though wine producers are increasingly turning to screw tops instead of corks as closures for the bottles, corks are still the traditional closure—and will probably be around for some time to come. So if you're going to drink wine at home, you'll need a corkscrew. There are hundreds—maybe thousands—of corkscrews available. But they fall into some general categories.

From the low-tech end of the spectrum are the "pullers." You probably have one in a drawer that some company gave you instead of a pen with the company logo on it. They take the form of a T-shape with a handle and a worm. There are no moving parts, which is why it depends on sheer force (yours) to get the cork out of the bottle.

The two-pronged puller requires less force but more finesse. It has no worm but two blades that you wedge into the bottle to grip the sides of the cork and pull. Professionals like it particularly for older corks that are in danger of crumbling. It's known as the "Ah-So," and it takes some practice to use.

Lever-type corkscrews can take a variety of forms from something you can put in your pocket to something you can mount on the wall. The most ubiquitous lever type is the butterfly corkscrew. It has a worm and butterfly-winged handles for leverage. The simplest lever corkscrew is the "waiter's friend"—so-called because it's the favorite among restaurant servers. It's got either a dual or single lever. Then there's the popular "rabbit" corkscrew with gripping handles on the sides and a top lever handle.

Vino Veritas

What is a worm?
The worm is not something you find at the bottom of the bottle as you do in certain tequilas. It's the curly metal prong found on most corkscrews that bores into the cork for removal. To avoid getting cork pieces into your wine while you're extricating the cork, be sure the worm doesn't go completely through the cork.

Before you can insert any corkscrew into the cork, you have to remove the capsule that surrounds the cork end of the bottle. Cut off the capsule with a small knife or with the foil cutter that comes with many corkscrews. To avoid wine dripping over the edge of the foil, be sure to cut it low enough on the neck of the bottle—under the second lip of the bottle.

Before You Fill the Glasses

Once the right glasses have been selected and the cork successfully pulled, the party is not necessarily ready to begin. Different wine styles require different serving temperatures. Some require decanting, others don't. Whether you are pouring just for yourself or for a room of twenty people, there are a few more considerations to make if you really want the wine to impress.

Serving Temperature

The proper storage temperature of a wine is not necessarily the proper serving temperature of that wine. Pouring a glass of young Cabernet Sauvignon at 53°F will cause you or your guests to cringe at the accentuated astringency from the tannins. Serving any wine too cold masks its aroma and flavor. On the other hand, serving a wine too warm will make it seem flat and dull and overly alcoholic.

The familiar rule for red wines is to serve them at room temperature. This maxim stops being relevant if you enjoy a room temperature of 80°F. For white wines, the wine is too cold if you serve it immediately from the refrigerator. Before you start sticking thermometers in everyone's wine, here are some guidelines:

- Sparkling wines and young, sweet white wines: 45 to 50°F
- Dry whites and rosés: 50 to 60°F
- Light-bodied reds: 55 to 65°F
- Bold reds: 62 to 68°F

Message in a Bottle

Before serving a white wine you think is too cold or a red wine you think is too warm, follow the Twenty Minute Rule. Twenty minutes before you serve your wines, remove the white from the refrigerator to warm it up a bit, and replace it with the red to cool that one off. The quickest way to chill a white wine is to submerge the bottle in a container of half ice and half water.

When to Let a Wine Breathe

Once you pop the cork, air is now that wine's best friend. Whether the wine is white, red, young, or old, a little air does a lot of good. After a few good swirls, the wine's aromas become more intense. In young red wines with high tannins, exposure to air "softens" the tannins and makes the wine less bitter and astringent. You may even enjoy that young Napa Cab even more an hour after pouring. Older wines are more fragile, of course, but a little air can blow off any initial off-aromas and release the glories underneath.

Savvy Sipping

Oops! You somehow got fragments of cork into the bottle of wine. Or you discover, just minutes before serving, that your wine has sediment. There's no time to let things settle. You can filter the wine into a decanter through clean fabric such as muslin or through a paper coffee filter with no adverse effects.

Some people have interpreted breathing as simply uncorking the bottle in advance of pouring. The truth is wine can't breathe in the bottle. The neck is just too small to let enough air inside. Studies involving wine experts have demonstrated that no one can really tell the difference between a wine that's been breathing in the bottle for minutes versus one that's been breathing in the bottle for hours. If you really want to aerate your wine, pour it into your glass or use a proper decanter.

Decanting Your Wine

A decanter is a thing, usually a glass carafe that can hold an entire bottle of wine. Decanting is a process, and aeration is simply one goal of that process. Decanting to remove sediment from older red wines is the other goal, and a more delicate process. Sediments consist of color and tannin molecules which have precipitated out of the wine over time.

To remove sediment successfully, first stand the bottle upright. Let it stand that way as long as possible so the sediment falls to the bottom of the bottle. A couple of days is ideal, but even thirty minutes is helpful. Remove the cork without disturbing the sediment.

With a candle or flashlight standing next to the decanter, slowly pour the wine in a steady stream into the decanter. The light should be focused below the neck of the bottle. That way you'll be able to see the sediment the exact moment it appears. That's your signal to stop pouring.

Organizing a Wine Dinner

A wine dinner, or any dinner party, is like a staging a play. When you plan your food-wine matches, you can start either with the food or with the wine. If you're a particularly good cook—or if you have a special recipe that you want to showcase—choose the wine based on how it will complement the food. If the food is to be the star, you'll want a wine in the "best supporting" role. If you have some exceptional bottles of wine that you've acquired and want to serve to an appreciative audience, choose foods with some subtlety.

Before You Enter the Dining Room

A dinner party should begin with a proper cocktail hour. A great way to welcome your guests and whet their appetites is to have crisp, refreshing wines available with light hors d'oeuvres. Many wines make great aperitifs, especially those with good acidity, as they get the salivary glands working.

- Dry Champagnes or sparkling wines are the best.
- A good still white wine is Sauvignon Blanc. If guests have a low tolerance for acidity, have smoother, creamier Chardonnay available.
- The best red aperitifs are Beaujolais wines, Côtes du Rhone, and the occasional Pinot Noir. Save your bigger reds for the dinner table.

Gathering at the Table

If you're serving more than one kind of wine with the meal, there's a general progression that works best for enjoyment. Serve white wines before reds, light wines before heavy ones, and dry wines before sweet ones. Yes, there are always circumstances that defy the rules. Perhaps you only served white wines as guests arrived and mingled. There is nothing wrong with serving only red wines with dinner, assuming they complement your dishes, of course.

How Much Wine to Buy

How many bottles of each should you buy for your dinner party? With so many variables—your friends' passion for wine, the number of courses you plan to serve, if you plan to have a different wine with each course, the pace of the evening—there's no definitive answer. Here's a chart to help you decide how long various wine bottle sizes will last, assuming your servings per person per course are four or five ounces.

▼ CONTENTS OF TYPICAL WINE BOTTLES AND CONTAINERS

Size	Ounces	5-oz. Servings	4-oz. Servings
187 ml	6.3	1	1
375 ml	12.7	2	3
750 ml	25.4	5	6
1 L	33.8	6	8
1.5 L	50.7	10	12
3 L	101.4	20	25
5 L	169.0	34	42

Dessert wines are a separate consideration altogether. You can serve them as an accompaniment to a dessert, or as the dessert itself. The serving size is much smaller, and the bottle size is half that of a table wine.

Learning About Wine While Enjoying It

Wine tasting parties do not have to be solemn gatherings of pompous individuals swirling, spitting, and uttering terms like "carbonic maceration" in reverential tones. A wine tasting party can be anything you want it to be. Start with your intention. Do you want your event to be educational in nature so that your guests come away having learned something new about wine? Would you rather assemble a bunch of different wines and let your guests learn something by guzzling the wines on their own? There's room for both of these approaches, and everything in between.

Savvy Sipping

When you're planning your wine purchases, remember that a "tasting" serving is much smaller than the typical four- or five-ounce glass of wine. About two ounces is the norm. You can get twelve servings from a standard bottle. Buy a little extra just in case one of your guests wants to come back for another taste.

"Traditional" Wine Tastings

Traditional wine tastings tend to have a structure, and they need a leader—someone knowledgeable about the wines being served who can facilitate discussion and answer questions. If you're not comfortable in that role, perhaps one of your friends would be thrilled to play host. (Make sure the person in the lead role has a sense of humor and is willing to go with the flow of your party.)

Whom do you invite? Anyone—regardless of their wine sophistication—who has an interest in sampling and learning about wine. How many wines do you serve? As many as you want—but five or six wines work well.

Message in a Bottle

Food has a place at a wine tasting. It can be as simple as some unsalted crackers for guests to cleanse their palates between wines. At a structured tasting, you don't want the food to interfere. But an alternative "theme" would be a food and wine tasting to see how certain flavors—salty, fatty, acidic—affect the taste of the wines.

Seat guests at a table with empty wineglasses in front of them—one for each wine if possible. It is possible to rent the proper glassware if you don't have enough. If want to taste both reds and whites, two glasses per person will work best. In any case, have a pitcher on the table to rinse the glasses between wines. And, of course, a dump bucket for the water (or, heaven forbid, a wine).

As with the sequence of wines for a dinner party, the general guidelines are white before red, light before heavy, and dry before sweet. In selecting the wines, you might want to consider a theme. Consider these traditional options:

- **Vertical tasting**—You serve several bottles of the same wine from the same producer, only from different vintages. For example, you could serve a Silver Oak Cabernet Sauvignon from Napa Valley from 1997, 1998, 1999, 2000, and 2001. The objective is to identify the wine's traits that appear from year to year—or the differences from one year to the next.

- **Horizontal tasting**—You serve the same kind of wine from the same year from the same general area but from different producers—say Pinot Noirs from Oregon's Willamette Valley from the 2003 vintage from different wineries.
- **Blind tasting**—You keep the identity of the wines secret while they're being tasted. That way no one is influenced by the reputation of a particular winery or region or vintage. Go ahead, include a jug wine in the tasting and see how it compares in the judging.

CHAPTER 16

Wine at Restaurants: You're in Charge

Restaurant wine lists have been known to render speechless the most articulate, high-powered business executives, so don't fret when your friends turn to you to order the wine. Of course, choosing the perfect wine can be intimidating, especially when each of your friends is ordering a different entrée and you see high price tags on bottles you might want. By the time you finish this chapter, you'll know what to order when, how to order it with confidence, and how to do it within your budget.

A Restaurant's Attitude Toward Wine

Restaurants have brand images to uphold, and these brand images are on display in everything they do, from the time they take your phone reservation to the moment they hand you the check. Wine is also an extension of a restaurant's image.

The Wine List

The first clue to a restaurant's wine personality—and to the kind of wine experience you're likely to have—is the "list." Some lists (if there is one at all) will only display a house red, a house white, and a house blush. This is not necessarily a bad thing: If you happen to be in a small ethnic restaurant offering some vino bianco from the homeland, this could be a wine night to remember.

At the other restaurant extreme, you will be handed a wine list that could easily be mistaken for an encyclopedia. The upside is that the establishment is serious about your total gastronomic experience; the downside is there are too many pages and too little time.

Vino Veritas

More than 3,300 restaurants worldwide have received Wine Spectator Awards for their wine lists. The award criteria include such things as regions represented and thematic match with the menu. Size also matters. Award of Excellence winners have at least seventy-five selections, Best of Award of Excellence winners have 350 or more, and Grand Award winners have 1,000 or more.

A restaurant reveals its personality or brand image not only by the number of wines on the list but by the range of producers it offers. Some lists will give you household names—highly advertised, popular, everyday wines. The goal here is comfort and dependability—again, not a bad way of doing things at all.

Restaurants that really care about the wine experiences of their guests will offer a varied selection—some familiar names, some unknown—

regardless of list size. You can decide for yourself whether you're in the mood for something classic or something more adventurous.

The Server

The wine list will be handed to you by the sommelier, your server, or the restaurant host. The sommelier is the restaurant's wine specialist (and not all restaurants have one) who creates the wine list and often serves the wine. Any restaurant with a sommelier truly cares about wine. Sommeliers have a reputation for being unapproachable, but this is not the case. They are knowledgeable, courteous, well-trained professionals who can guide your wine selection based on preferences, food pairings, and price. Chances are a sommelier will make your decision-making effortless.

Without a sommelier, you should direct wine questions to the server. Depending on the establishment, servers will be familiar enough with the wines to describe them and recommend dishes to complement them. Sometimes, you will have to make your own decisions.

Servers ill-equipped to provide knowledgeable wine recommendations reflect the personality of the restaurant in other ways. Look for these clues on your next night out:

- Is your server trained to present and pour according to long-standing wine traditions?
- Is your server attentive to you when your glass is empty?
- Is your server overly zealous in pouring by prematurely topping off the glasses so you run out of wine before your entrée is served—necessitating another bottle?

Glassware

If you went to a restaurant and ordered a $30 steak only to have it served on a paper plate, you would be furious. Sadly, that is the kind of treatment most of us have come to accept when we order fine wine: It is too often served in cheap glasses!

The typical glassware is either too small, too thick, or too warm. Sometimes the glasses have no stems—which may be acceptable for a theme restaurant—but an eatery that makes wine a priority respects its customers by using appropriate glasses.

Wine by the Glass

Ordering wine by the glass has made it so easy—and relatively inexpensive—to try new and unfamiliar wines. Be attentive, though, to how a restaurant treats its opened bottles.

As soon as a bottle is uncorked, the wine begins to deteriorate because of contact with the air. Proper storage, then, is paramount. If you sense that the restaurant does not have a preservation system that keeps its wines-by-the-glass fresh, it is perfectly acceptable to ask your server when the bottle was uncorked. If the wine has been hanging around for a day or two, you might be well served to make another selection.

One of the advantages of ordering by the glass is that a restaurant is usually willing to give you a taste before you buy. More than likely, the bottle is already open. Your server's attitude will quickly sour, however, if you ask to sample every wine-by-the-glass on the list.

Deciphering the Wine List

The best wine lists are not only comprehensive but user-friendly. One of their goals should be to aid your decision-making. Wine lists come in all shapes, sizes, degree of description, and degree of accuracy.

Basic Classifications

Most often, wines will be listed under general headings of red, white, sparkling, and dessert. This presentation is limited in its usefulness, but it does come in handy for unfamiliar Old World wines that are named after geographical locations with no mention of grape variety. You will learn that Château Canon La Gaffelière Saint Emilion is red and that Lemberger, an obscure European grape, is red too.

Generic wine lists will occasionally include after-dinner drinks in their dessert wine section. So, in addition to Sauternes and ports, you may find liqueurs and single malt scotches.

Listing by Country or Varietal

More detailed lists may be subdivided by country, region, or varietal. In this scenario, wines might be listed under French Reds, Italian Reds, and American Reds or specified further by Bordeaux, Campania, and California. With varietal listings, likely headings in the white wine section are Chardonnay, Sauvignon Blanc, and Pinot Grigio.

"Stylish" Wine Lists

Words such as "big," "full-bodied," "fresh," "oaky," and "dry" may be more meaningful than geographical and varietal headings to someone not acquainted with a particular wine. Many restaurants organize their wine lists in just this way. Under a white heading of "Dry and Crisp," you could find a Pinot Grigio alongside a Sancerre and Chablis. A short but descriptive "Big Reds" list might include a California Cabernet and an Italian Barolo. When you have no clue about a wine's grape heritage or region of origin, you will get the general idea of taste from this sort of listing.

Vino Veritas

How much wine should I order for a group?
The rule of thumb is about a half bottle per person—although that could go up or down according to your group's drinking profile. For a group of three or more whose wine preferences you don't know, it's always safe to order both a red and a white.

Progressive Lists

Some lists will put wines in sort of a progressive sequence—such as from lightest in style to richest. In such a list you could expect to see a Beaujolais at or near the top, perhaps a Chianti in the middle, and a Cabernet at the end. Another progressive technique is listing the wines by price—either cheapest to most expensive or the reverse. This is helpful to the cost conscious and the status conscious alike.

Strategies for Choosing a Wine

If your last restaurant meal was somewhat forgettable, it was probably not the wine's fault. Indeed, some wine and food matches are not exactly ethereal, but, in all likelihood, the meal was not a total bust. You may have had to enjoy the food and wine separately, but at least you learned a lesson about what not to order in the future. Three specific strategies will help you choose a bottle everyone can enjoy on your next night out.

Strategy #1: Keep It "Friendly"

Certain wines are known to be food-friendly. They simply have the ability to complement just about anything. When each person in your party of eight is ordering a different entrée, it only makes sense to choose such a wine.

Among the food-friendliest wines are Pinot Noir (red) and Riesling (white). How easy can it get? You'll find terrific Pinots from Oregon and California, and, of course, the Burgundy region of France. If your group prefers white, try an exceptional Riesling from upstate New York, Washington, Germany, or Alsace.

Strategy #2: Get a Sneak Preview

The most reliable way to choose a wine with confidence and impress your dining partners with your knowledge and sophistication is to study the wine list before you get to the restaurant. In the quiet and comfort of your own home, you can choose the style of wine you want at the price you are willing to pay. Along the way, you can also learn to pronounce Pouilly-Fuissé (poo-yee-fwee-SAY).

Savvy Sipping

Be careful about ordering older vintages. They can be risky choices. First of all, they're expensive. Second, they're more fragile. They're on the list for a reason, of course, but unless you really understand how wines change as they age, stick with younger vintages.

Many restaurant websites include links to their wine lists (in whole or in part). If you cannot find what you need there, most restaurants will be pleased to fax you the list, provided you're not calling them during their peak business hours and you're not requesting to see their entire two-hundred-page list. A better idea might be to visit the restaurant in person a day or two ahead of your reservation to study the list.

Strategy #3: Ask for Help!

There's no shame in asking for help. In fact, it shows a good deal of self-assurance. The person to ask is the sommelier or wine director, if the restaurant has one.

Vino Veritas

The sommelier of yore had a silver cup hanging around his neck on a ribbon. Called a *tastevin* ("taste wine" in French), it dates back to the cellar masters of Burgundy who used them to sample wines in near-dark cellars. The dimples in the metal reflected what light there was and made it possible to check the wine's appearance.

Today's sommeliers are often young, cordial, and just as likely to be a woman as a man. They're more like tour guides than professors. They'll ask you several questions about the kinds and styles of wines you like, what you might be ordering to eat, and whether you are willing to try something new and different. During your conversation, the sommelier will probably get a feeling for how much you plan to drink and how much you want to spend.

Sommeliers know their wine lists intimately because, in most cases, they have created them. They have chosen the wines, negotiated the purchases, overseen the storage, written the descriptions, and trained the staff to serve them. Sommeliers are enthusiastic about sharing their wine finds. Sometimes they've been able to buy bottles that are not available in any retail store. This could be your night to sip something truly remarkable.

Wine Etiquette

For a beverage that dates back thousands of years, you would expect a myriad of traditions to accompany the consumption of wine. Nowhere is that more obvious than inside a restaurant.

Presentation of the Cork

Before wine bottles had labels, there was no real proof that a particular bottle of wine came from the winery to which it was attributed. Some unscrupulous restaurateurs would pass off common French wine as having come from the famous châteaux. To maintain their good reputations, the châteaux began branding their corks. Restaurants then began presenting the corks to customers to verify the wine's origin.

The practice continues to this day, long after the need to do so has passed. So, what are you, the diner, supposed to do with the cork once the waiter has plopped it down in front of you? Anything you want. Ignore it. Examine it if you prefer. Sniff it if you feel like it. Slip it into your pocket to take as a souvenir. The cork won't tell you anything that won't be evident in the glass.

Savvy Sipping

Corks that are either dry and crumbly or completely wet are a clue that air may have crept into the bottle and spoiled the wine. A taste will tell you. Occasionally, harmless tartrate crystals are visible at the end of the cork that had contact with the wine. They have no effect on taste.

Presentation of the cork will become less of an issue as more wineries opt for screw cap closures. Unless there's a winning sweepstakes number inside the cap, the screw cap probably won't be presented for inspection.

The Tasting Ritual

Back in the days before modern winemaking methods, wine would often go bad, so restaurant patrons were offered the opportunity to sample their wine before drinking it. That's still the reason for the ritual. It's not merely to see if the wine meets your expectations. It's not to test your wine knowledge and show you up as a rube. It's simply to make sure you're getting the wine you ordered and that the wine is in good condition.

Here are the steps in the routine. The waiter presents the bottle for you to visually inspect. You check that it's the same wine and same vintage that you ordered. If not, speak up. If the wine you ordered isn't available, your server should make a recommendation for a similar wine in the same price range.

The waiter cuts the capsule and removes the cork. He puts the cork on the table in front of you. You've already mastered this step.

The waiter pours a small amount of wine into your glass. You admire it. Study the wine against a white or light background, such as the tablecloth or napkin.

If the wine's color and clarity have met with your approval, it's time to swirl. Now stick your nose right into the glass and inhale deeply.

Assuming the aromas have been pleasing, take a sip. Hold the wine in your mouth. Roll it around on your tongue before you swallow.

Now to the big finish. The wine is acceptable, and you nod to the waiter. That's his signal to pour for the group.

That's all there is to it. Take a bow.

When you order a second bottle of a different wine, the waiter brings clean glasses, and you repeat the ritual. When the second bottle is the same wine, the waiter brings one clean glass and offers you the opportunity to taste again. It's up to you. The restaurant is under no obligation to bring clean glasses for everyone, but it's a nice gesture.

Sending a Wine Back

If the wine is clearly flawed, do not hesitate to send it back. The wine could be corked, oxidized, or maderized. In other words, if it smells like wet cardboard, nail polish remover, or Sherry (when you didn't order Sherry), something is wrong.

Calmly yet confidently, simply say, "I'm afraid this is a bad bottle, and I'd like to send it back." A server who knows wine will probably smell it for himself and cart off the offending bottle. He'll return with a replacement. Even if you're the only one who perceives the flaw, the waiter will most likely replace the wine anyway.

Rejecting a bottle is hardly a financial hardship for the restaurant. The restaurant will, in turn, send the bottle back to the distributor for replacement.

Sample Before You Order

The tasting ritual is all about the condition of the wine, not whether you are happy with your selection. In some instances, there are ways to sample a bottle before you buy it. Simply flip back to the wines-by-the-glass section of the list, and see if the bottle you want appears there.

A restaurant isn't about to open a bottle of wine just for you to taste. It would be too wasteful—and expensive—if you didn't like it. If the wine you wish to taste is also available by the glass, your server will likely give you a small sample to try. If that is not possible, simply purchase a glass. It is always preferable to purchase a glass and not like it than to purchase an entire bottle and not like it.

The Corkage Fee

Some restaurants, including many famous ones, will allow you to bring a bottle of wine with you to dinner. You can pick out something special from your cellar or stop at a wine shop on the way and pick up something from the closeout shelf. You don't pay restaurant markups, but you can expect to pay a corkage fee to cover the costs of wine service and use of the restaurant's glassware. The fee is usually a per-bottle charge and can vary dramatically.

There are some rules of etiquette to follow when you want to take a bottle to a wine-serving restaurant. Never take a bottle that is already on the restaurant's wine list. Call in advance to check. In fact, calling ahead is always a good idea. When you explain that you've been saving this special wine for ten years to drink in celebration of your tenth wedding anniversary, what restaurateur wouldn't be charmed?

At tipping time, don't forget to do the right thing: Tip your waiter according to what the bill would have been had you ordered the wine from the restaurant's list.

Getting the Most for Your Money

Money is often the top priority when choosing a wine. If you had unlimited financial resources, you could order anything that struck your fancy. If you didn't care for it, you could order something else. For most of us, the goal is to get the best possible wine for the most reasonable price—in other words, the best value for your money.

How Restaurants Price Wines

Pricing policies are as different as the restaurants themselves, but here's a general rule of thumb: If the wholesale price of a bottle of wine is $10, a retail wine shop will charge $15. A typical restaurant will charge $20 to $30 for the same bottle.

The markups vary from wine to wine—the biggest markups being at the low and high ends of the list. At the low end, the wines are cash cows. Some customers want their wine and they want it cheap, and they're not too picky about what they get. This clientele practically keeps the restaurant open.

At the other end of the list, you have a different scenario. The restaurant is selling either to the extremely well-heeled or to expense account diners who are indifferent to what the wine costs. At the middle of the list, the wines usually have lower markups, and that is where you tend to find the best values.

Some restaurants—especially those committed to encouraging the public to drink wine—have another approach. Their objective is to get their customers to try higher quality wines, and they achieve this through a pricing strategy of adding about $10 to the retail price of the wine. Even with these modest markups, the restaurant still makes money, and it attracts faithful customers.

Vino Veritas

Flights of wine are small tastes of wine (about two ounces each) served by a restaurant as a series. The four to six offerings are often based on a theme—Italian reds, for example, or whites with oak or wines with funny names. The purpose is to present wine lovers with an opportunity to experiment with new wines at a reasonable cost.

More Tips for the Value Conscious

No one wants to be regarded as a cheapskate, but common sense dictates that if you maximize value, you can order more bottles for less money. Here are some ways to do that:

- Unless you're familiar with the house wine, skip it in favor of something else. The restaurant probably bought it on the basis of price and gave it the highest markup.
- Buy by the bottle. A standard bottle contains four to six glasses of wine, depending on the size of the pour. Once you've purchased three wines by the glass, you've paid for a whole bottle.
- Choose a wine from the same region as the restaurant's food specialty. A good Italian restaurant, for example, will have a creative—and usually value priced—selection of Italian wines.
- Look for varietals that aren't all the current rage. Chardonnays, Cabs, and Merlots have been hot sellers in the past and have commanded higher dollars. Cast your eyes elsewhere for varietals such as Chenin Blanc, Pinot Gris, or Malbec.
- Experiment with wines from parts of the world where the land itself is less expensive (and, hence, the end cost of the wine is less expensive). A perfect place to start is South America, home to Chile and Argentina.

CHAPTER 17

All Things Bubbly

Champagne rings in each new year, launches mighty ships, and celebrates newlywed vows. Bubbles are consumed to commemorate auspicious occasions—from royal coronations and corporate mergers to the birth of a child. Sparkling wine is synonymous with celebration, but these days, it's become the partner to everyday events as well. Bubblies come by different names, in lots of styles, and from places far removed from France. The informed wine drinker knows how to choose the right one for any occasion.

Champagne vs. Sparkling Wine

The term "champagne" is used generically to mean all sparkling wines. However, thanks to international treaty, the term "Champagne" can only appear on bottles produced in the Champagne region of France, north of Burgundy. Most bottles of wine produced in the Champagne style in the United States will say "sparkling wine" on the label.

The French only sought to protect this name a few decades ago. Before Champagne became legally protected, a California winery called Korbel used "champagne" on its labels. They can still use the name, but it must appear right next to California on the bottles.

Making the Bubbles

Whether it is called Champagne or sparkling wine, this bubbly beverage is more difficult to produce that still wines. The process, called *méthode champenoise*, is time consuming and labor intensive. Some wineries take shortcuts, but the authentic *méthode champenoise* can be condensed into seven basic steps:

1. Grape juice is fermented, just like any other wine.
2. After fermentation, in a process called *assemblage,* the producer blends various lots of still wine together to achieve a certain style, namely the house style. This final blend is called the cuvée.
3. *Liqueur de tirage,* a combination of yeast and cane or beet sugar, is added to the cuvée, and the wine is bottled. A second fermentation takes place in the bottle itself over the next twenty to forty-five days, producing carbon dioxide in the form of bubbles.
4. When the yeast cells have completed their work, they sink into the neck of the bottle. The wine ages in the bottle in contact with the dead yeast. This is called *sur lie* aging.
5. The bottles are rotated from a horizontal position to a vertical, upside-down, position. This allows the sediment of dead yeast cells to collect in the neck of the bottle close to the cork so that it can be removed easily and quickly. Rotating the bottles is called riddling.
6. The neck of the bottle is frozen and the sediment (in the form of a frozen plug) is removed, called disgorging.

7. After disgorgement, the producer adds the dosage, a combination of cane sugar and extra wine, the latter of which makes up for what was lost during disgorgement. The amount of sugar added depends on how sweet the producer wishes his product to be. In some cases, the producers leave the sugar out entirely. The bottles are recorked.

Another sparkling process, the transfer method, is similar to *méthode champenoise* except that, instead of riddling and disgorgement, the wine is transferred after the second fermentation to pressurized tanks and filtered. You have to read the fine print on the label to know. "Fermented in this bottle" means traditional method. "Fermented in the bottle" means transfer method.

Savvy Sipping

The bubbles will tell you something about what method was used. *Méthode champenoise* produces tiny bubbles that float upward in a continuous stream. Cheaper bubbles are large and random and don't last as long. Bubbles from carbonation aren't integrated into the wines like in Champagne—so they'll quickly disappear, much like the bubbles in your can of Coke.

Cheap Bubbles

The *methode champenoise* is not only a time consuming process; it is also expensive. You can bet that when you buy a $5 bottle of sparkling wine, it was produced another—cheaper—way. The Charmat method (also known as the tank method or *cuve close*) was likely used. It involves conducting the second fermentation in large, closed, pressurized tanks. With this process, you can produce a lot of wine in a short period of time—so the sparkling wine is ready to drink not long after harvest, in maybe only a few weeks. The downside is that this method produces wines that taste more like still wines with bubbles rather than actual Champagne. Here's what happens:

1. Still wine is put into closed, pressurized tanks, and sugar and yeast are added to facilitate the second fermentation.

2. The wine is filtered under pressure to remove any solids.
3. Dosage is added to adjust to the sweetness level desired, and the wine is bottled using a counter pressure filler.

An even less expensive technique is sometimes used that simply injects carbon dioxide into the wine—like a carbonated soft drink. If that's the case, the label on the bottle will say "carbonated."

Grapes Matter

Authentic Champagne is made from three traditional grapes: Pinot Meunier, Pinot Noir, and Chardonnay. Pinot Meunier contributes a youthful fruitiness. Pinot Noir gives Champagne its weight and richness and is responsible for its longevity. Chardonnay adds lightness.

One of the most important decisions a Champagne maker has to make is how to blend these grapes to make the base wine. Wines from the different varieties and vineyards are kept separate. The producer then blends the wines (including wines from past years) in varying proportions to create its distinct cuvée. This is what distinguishes the ultimate taste of one producer's Champagne from his competitor's.

History of Champagne

Until the mid-1600s, Champagne as we know it didn't exist. The region produced still wines, which were very popular with European nobility. But Champagne had yet to be discovered. The Champagne region in northern France has a cold climate, posing problems for growing grapes and winemaking. Cold winters and short growing seasons mean that grapes had to be harvested as late as possible to get them as ripe as possible. That meant just a short time for fermentation, because the cold temperatures of winter paralyzed the yeast cells. So the wines were bottled before all the sugar had been converted to alcohol.

Then spring would arrive, and fermentation would begin again—this time in the bottle. When the bottles didn't explode from all the pressure that had built up from the carbon dioxide produced naturally during fermentation, the wines had bubbles. To the winemakers of the time, bubbles were a sign of poor winemaking.

Dom Pérignon, the Benedictine monk who's often called the inventor of Champagne, was one of those winemakers. He spent a good deal of time trying to prevent the bubbles. He wasn't successful, but he did develop the basic principles used in Champagne making that continue to this day:

- He advanced the art of blending to include different grapes and different vineyards of the same grape.
- He invented a method to produce white juice from black grapes.
- He improved clarification techniques.
- He used stronger bottles to prevent explosions.

When Dom Pérignon died in 1715, Champagne accounted for only about 10 percent of the region's wine, but it was fast becoming the preferred drink of English and French royalty. A royal ordinance in 1735 dictated the size, weight, and shape of Champagne bottles as well as the size of the cork. Two historic Champagne houses came into existence: Ruinart in 1729 and Moët in 1743. By the 1800s the Champagne industry was in full swing.

Vino Veritas

Madame Clicquot, a young widow who ran her husband's Champagne house after his death in 1805, was the first to solve the sediment removal problem. She cut a series of holes in her dining-room table so that the bottles could be positioned upside down at 45-degree angles. After several weeks of turning and re-angling the bottles, all the sediment collected in the neck.

Champagne Houses

Unlike other French wines that are named after growing regions, Champagnes are named for the houses that produce them. The houses, in turn, produce various brands of Champagne—called marques. The largest and most famous of the houses are known as the Grandes Marques. Many belong to a union called the Syndicat de Grandes Marques de Champagne. Here are some of the more recognizable members:

- Bollinger
- Pol Roger
- Charles Heidsieck
- Pommery & Greno
- Krug
- Louis Roederer
- Laurent-Perrier

- Ruinart
- Moët et Chandon
- Taittinger
- G. H. Mumm
- Veuve Clicquot-Ponsardin
- Perrier-Jouët

Beginning with Moët et Chandon in 1974, a number of French Champagne houses opened up shop in California. These New World facilities produce sparkling wines the traditional way using the same grape varieties as in France: Pinot Noir, Chardonnay, and Pinot Meunier. The French-American productions include Domaine Carneros (owned by Taittinger), Domaine Chandon (owned by Moët et Chandon), Mumm Cuvée Napa (owned by G. H. Mumm), Piper Sonoma (owned by Piper-Heidsieck), and Roederer Estate (owned by Louis Roederer).

Vino Veritas

Madame Lilly Bollinger, a young widow who took control of the esteemed Bollinger Champagne house, had this to say about bubbly: "I only drink Champagne when I'm happy and when I'm sad. Sometimes I drink it when I'm alone. When I have company I consider it obligatory. I trifle with it if I am not hungry and drink it when I am. Otherwise I never touch it—unless I'm thirsty."

Grower Champagne

While some of the major Champagne houses have sizeable vineyard holdings, they still buy most of their grapes from the 20,000 or so small growers in the Champagne district. The small growers, who collectively own about 90 percent of the vineyards, are increasingly making their own Champagnes. About 130 of these grower Champagnes are available in the

U.S. market (out of the thousands sold in France). You've probably never heard their names (they can't afford to pay for promotion and advertising like the big guys), but they offer high quality and bargain prices.

How do you recognize a grower Champagne? It's on the label. In the lower right-hand corner of the front label are two letters followed by some numbers. The only letters that signify it's a grower Champagne are either "RM" or "SR." Here are all the possible letters and what they mean:

- **NM (Négociant-Manipulant)**—The term means merchant-distributor. These are the big houses. They buy grapes in volume from independent growers.
- **RM (Récoltant-Manipulant)**—The term means grower-distributor. This is a grower that makes and markets its own Champagne.
- **MA (Marque d'acheteur)**—This term is used for a brand of Champagne not owned by the actual producer of that Champagne.
- **CM (Cooperative-Manipulant)**—This is a cooperative of growers who bottle their product together—although these wines can include purchased grapes.
- **RC (Recoltant-Cooperateur)**—This means a grower sends its grapes to a cooperative to be made into wine. The grapes can be blended with other wines in the cooperative.

Choosing a Champagne

A Champagne house establishes its reputation based on a particular style. Many factors influence the style, including grape varieties, vineyards, blending choices, tradition. The objective of each house is to provide consistency from one year to the next. When you find a Champagne that you like, you can be sure it will have the same characteristics year after year.

Vintage Years

Champagne is produced every year. But "vintage" Champagne is only produced in the best years. Like in all other regions, some grape harvests in Champagne are better than others. In exceptional years, a house will decide to make its bubbly using only the grapes from that harvest—and will date the bottle with that year. In the years in between, the house blends wines from multiple years, producing nonvintage (NV) Champagnes. Blending across years is one reason you can expect uniform quality.

Vino Veritas

For a Champagne to qualify for a vintage date, 100 percent of the grapes used in its production must have been harvested that year. A vintage Champagne also must age for three years before its release but can be, and often is, aged longer.

Nonvintage Champagne represents most of a house's production—80 percent or more. They're usually lighter, fresher, and less complex than their vintage counterparts.

From Dry to Sweet

The amount of sugar to add to the dosage before bottling is one of the most important decisions a Champagne producer must make. It can drastically change the style of that wine. There are six categories of Champagne based on their sweetness levels. Here they are, progressing from dry to sweet:

- Extra Brut (0 to 0.6 percent sugar)—driest, but not a common style
- Brut (less than 1.5 percent sugar)—very dry, the most popular style
- Extra Dry (1.2 to 2 percent sugar)—off-dry
- Sec (1.7 to 3.5 percent sugar)—lightly sweet
- Demi-Sec (3.3 to 5 percent sugar)—sweet
- Doux (more than 5 percent sugar—very sweet

Variations on a Theme

Once you know how sweet you want your next bottle of Champagne to be, you must then choose a type of Champagne. A *blanc de blancs* is made entirely from the Chardonnay grape. These Champagnes are light, elegant, and refreshing. A richer style is the *blanc de noir* ("white from black"), made entirely from Pinot Noir and Pinot Meunier grapes. This Champagne will have a dark gold color with perhaps the slightest tinge of pink. A bottle lacking these terms is made from all three grapes.

Then there is rosé Champagne, the accompaniment to romance. Rosé Champagne gets its pink color in one of two ways. The winemaker can leave the skins of the grapes in brief contact with the grape juice during the first fermentation, or add a little Pinot Noir wine to base the wine blend. Rosé Champagne is not necessarily sweet—most are dry—but this association is understandable given that most blush wines in the American market are sweet. Rosé Champagne is available both as a vintage wine and as nonvintage.

Name Your Size

Have you ever noticed those super-large Champagne bottles on display at wine stores and restaurants? Well, they're not just some marketing tool. They're real. Champagne is bottled in nine different sizes, shown in this table.

▼ **CHAMPAGNE BOTTLE SIZES AND NAMES**

Measure	Size Equivalent	Servings	Popular Name
187 ml	quarter bottle	1	split
375 ml	half bottle	2	half
750 ml	standard	4	fifth
1.5 L	2 bottles	8	magnum
3 L	4 bottles	17	jeroboam
6 L	8 bottles	34	methuselah
9 L	12 bottles (1 case)	50	salmanazar
12 L	16 bottles	68	balthazar
15 L	20 bottles	112	nebuchadnezzar

Only the half bottle, standard bottle, magnum, and jeroboam contain Champagne that's undergone the second fermentation in the bottle. The three largest sizes are rarely made anymore.

Savvy Sipping

Champagne splits are handy because of their size—about a serving and a half. But, even though they are corked just like their bigger brothers, they don't keep as well. So drink them up right away before they lose their freshness.

Champagne by Any Other Name

The fact that a sparkling wine is produced outside of the Champagne region of France doesn't mean that it's inferior. It's just a little different. Some sparkling wines are made with the exact same grapes and by employing *méthode champenoise*. They will be different by virtue of their place of origin—Napa Valley does not have the soils and weather of Champagne—and the blending choices of the winemaker. Many experts have failed to recognize the difference between well-made sparkling wines from inside and outside the Champagne region.

French but Not Champagne

Even in the Loire Valley (so close to Champagne), they can't use the Champagne name on the labels of their sparkling wines. The region known, in part, for its use of Chenin Blanc grapes in Vouvray uses the same grapes for its sparklers. The effect is refreshing and creamy.

The eastern regions of France, including Alsace, are known for blending Pinot Noir, Pinot Blanc, and Pinot Gris for their crisp sparkling wines. French sparkling wines produced outside of Champagne are labeled "crémant".

Spanish Bubbles

It used to be called Spanish Champagne. Then in 1970 the European Union banned the use of the term outside of Champagne. From then on Spanish sparkling wines have been known as Cava. The word is Catalan for cellar, referring to the underground cellars where the wines are aged.

Vino Veritas

Using atomic spectrometry to measure metal concentrations in the wines, researchers at the University of Seville in Spain correctly identified bottles of Champagne versus bottles of Cava 100 percent of the time. The measurements reflected the trace metal content in the soils where the grapes were grown. This technique could be used in the future to detect wine fraud.

To qualify as a Cava, the sparkling wine has to be produced according to *méthode champenoise* using specified grape varieties. The list includes Chardonnay and Pinot Noir, which are used in the best wines, but producers still use the "big three" indigenous grapes: Macabeo, Xarel-lo, and Parellada. The bottles must be cellared for a minimum of nine months, aging *sur lie*, to qualify for the Cava designation.

Cavas are usually light and crisp and inexpensive. Look for:

- Freixenet Cordon Negro Brut
- Segura Viudas Aria Brut
- Mont-Marcal Brut
- Codorniu Brut
- Paul Cheneau
- Fleur de Nuit

Italy Sparkles

Italy produces oceans of sparkling wine, and one of the most famous is Prosecco. It's made from a grape of the same name in the Veneto region of northeastern Italy. Prosecco comes both fully sparkling (spumante) and lightly sparkling (frizzante). They're crisp and dry and inexpensive. They've become very popular, and you see more and more of them on restaurant wine lists.

The more familiar Asti (in the past known as Asti Spumante) comes from the Muscat grape. Its second fermentation takes place in pressurized tanks in a modified version of the charmat method, and its taste is semi-sweet to sweet. Asti Spumate's cousin is Moscato d'Asti, which differs from the former in that it is frizzante instead of spumante, sweeter, lower in alcohol, and is corked like a still wine. Both should be drunk young and fresh.

Lambrusco is another Italian option. Most Americans know it as pink, semisweet, and frizzante, but white and dry versions do exist.

Sparkling Wine in the United States

California and New York produce more sparkling wine than any other states. In California, particularly in the cooler climates of Sonoma and Mendocino counties, Pinot Noir, Chardonnay, and Pinot Meunier can flourish, perfect for sparklers. Many producers have no French ties, such as Gloria Ferrer and Schramsberg. While California gets most of the attention, sparkling wine has been a mainstay of New York winemaking since before the Civil War when French Champagne makers were recruited by local wineries.

Some sparkling wine recommendations from around the United States:

- Château Frank Brut (New York)
- Argyle Brut (Oregon)
- Domaine Carneros (California)
- Gruet Brut (New Mexico)

Storing and Serving Bubbly

You never know when you'll need a bottle of Champagne to celebrate an event, big or small. Champagne has practically become the universal beverage. Keeping a supply just makes good sense.

How to Keep It When You're Not Drinking It

Champagne is sensitive to temperature and light. Like other wines, it does best stored in a cool, dark place without big temperature fluctuations. You don't need an expensive cooling unit—a 50°F basement usually works fine. Champagne is ready for immediate consumption as soon as it leaves the Champagne house, but if you provide the right conditions for your typical sparkler, it should last for three to four years, if you haven't drunk it by then. Storing it in the refrigerator will not do any damage.

Message in a Bottle

Bubbly is best served between 45° and 50°F. It will take three to four hours in the refrigerator to cool a bottle. But you can quick-chill your Champagne in about twenty minutes by immersing the bottle in ice water. It's faster than ice alone. Half ice and half water in an ice bucket is the way to go. No bucket? The kitchen sink will do.

Popping the Cork

Popping the cork is a great way to grab the attention of the entire room, but it wastes bubbles. The cork should be removed so the sound you hear is a soft sigh. Removing the cork in this slow manner also reduces the risks of killing someone nearby. (After all, there are seventy pounds-per-square-inch of pressure in that bottle!) Here's how to safely open your bottle of Champagne:

1. Remove the foil covering.
2. Stand the bottle on a table or counter for support. (It's safer than holding the bottle in your arms and possibly pointing it at someone.)
3. Get a towel. Keep one hand over the top of the cork with the towel between your hand and the cork. Untwist the wire cage. Remove the wire.
4. Keep the towel on top of the cork with one hand and put your other hand on the bottle at a point where you have a good grasp.
5. Turn the bottle—not the cork. You'll feel the cork loosen a bit. Keep a downward pressure on the cork as it completely loosens and finally releases.
6. Hold the cork over the opened bottle for a few seconds to ensure the Champagne doesn't escape.
7. Pour!

Vino Veritas

Germany may not be known for sparkling wines, since most of it is consumed within its own borders. Theirs is called Sekt, and it's made using the charmat method. Riesling is used for the better wines. If the bubbly has been made using just one variety, the grape name will be on the label.

Pour Champagne slowly. Because of the bubbles, the liquid rises quickly, and you can end up with overflow (and wasted Champagne) before you know it.

Drinking Vessels

You've undoubtedly seen the sherbet-style glasses that were popular in the 1950s. These glasses are still everywhere, but long-stemmed flutes are the glassware of choice for sparkling wines. The elongated shape and slight narrowing at the rim enhance the flow of bubbles and keep them from escaping.

Vino Veritas

Because of its rougher surface, crystal produces more bubbles than ordinary glass. If you want the effect of crystal without the expense, do what restaurants do. Lightly scratch an X in the bottom of the inside of the glass with the tip of a knife. This gives the bubbles something to cling to—just like the crystal.

There's no need to chill the glasses. If you do, they'll just fog up and cloud your view of the bubbles. Also, make sure the glasses are spotlessly clean. Detergent residue can interfere with the bubbles.

Champagne Leftovers

On the rare occasions that the bottle of sparkling wine hasn't been emptied, your main objective is to save the bubbles for another day. Your best bet to preserve the effervescence is a Champagne bottle stopper. It's made of metal with a spring and special lip to grab the rim of the bottle. They're available in most kitchen stores and wine shops. A good backup procedure is to wrap the bottle opening with two layers of plastic wrap and secure it with a rubber band.

For quality Champagnes, you can usually stick the uncorked bottle back in the refrigerator overnight and still have bubbles in the morning. The inert and heavy carbon dioxide gas from the bubbles forms a protective layer on top of the wine, preventing oxidation and containing the bubbles below. But a day—maybe two—is about as long as the protection will last.

CHAPTER 18

Dessert Wines and Fortified Wines

Historically, no wines have been both loved and maligned more than dessert wines and fortified wines. In one culture, they are treasured by kings and queens; in others, they are the stuff of skid row. Some were discovered through accidents of nature, others through human oversight. In any case, many of them deserve a place among the world's greatest wines.

Sweet Wines in History

Sweet wines go back to ancient times. The most acclaimed wines in Rome were sweet and white. When ancient winemakers let their grapes raisin on the vine, or when they dried their grapes on straw mats, they knew the resulting wines would be sweeter and more concentrated in flavor. These wines were also more likely to withstand transportation to outlying areas.

Vino Veritas

Not all wines that start out with the grapes dried on mats are sweet. Recioto della Valpolicella Amarone—better known as just "Amarone"—is a dry wine made by fermenting to completion the juice inside these dried grapes. The name Amarone translates to "strongly bitter."

In the Middle Ages, vintners in Venice and Genoa exported sweet dried grape wines to northern Europe. In addition, sweet wines from Hungary (Tokaji) and from South Africa (Constantia) were on every royal table in Europe.

Late Harvest and Noble Rot

Every country famous for producing a luxurious sweet wine has a story (or legend) for how that wine was discovered. Germany makes the most famous late harvest sweet Rieslings in the world, and their story goes something like this: In 1775 a messenger was sent to Schloss Johannisberg in Germany's Rheingau region to give the official order to start harvesting the grapes. He was robbed on the way and delayed. By the time he got to the wine estate, the grapes had begun to raisin on the vine. They were picked anyway and produced astonishingly delicious sweet wine. There is evidence that sweet late harvest wines had already been produced throughout Europe in the previous century, but wouldn't you rather believe this account?

Late Harvest Wines

The term "late harvest" means that the grapes were picked late into the harvest season, after they had surpassed the sugar levels required for ordinary table wine. The extra ripening time—which can be weeks—adds sugar, but it also creates stress for the winemakers as damage from rain, rot, and birds becomes more likely. The high sugar content of the grapes can translate into a wine that's sweet or a wine high in alcohol—or both.

Late harvest wines are known for their rich, honeyed flavors. Riesling grapes (the variety used for most late harvest wines) have the ability to develop high sugar levels without losing their acidity. That's why they can make unbelievably sweet wines that are not also cloying. The acidity also helps these white wines to age well. Famous late harvest wines also originate from Sauvignon Blanc, Gewürztraminer, Sémillon, and even Zinfandel grapes.

Noble Rot

While the Germans have their legend for "inventing" late harvest wines, the French have their own legend for their famous Sauternes wines. It seems a château owner told his workers not to pick his grapes until he returned from a trip. By the time he returned, the grapes had become infected with a fungus that shriveled them. Despite their disgusting appearance, the grapes were picked and turned into wine. The taste was so exquisite that the owner declared his grapes would thereafter always be picked after the fungus had arrived.

The friendly fungus of the legend is *Botrytis cinerea*, known affectionately as the noble rot. It dehydrates the grape, leaving a more concentrated sweet juice behind.

Savvy Sipping

Botrytis is a finicky fungus. Under the wrong conditions, gray rot forms instead and spoils the grapes. If the weather is unremittingly hot and dry, the fungus won't develop at all. The result is a sweet but much less complex wine.

A wide range of grapes can benefit from the positive effects of noble rot: Riesling, Chenin Blanc, Gewürztraminer, Sauvignon Blanc, Sémillon, and Furmint. Three areas in particular are historically famous for their botrytized wines.

- **Sauternes**—The French wine by the same name is made mostly from Sémillon but usually includes some Sauvignon Blanc and sometimes Muscadelle. The sweet Sauternes aren't necessarily made every year. If the grapes don't ripen properly and if Botrytis infection doesn't set in, the winemakers must wait until the following year.
- **Germany**—German winemakers use Riesling to produce their Beerenauslese and Trockenbeerenauslese wines.
- **Hungary**—Tokaji (also referred to as Tokay) comes from an area around the town of Tokaj. The Furmint grape is responsible for these beauties.

Vino Veritas

Château d'Yquem is in a class all by itself in the world of Sauternes. Harvesting the 245-acre estate can take eight to nine weeks because winemakers only want the most perfectly botrytized grapes. Pickers make an average of five passes, or "tries," through the vineyard. This is the main reason why Sauternes are so coveted—and expensive.

Ice Wines

Ice wines are made from frozen grapes. As the story goes, the discovery of ice wine dates back to the winter of 1794 when producers in Franconia, Germany, had frozen grapes on their hands and decided to go forward with the pressing. When they finished, they were startled by the high sugar concentration of the juice.

When grapes freeze, the first solid to form is ice. As the grapes are crushed, the ice is left behind with the other solids—the skins and seeds. This leaves behind a very sweet juice. For example, if the sugar content of the juice is 22 percent when pressed normally, it would be 50 percent or more after freezing and pressing.

In order for the grapes to freeze, they have to be left on the vine well into the winter months, when freezes of 18 degrees Fahrenheit are typical. Waiting for them to freeze can be risky business. If the weather doesn't cooperate and the grapes don't freeze, a grower can lose his entire crop. Harvesting takes place by hand in the early (and necessarily cold) morning hours when acidity levels are at their highest. Pressing produces only tiny amounts of juice—one reason for the extremely high prices of ice wines.

Who Makes Ice Wine

Germany and Austria were the traditional producers of ice wine (Eiswein in German), but in the last ten years Canada has taken over as the largest producer. Canadian winters are much more predictable. The Canadian versions use a variety of grapes besides Riesling, including some lesser known varieties such as Vidal, a French hybrid.

Canada, Germany, and Austria strictly regulate the making of ice wines. Among other things, there are standards for sugar levels and temperature at harvest. Ice wines produced in the United States—particularly in Washington State, in New York's Finger Lakes region, and in states near the Great Lakes such as Michigan and Ohio—are not bound by such strict standards.

Some maverick producers use an alternate method for making ice wine: They stick the grapes in the freezer before pressing them. The lower prices for these ice wines reflect the easier production.

Serving Ice Wine

Ice wines and sweet late harvest wines come in small (375 ml) bottles with big price tags. It isn't unusual to pay $60 to $200 for a half bottle. Fortunately, you serve less of them—two to three ounces—than you would a table wine. They're best served chilled and in proper stemware.

Port

The origins of port—the great fortified red wine—go back to the seventeenth-century trade wars between England and France. The British had developed a real affection for the wines of Bordeaux, but import bans and high taxes forced the English merchants to look elsewhere for their red wines. That "elsewhere" was Portugal. They found wines to their liking along the Douro River. To make sure that the wines survived the trip to England, merchants added brandy to stabilize them before shipping.

As for the discovery of the winemaking technique that results in port, there is a legend. In 1678 a British wine merchant from Liverpool sent his sons to Portugal to seek out some wines for transport. They ended up at a monastery in the mountains above the Douro where the abbot added brandy to the tank before the natural end of fermentation. The alcohol stopped the fermentation process, leaving a sweet, high-alcohol wine. The secret to making port was now out.

What's in a Name?

English merchants set up trading companies in the city of Oporto to ship these fortified wines back home. The wine itself thus became known as Porto, and, to this day, that label designation means that the contents are authentic port. These merchants are also responsible for the English names of so many port producers.

The quality port producers that are of British descent are Cockburn, Sandeman, Croft, Taylor, Syington, Dow, Graham, and Warre. The "Grand Dame" of port is Ferreira. Equally good port houses are Fonseca and Quinta do Noval.

Much like the rules governing the use of the name Champagne, port wine must come from a specific place—the Douro region of Portugal. Port-styled wines are made all over the world, but they're not true port.

Port-styled wines are made in areas such as California, Washington State, Canada, Australia, and South Africa. By law these wines must include the area of production alongside the port name. Producers tend to use grapes from their own areas in the blends, not necessarily the traditional grapes of Portugal.

The regulations governing port's production allow eighty different grape varieties to be used. In practice, though, it really comes down to a handful. There are only five classic port varieties:

- Tinta Roriz (the same as Spain's Tempranillo)
- Touriga Nacional
- Tinta Barroca
- Tinto Cão
- Touriga Francesca

Ports come in a head-spinning number of styles. Most of them are red and sweet, but some are white. The style varies according to the quality of the harvest, how long the wine ages in wood before bottling, and whether the wine is from a single year or blended with wines from other years.

Top of the Line: Vintage Port

Vintage port is not made every year. On average, only about three years in ten are suitable enough for vintage port. Even in those years, only about 10 percent of the total production will be bottled as vintage port. The rest will be used for other types of port.

Vintage port is aged in the bottle for most of its life. It spends two years in cask before bottling, which for port is not a long time. When it is bottled, its tannins are still quite fierce, so a long bottle aging is in order. Vintage port often requires at least twenty years of aging, and it can continue to improve for decades after that.

Vintage port is bottled unfiltered and unrefined, so a discernable crust will be visible in the bottle once opened. Taking time to decant the port will remove the accumulated sediment.

Vino Veritas

Single Quinta (meaning "single farm") ports emerged in the 1980s and have become very popular. They're made from grapes from single-vineyard sites, and they can be produced in years when vintages have not been declared. The producer has deemed the quality of the wine from that location to be exceptional.

Late-Bottled Vintage Port (LBV)

LBVs are probably the next best thing to vintage port. They're vintage dated and made from a producer's best grapes, but they come from undeclared years. The grapes can originate from several vineyards or farms. LBVs are bottled four to six years after harvest, meaning they've aged in cask longer than a vintage port, and are ready to drink upon release.

Tawny Port

Tawnies are aged in wood for years—as long as forty—until they fade to a tawny color. They're a blend of wines from several years and are ready to drink immediately. Once opened, they can retain their vitality for a few weeks.

A tawny port will often be categorized by age, which appears as "10 Year Old," "20 Year Old," "30 Year Old," and "40 Year Old" on the label. The number is really an average age because older, more complex wines are blended with younger, fruitier wines. Colheita ports are tawny ports from a single year (*colheita* is Portuguese for "vintage").

Ruby Port

Ruby port is one of the least expensive ports. It consists of wines from various vintages which have been aged two or three years in vessels ranging from oak barrels to stainless steel tanks. It retains its dark ruby color and has a limited shelf life.

Message in a Bottle

Vintage Character ports are ruby ports made from higher quality grapes. They are blends from several harvests, and you won't see the term "vintage character" on the label. These wines are given proprietary names like Bin 27, Six Grapes, and Boardroom.

White Port

White port is produced just like red port except It's made from white grapes—principally Malvasia Fino, Gouveio, and Rabigato grapes. Many white ports are dry, and these are typically served as an apéritif.

Sherry

Sherry is a dry or sweet fortified wine from the Jerez region of southern Spain, though its name makes you think of England. It is produced from three main grape varieties: Palomino, Pedro Ximenez, and Moscatel. Making sherry is complicated, but the results can be sensuous.

Relying on a Finicky Yeast

Most sherries begin with the white Palomino grape. At the end of the aging process, Moscatel may be added for color and Pedro Ximenez for sweetness. Before aging, of course, comes fermentation, just like any other wine. After fermentation, the base wine is fortified through the addition of a grape spirit and barreled. For those sherries destined to become Finos, Manzanillas, or Amontillados, a yeast called flor forms on the surface of the wine in the barrels. The flor influences the wine's flavor, producing compounds called aldehydes, and creates a protective layer like a crust on top of the wine, slowing oxidation. For the flor to form, the wine must be high in acidity (food for the flor), and the environment must be humid.

The flor plays no role in sherries destined to become Olorosos or one of the sweet versions. Olorosos develop their unique flavors through controlled oxidation.

The Solera Method of Blending

As the sherries age in barrel, they are subjected to one of the most fascinating blending operations in all of winemaking, known as the solera system. Imagine rows and rows of casks all stacked on top of each other—up to fourteen tiers. The oldest wines are on the bottom and the youngest on top. Producers remove about a quarter to a third of the wine from the bottom barrels and bottle it. They replace what they just removed with a wine from the next oldest, one tier up. This cascading of sherry from the younger to the older continues all the way to the top. By blending all these wines together, you get an enormously complex product. Sherries are not vintage dated, so it's perfectly fine to blend wines together from different years.

Vino Veritas

The most decadent sherry in the world is Pedro Ximenez, made exclusively from grapes of the same name. First the grapes are dried under the hot Spanish sun, concentrating the sweetness and flavor. The rich juice is then fortified and aged in solera. When finished, the aromas of the wine are reminiscent of molasses and raisins.

Types of Sherry

Not all sherries are created equal. They range in style from bone dry to so syrupy sweet you could pour them over ice cream. Here are the ones to know:

- **Fino sherries** are produced with the help of flor. They are typically pale and dry with aromas that might remind you of roasted almonds.
- **Manzanilla sherries** are basically fino sherries, but the type of flor yeast used in their production is unique and gives the wines a more aromatic character. The yeast is *Saccharomyces beticus*, and it thrives in the more humid climate of Sanlucar de Barrameda, a town in the Jerez region.
- **Amontillado sherries** are unique because they continue to age in barrel after the flor dies, picking up added personality through oxidation. Pale cream sherries are amontillados.
- **Olorosos** develop completely without the influence of flor. Dry olorosos do exist, but many of the famous ones are sweet.
- Many **sweet sherries** are made from the fermented juice of the Pedro Ximenez or Moscatel grapes. Flor does play a role in these wines. Palomino is often nowhere in sight, although winemakers are perfectly free to add dry sherry made from the Palomino grape to these wines to enhance their personality.

Madeira

Madeira is just about indestructible. While almost all other wines can't take heat and motion and won't last more than a couple of days once the bottles are opened, Madeira can survive all those things. In fact, Madeira thrives on heat; without heat it wouldn't exist.

Madeira is a Portuguese island four hundred miles off the coast of North Africa. It was perfectly situated in the Atlantic to become a thriving port for ships traveling to South America and around Africa to Asia. Transporting wine was difficult because it was undrinkable by the time the ships arrived at their destinations. Shippers added brandy or a neutral grape spirit to stabilize the wines.

After enough trips, it was discovered that the wines tasted better after the voyages than before, and Madeira, as it came to be called, that had made a round trip was better than Madeira that had traveled only one way.

Shippers began putting wine in the holds of ships for the sole purpose of developing their flavors. This proved too expensive, so winemakers had to come up with other ways to simulate the journeys. Subjecting the wine to heat did the trick.

Madeira usually starts out like port. After fermentation and fortification it spends several months in heated tanks or rooms or is left exposed to the sun. As the wine literally cooks and oxidizes it develops a caramel color and nutty flavors.

Savvy Sipping

When table wines not intended to become Madeira are exposed to heat and damaged, they pick up characteristics of Madeira. When a wine connoisseur says that a Merlot is "madeirized," it is not a compliment.

Like sherry and port, there are different types of Madeira. These types share the name of the primary grape used to make them:

- Sercial is the driest style. It has high acidity and might remind you of almonds.
- Verhelho is smoky and moderately sweet. It is suitable as an apéritif.
- Buals have a raisiny sweetness.
- Malvasia Madeiras, more frequently called Malmsey Madeiras, are the sweetest of them all and have a pronounced nutty flavor.

Marsala

Marsala wine is not just for cooking! In truth, Marsala is the famous port-styled wine of Sicily. It is made from the indigenous grape varieties of Catarratto, Grillo, and Inzolia, and can be produced in dry or sweet styles.

Marsala is unique in that it can be aged and blended according to the sherry solera system. However, the flor yeast never plays a role, so the wine will have a character all its own.

CHAPTER 19

Wine and Health

Wine has been associated with good health for thousands of years. Clay tablets dating back to 2100 BC show wine being used as medicine. In 450 BC Hippocrates recommended wine to relieve fevers, disinfect wounds, and supplement nutrition. In 1680 the doctor for Louis XIV urged the king to regularly drink Burgundy to maintain his health. In the nineteenth century, European wine drinkers escaped the ravages of cholera, scientists believe, because the wine wiped out the bacteria causing the disease. Today, researchers are trying to find out just how wine interacts with the human body.

The French Paradox

It was a Sunday evening in November 1991 when 33.7 million Americans turned on their TVs to watch *60 Minutes* and saw Morley Safer report on an odd phenomenon in France. The French people, he said, ate high-fat, cholesterol-laden foods—such as cheese, butter, eggs, organ meats—yet they had a much lower rate of heart disease than supposedly healthier-eating Americans. He went on, "Obviously, they're doing something right—something Americans are not doing. Now it's all but confirmed: Alcohol—in particular red wine—reduces the risk of heart disease."

This phenomenon became known as the French Paradox and, within four weeks of the television show's broadcast, U.S. sales of red wine soared by 40 percent. The report prompted a change in thinking of wine as a toxin to wine as a potential healer, and it encouraged research projects to investigate how wine consumption affects the heart, lungs, brain, bones—and our overall health.

Does the French Paradox still stand up?

Wine vs. Beer and Spirits

While the research is ongoing, studies conducted around the world seem to confirm that wine and other alcoholic beverages—consumed in moderation—reduce the risk of coronary heart disease by 20 to 40 percent. With all the research analyzing the effects of wine, beer, and spirits on various parts of the body, the unique health benefits of wine in isolation from other alcoholic beverages are gradually coming to light. If nothing else, these unique benefits may be at least partially linked to way wine is consumed. Unlike consumers of beer and spirits:

- Wine enthusiasts tend to drink wine with meals rather than on empty stomachs.
- Wine drinkers tend to sip more slowly.
- Wine drinkers tend to spread their drinking out over an entire week rather than binge on weekends.

The upshot is that, for wine drinkers, the alcohol may be absorbed more slowly and over a longer period of time, and the resulting health effects might be different.

What the Studies Say

It's hard not to be confused by all the scientific studies that are released every day. The information is often complicated, incomplete, or even contradictory. What is universally accepted is that excessive consumption of alcohol creates serious health risks—liver damage and hypertension among them. At the same time, evidence is emerging that moderate wine consumption can be beneficial in a number of areas.

Vino Veritas

What is "moderate" consumption?
The U.S. government defines it as no more than two drinks a day for men and one drink a day for women. One drink is the equivalent of five ounces of wine, twelve ounces of beer, or one shot (about 1.5 ounces) of spirits like scotch or vodka. Other countries define "moderate" more liberally.

Heart Disease and Stroke

Individuals who drink alcoholic beverages in moderation have a lower risk of coronary heart disease than heavy drinkers or abstainers. It doesn't seem to matter whether the alcohol comes from an expensive Bordeaux, a Budweiser, or a dirty martini. The alcohol increases the level of "good" cholesterol (HDL) in the body. HDL acts like a detergent, removing excess fat in the blood and carrying it to the liver where it is metabolized.

Much the same holds true for preventing strokes. In addition to increasing the level of good cholesterol, the blood is prevented from clotting—which reduces the risk of ischemic strokes.

Diabetes

Observational studies indicate that diabetes occurs less often in moderate drinkers than in abstainers. The Harvard School of Public Health conducted a study of 100,000 women over fourteen years. The women were divided into three levels of alcohol consumption. After factoring for family history of diabetes and smoking, the results showed that the women who drank moderately and regularly had a 58 percent lower risk of developing diabetes than abstainers. Women who drank more or less still had a 20 percent lower risk than nondrinkers. Results applied to both wine and beer drinkers—but not spirits drinkers.

Alzheimer's Disease and Dementia

Studies around the world have shown that moderate drinkers are less likely to develop dementia. Research on elderly participants have documented that the moderate drinkers performed better on memory and cognitive tests than nondrinkers.

In a Danish study designed to screen for signs of mental decline, researchers found that participants who drank at least one glass of wine a week were much less likely than those who drank no wine to develop dementia. Beer and spirits failed to produce the same results.

Bone Mass

It was once accepted that alcohol lowers a woman's bone mass, leading to osteoporosis. However, a couple of recent studies have indicated otherwise. One study was conducted to determine the effect of alcohol consumption on the bones of elderly women and how that might differ from the use of estrogen-replacement therapy. Moderate drinkers, it showed, had the greatest bone mass followed by light drinkers and followed, finally, by nondrinkers.

In a study of twins in England, it was determined that moderate-drinking individuals had significantly greater bone mass than their infrequently drinking twins.

Longevity

The American Cancer Society conducted a survey of a half million people over nine years to examine "total mortality"; that is, the risk of dying of any cause. The risk was greatest among both abstainers and people who drank six or more alcoholic beverages a day. Moderate drinkers (those who had one-half to two drinks a day) had a 21 percent lower risk than nondrinkers.

Patterns of Consumption

Current thinking is that the health effects of alcohol consumption depend on both how much you drink and your drinking patterns. Because many of the biological effects of alcohol are short-lived (lasting only twenty-four hours), the best advice seems to be, if you're going to drink, do it moderately every day. Don't save it up for weekend partying.

Savvy Sipping

Obviously, drinking alcoholic beverages is always inappropriate at certain times, such as when you're going to be behind the wheel of a car. If you are pregnant, talk to your doctor. Fetal alcohol syndrome is caused by heavy drinking.

A recent University College London study of civil servants found frequent drinking was more beneficial for cognitive function than drinking only on special occasions. Research on hypertension at the Worcester Medical Center in Massachusetts determined that men who drank monthly had a 17 percent lower risk of cardiovascular disease than nondrinkers. Weekly drinkers had a 39 percent lower risk, and daily drinkers had a 44 percent lower risk.

Although the explanations have yet to be conclusively determined, consuming alcoholic beverages with food seems to be beneficial as well.

Health Components in Wine

Wine in some cases goes beyond just the alcohol in producing health benefits. Recent research focuses on identifying specific components in wine and explaining how they work. Much of the emphasis is on antioxidants, which inhibit the oxidation of LDL cholesterol in the blood. This oxidation has been linked to clogged arteries, blood-clot formation, and tumor growth.

Antioxidants

Antioxidants in wine come in the form of phenolic compounds such as tannins and flavonoids. The flavonoids in red wine are especially powerful, more than twenty times more powerful than those in vegetables.

The antioxidant that's getting most of the attention these days is resveratrol. Resveratrol is produced in the skins of grapes in response to fungus attacks and stress. Because red wines are fermented in contact with the skins, they acquire more resveratrol than white wines and carry more potential benefits than either white wines or other alcoholic beverages.

Grapes from cold, damp climates that have to fight harder to survive produce more resveratrol than those in warm climates, and grapes that are more sensitive to growing conditions—such as Pinot Noir—seem to have more resveratrol than their hardier counterparts—such as Cabernets.

Vino Veritas

The antioxidants found in wine come from the grapes. But the antioxidants aren't exclusive to grapes. The same ones are also found in allium vegetables—onions, leeks, garlic, shallots—and in broccoli, spinach, blueberries, strawberries, tea, and chocolate!

Wine and Weight Loss

Confusion reigns when it comes to the effect of wine (and other alcoholic beverages) on weight loss. Wine has plenty of calories—about 100 calories a glass. So it would just seem logical that if you cut out wine, you'd lose weight. However, there's no evidence that giving up wine on your diet will necessarily help you shed the pounds. A 2010 study published in the Archives of Internal Medicine monitored the alcohol consumption of 20,000 trim middle-aged and older women. Those who drank alcohol in moderation over time put on less weight and were less apt to become overweight compared to nondrinkers. This was true even after taking into account various lifestyle and dietary factors that might influence a woman's weight.

Wine's calories come primarily from the alcohol. Most of the sugar was converted to alcohol during fermentation. The exceptions are fortified dessert wines, which have both higher sugar and higher alcohol contents. You may notice, too, that even some slightly sweet wines such as White Zinfandel have more calories than fully dry table wines.

Message in a Bottle

Calories in wine are directly related to the alcohol content. To determine the number of calories in a glass of wine, multiply the percentage of alcohol (found on the label) by the number of ounces you pour into the glass, and multiply that by 1.6. For example: 13 (percent alcohol) × 5 (oz.) × 1.6 = 104 total calories.

There are numerous variables that affect how wine will fit into your weight loss regimen:

- Whether you use wine to replace food or drink it in addition to food
- How much wine you consume
- How your body is genetically predisposed to process alcohol
- What foods you eat
- How much exercise you get

Wine and Carbohydrates

Wine labels are now allowed to include calorie and carbohydrate counts. Low-carb diets have been so popular that some wine companies were quick to jump on the bandwagon of low-carb wines. Wines, of course, are inherently low in carbohydrates. The residual sugar left over after fermentation determines the number of carbohydrates. Compare the amounts to other beverage choices.

▼ **CARBOHYDRATE COUNTS IN SELECTED BEVERAGES**

Beverage	Amount	Carb Grams
Red Wine	1 glass	0.4–2.3
White Wine	1 glass	0.8–1.0
Dessert Wine	2-oz. glass	7.0
Beer	1 bottle	9.0–12.0
Light Beer	1 bottle	3.0–8.0
Spirits	1.5-oz. shot	0–0.1
Coca-Cola	1 can	40.0
Diet Coke	1 can	0.3

Too Much of a Good Thing

Overindulging on any alcoholic beverage leads to the classic symptoms of queasy stomach, shaking hands, and pounding headache. Scientifically, here is what really goes on inside your body when you ingest alcohol.

How Wine Moves Through the Body

Once you take a sip of that incredible Amarone, it goes into the stomach, where 20 percent of the alcohol is absorbed. The rest moves on to the small intestines, where most of the rest is absorbed. The alcohol is delivered to the liver, where enzymes break it down. Now, the liver can only process a limited amount of alcohol at a time—about one drink an hour. When you consume more, the alcohol is in a holding pattern—in your blood and body tissues—until the liver can metabolize some more.

Vino Veritas

The alcohol that remains unmetabolized can be measured in breath and urine as "blood alcohol content" (BAC). BAC peaks within thirty to forty-five minutes after consuming a drink. BAC is measured as a percentage. In most states, .08 percent is considered legally drunk.

Men and Women Process Alcohol Differently

A man and a woman can be the same height and weight, but they will still handle that glass of wine differently:

- Women have less body water—52 percent compared to 61 percent for men. The man's body will be able to dilute the alcohol more readily than a woman's body can.
- Women have less of the liver enzyme (dehydrogenase) that breaks down alcohol, so a woman will metabolize alcohol more slowly.
- Hormonal factors have an impact. Premenstrual hormones cause a woman to get intoxicated more quickly. Also, birth control pills and estrogen medications will slow down the rate that alcohol is eliminated from the body.

The Hangover

A hangover is the body's reaction to alcohol poisoning and withdrawal. It starts from eight to twelve hours after your last drink. The severity may vary from one person to the next, but, fundamentally, it's based on how much you consumed. The symptoms might be as mild as thirst and fatigue, or as acute as headache, depression, nausea, and vomiting.

Savvy Sipping

> Heavy drinking causes brain shrinkage. Overindulging has more lasting effects than hangovers. The brain shrinks as a natural part of aging, but excess alcohol speeds it up and causes damage to the brain's frontal lobe, the part that controls cognitive functions.

There are few things you can do to cure a hangover. Time and water are your best friends at that stage, but there are some measures you can take to prevent a hangover (besides not drinking as much).

- Before you start drinking, eat something high in fat. It will delay absorption of the alcohol.
- While you're drinking, drink a glass of water between each glass of wine. It will keep you hydrated and minimize intoxication.
- While you're drinking, don't be afraid to snack.
- Before you go to bed, eat something salty to replenish what the alcohol has flushed out of your body, and then drink more water.

Wine and Headaches

For many people, wine leads to headaches even if they keep their consumption levels in check. You may be sipping a perfectly exquisite Cabernet, appreciating its maturity and its velvety texture, and suddenly the throbbing in your head starts and doesn't abate. What causes these types of headaches?

Sulfites usually get the blame. After all, the label on the wine bottle has a bold, cautionary warning: "Contains sulfites." In reality, only 1 percent of the general population has a genuine sulfites allergy, usually individuals with asthma or those on steroid medications. If you are part of that 1 percent, you'll more than likely develop rashes, abdominal pain, or extreme breathing problems from the wine. If you take a sip of Chianti and get a headache but not a rash, you cannot blame sulfites for your condition.

Message in a Bottle

Sulfites are present in lots of foods—and at usually higher concentrations than in wine. They're contained in dried fruits, jams, baked goods, canned vegetables, frozen orange juice, bacon, dried noodles, and pickled foods.

The Sulfite Story

In wine, as in other foods, some sulfites are naturally present. The primary element of sulfites, sulfur, is abundant in various forms in all living things. In winemaking, manufactured sulfites are added to wine to prevent bacterial growth and to protect against oxidation. The practice of using sulfites as a preservative isn't new, and winemakers worldwide continue to add them. Only when their wines are sold in the United States do they have to be labeled with the sulfite warning. Before that bottle of Chianti hits the shelf at Costco, an extra or new label goes on.

The amounts of added sulfites are small. They are measured in parts per million (ppm). The legal limit for some foods goes as high as 6,000 ppm. For wine the maximum allowed is 350 ppm, but most wines contain much less—typically from 25 to 150 ppm.

The law says that if a wine has a sulfites concentration of 10 ppm or higher, the label must carry the sulfite warning. To be labeled a "no sulfite wine," it can contain no more than 1 ppm. Because those wines are very perishable, they should be consumed sooner rather than later.

In general, white wines will have more added sulfites than reds. When grapes are crushed to make white wine, only the juice goes into a tank for fermentation. Red wines must be in contact with red grape skins during fermentation, and besides imparting color, the skins pass on tannins, which act as natural preservatives.

The Blame Game

Even if sulfites are not the cause of your headache, this information does little to remove it. Here are five possible sources of your wine headache:

- **Histamines**—These are chemical substances found in aged and fermented foods such as wine, cheese, and salami. They also occur naturally in eggplant. Histamines are the substances behind allergic reactions. Among other effects, they can dilate the blood vessels in your brain. Red wines usually have a higher level of histamines.
- **Tyramines**—These are chemical substances found in cultured foods such as cheese and yogurt; fermented foods like wine, dark beer, and soy sauce; and chocolate, vanilla, nuts, and beans. Tyramines are toxic, and the liver works to remove them from the body. Scientists believe that alcohol slows the rate at which the liver processes tyramines, thus resulting in wine headaches.
- **Congeners**—These organic compounds are by-products of fermentation that help give wine its characteristic flavor. When congeners enter the bloodstream, your immune system recognizes them as poisons and releases cytokines (the same molecules that fight off the flu) to eliminate them. Generally, darker beverages (red wine, bourbon) have more congeners than lighter ones (white wine, vodka).
- **Prostaglandins**—These are naturally occurring compounds in grape skins, and some people have difficulty metabolizing them. Ibuprofen blocks prostaglandins, so take one before your day of wine tasting.

Wine-Health Challenges

Real wine enthusiasts, rather than casual drinkers, look for ways to keep wine an integral part of everyday life, in spite of occasional challenges. Headaches are major challenges, of course, but there are other less-severe examples that can be managed more easily.

Purple Teeth

You may not be a professional wine taster who samples hundreds of wines in a day's time, but that does not make you immune to the discoloring effects of red wine. The stains usually are not permanent and disappear when you brush your teeth. Some serious red wine connoisseurs do notice that over time mere brushing does not remove the purple color completely. A trip to the dentist for a professional whitening procedure might be in order. However, there are some measures you can take to prevent and fix the situation.

- Wait an hour or so after drinking wine to brush. The high acidity in wine can leave your teeth sensitive to abrasion. Brushing prematurely could damage your tooth enamel.
- Drink water between sips of wine. It will help eliminate the acid.
- Before brushing, dissolve a half teaspoon of baking soda in a glass of water and take as you would a mouthwash.
- Use a fluoride rinse two to three hours before winetasting.

No Alcohol, Please

When you really like wine but have to stay away from alcohol, are you out of luck? Alcohol-free wines are available, but their resemblance to ordinary table wine, both in aroma and flavor, depends on how the producer removed the alcohol.

Historically, winemakers used steam distillation or reverse osmosis to remove the alcohol, but these processes tended to degrade the wine's flavor and aroma. Many alcohol-free wines are still made in this way, but the best are made using the spinning cone column. The winemaker sends the wine through the spinning cone, and centrifugal force basically pulls the wine apart, drastically increasing its surface area. While this is happening, nitrogen is injected into the bottom of the cone, and as it rises, it traps all the delicate compounds controlling the wine's aroma and flavor. These compounds are then condensed and added back to the dealcoholized liquid. Unfermented grape juice is often added at the end to enhance the overall beverage.

One thing you should know is that alcohol-free wines are not necessarily totally free of alcohol. If you check the label, you will usually find an alcohol level of .5 percent. One of the best alcohol-free wines is Fre, produced by California's Sutter Home Winery.

Get the Lead Out

Lead crystal is beautiful, and your crystal glasses and decanters can make your wine appear particularly elegant. Over time, however, wine can absorb some of the lead. Never store wine in lead crystal decanters, especially more durable wines such as sherry. Of course, using your lead crystal glasses every so often for a dinner party is harmless.

For new crystal, soak it in vinegar for twenty-four hours and then rinse. Stay away from harsh detergents as well, for these can increase the release of lead.

CHAPTER 20

The World of Wine Tourism

People have been making and drinking wine for thousands of years, but only recently have wineries and wine regions begun to create experiences for tourists wanting to see where their favorite bottle of red wine was made. Tours and tastings were only the beginning; now wineries from South Africa to Australia are becoming centers of culture where wine, food, hospitality, and the arts come together in fresh and exciting ways.

Four Pioneers of Global Wine Tourism

It is no secret that wine lovers have visited wineries throughout the ages. Thomas Jefferson was perhaps the most famous early wine tourist. He had a passion for Bordeaux, especially for wines from "Chateau de la Fite" and "Chateau Margau," as he wrote in his journals. Today these estates are called Chateau Lafite and Chateau Margaux, and they make some of the world's most coveted wine. However, it wasn't until the latter part of the twentieth century that wineries began to be built with hospitality in mind. This was a revolutionary concept, and these four individuals were at the forefront of this new movement.

Robert Mondavi
Robert Mondavi Winery, Napa Valley, California

Robert Mondavi died in 2008 at the age of 94, and he will be remembered not just as the father of California wine but also as the father of wine tourism. When he built his winery in 1966, the first in Napa Valley since the end of Prohibition, the cards in many ways were stacked against him. Americans were not drinking much quality wine at the time, and thanks to the devastating effects of Prohibition, the rest of the wine world had practically forgotten about California wine.

Mondavi knew he had to find an innovative way to bring people to his winery, so he designed it with hospitality in mind. He began offering free tours to the public, instructing them on the finer points of grape growing and winemaking, and promising them a tasting of his wines at the end. He or one of his sons would often stand at the winery entrance motioning to cars speeding along Highway 29 to pull in to the winery.

Robert Mondavi didn't stop there. So successful was his tour program that he began offering cooking classes, in which great chefs would prepare fine cuisine in the winery kitchen and explain how it complemented a variety of wines. He also instituted a summer jazz series in 1969 to promote not just his winery and Napa Valley as a whole but to raise money for charity. The Robert Mondavi Winery Summer Festival, as the jazz series is now called, continues to this day.

Mondavi's goal was nothing less than to rebuild a wine culture in the United States. In the process of achieving this goal, he unintentionally created a model for how wineries and wine regions could reach out to savvy wine lovers and prospective wine lovers.

Jean-Michel Cazes
Chateau Lynch-Bages, Bordeaux, France

The French have no problem making extraordinary wines, but they have been a bit slow to incorporate tourism into the day-to-day life of their winemaking regions. In the 1950s a passionate Russian-born, French-educated wine merchant named Alexis Lichine purchased a Bordeaux property which he dubbed Chateau Prieure-Lichine and advertised his new tasting room on billboards outside. The neighbors were horrified.

Jean-Michel Cazes was more successful. After overhauling the winemaking at Chateau Lynch-Bages in the 1970s, Cazes purchased a neighboring estate and turned it into a hotel complete with a restaurant staffed by a world-class chef. Cazes was also instrumental in turning the sleepy village of Bages into something more dynamic by helping establish a literary competition, a marathon, and even the occasional concert. His inspiration was Robert Mondavi, whom he met in 1978.

Bordeaux will never be like Napa Valley, and this is not necessarily a bad thing. Napa's winemaking tradition is a century old; Bordeaux's goes back 1,000 years. When visiting Bordeaux or any other region in France, it is important to appreciate this history, and thanks to innovators such as Jean-Michel Caves, you can appreciate this legacy in style.

Denis Horgan
Leeuwin Estate, Margaret River, Australia

Before Denis Horgan took possession of 500 acres of land near Margaret River in Western Australia in the 1960s, this area was mainly known for its surfing, and beer, not wine, was the beverage of choice. Then he received word from a friend that a California vintner named Robert Mondavi was looking to invest in the region, as it had recently been deemed excellent for grape growing.

Horgan began planting vines, and soon his Chardonnays were catching the attention of the global wine press. Like Chateau Mouton-Rothschild in Bordeaux, he recruited different artists to design the labels of select bottles each year. Horgan also built a restaurant, one of the first winery restaurants in Margaret River to serve dinner on Saturday nights.

Horgan will arguably best be remembered for bringing world-class entertainment to his Leeuwin Estate, a winery so far removed from metropolitan areas that in the early years of his now famous concert series he pitched tents to house some of his visitors. He recently built an airstrip to handle all of his visitors, and future plans include a golf course and hotel.

Charles Back
Fairview Wines, Stellenbosch, South Africa

Even though the policies of apartheid have been officially repealed, the cultural damage still lingers, and it has kept many tourists away from this stunningly beautiful wine region.

Charles Back refused to let history deny him his ambitions. Since the 1930s his family has farmed a property north of Stellenbosch called Fairview, and by the late 1970s, wine grapes dominated the estate. Back's stroke of genius was his sense of humor, and this is most evident in wines he created with names similar to their more famous counterparts. He released wines called Bored Doe (Bordeaux), Goats do Roam (Cotes du Rhone), and Goat Door (Cote d'Or-Burgundy), and they have become the bestselling South African wines in the Untied States.

The French did sue Back for trademark violations, as his wines' names sounded so similar to theirs. Back prevailed, and his goats are still roaming.

Keeping with the goat theme, Back's Fairview Wines estate has a goat tower which welcomes guests to the property. There is also a restaurant, and it is packed most nights, but it is Back's unique combination of marketing prowess and quality wines that have propelled Fairview Wines into one of South Africa's most visited estates.

Do All Wineries Receive Guests?

As of November 2009, the United States had 6,223 registered wineries, and that number continues to grow. California alone has more than 3,000, and tiny Napa Valley has surpassed 400. When you take into account the rest of world, you literally have tens of thousands of wineries around which to plan your next vacation. Not all wineries are created equal, however. Some wineries are huge enterprises while others may have only two employees: the winemaker and the bookkeeper. Many wineries do not entertain visitors at all, some because they cannot afford to employ a hospitality staff, and others because they sell so much of their wine through mailing lists or distribution that they don't really need a visitor center. Many wineries that do welcome visitors have drop-in tasting rooms, while others require an appointment.

Savvy Sipping

If you plan to bring your children along for your trip to wine country, have planned activities for them while you are tasting. They can become easily bored. Be sure to keep them away from breakable objects in the tasting room.

The bottom line is that advanced planning is critical if you wish to get the most out of your wine excursion. Whether your winery visit includes a tour and tasting with the winemaker or with a trained hospitality specialist, you will be welcomed warmly and passionately immersed in the story of that particular estate.

Planning Your Trip

With so many options, far and near, the most difficult part of your trip will be choosing which wine region to visit. Geographical location, obviously, is the first variable. Do you want to take a day trip close to home—or will you plan a whole vacation around a trip to the wine country of Bordeaux or Napa or Rioja?

Depending on your chosen location, you may have to narrow down the list of wineries you wish to visit. All fifty American states have wineries, but if you want to tour the wineries of Tennessee (38) or Arizona (36), you'll have fewer alternatives (and an easier decision) than if you're in Oregon (453) or Washington (564). Faced with a multitude of possibilities, one strategy is to base your selection on the wines you enjoy. If you prefer Cabernet Sauvignon, choose wineries known for this varietal. If you prefer wines from a particular winery, your trip planning just became much easier. Be sure to visit both large and small wineries, as each can offer distinct yet superlative experiences.

Vino Veritas

In Australia most of the wineries are open to the public. But don't look for signs for the tasting room, because they go by another name. Australians call tasting rooms "cellar doors." Australian producers can make a dizzying number of wines—so there's plenty to sample.

When to Go

When to go is another variable. During the winter months, wineries (particularly those in the more popular wine regions) are much less crowded. Traffic is minimal. Of course, the vines are dormant—so you'll see bare trellises in the vineyards.

In the summer the vines are fully awake and the grapes are well on their way to getting ripe. You'll enjoy better weather but more crowded wineries and restaurants. The busiest time of the year by far is autumn—harvest time—and some wineries will host special events to mark the occasion. To avoid the biggest crowds during this time, visit your chosen wineries on weekdays or in the morning. Each season, then, has it advantages.

Finally, remember that the dead of winter in the Northern Hemisphere is the beginning of summer in the Southern Hemisphere. This means that if you live in the United States and wish to experience the grape harvest in New Zealand, visit in late February or early March, a time when California vineyards are just beginning to wake up from their winter dormancy.

Be Prepared

Once you've arrived at your destination, following these tips will make your outing more memorable—for all the right reasons.

- Don't be too ambitious. Three to five wineries in one day is plenty for the best of wine tourists. Part of the fun is soaking in the beauty and personality of each estate.

- If in doubt, call ahead to the wineries to confirm their tasting room hours, just in case a winery only receives visitors by appointment. It also helps to find out what wineries charge for tastings and tours. Very few wineries these days offer complimentary tastings.
- Designate a driver. Spitting is not considered a bad habit at wineries. Spittoons should be available in each tasting room. If nobody in your group wishes to spit, then arrange for a limousine or private bus to escort you from place to place.
- Dress sensibly. Wear comfortable shoes if you've scheduled vineyard walks, and dark colors for potential wine spills.
- Leave your perfume or cologne at home. You may not smell it, but the person next to you trying to catch the bouquet of her wine will be painfully aware of it.
- Take a cooler. If you buy wines on your trip, you'll need a place to store them during the day. Tossing them in a hot trunk might cook them before you get them home. Imagine the disappointment.
- Take a notebook. Many wineries will give you a list of the wines you have tasted. If such lists are not available, you will want to jot down the name of that Riesling you enjoyed.

Tasting Rooms

The tasting room will likely be your first stop. Wineries with extensive visitor programs may have a reception area set apart from the tasting room. If you have booked a tour, visit the reception office first.

Winery tasting rooms are not necessarily located at the wineries themselves. Some wineries pool their resources and open cooperative tasting rooms in nearby towns. In addition to wine tasting, many tasting rooms will also have souvenirs available for purchase. Larger wineries will have a separate retail store. If you do choose to purchase a bottle of wine after your tasting, some wineries will apply the tasting fee toward your wine purchases. Larger wineries may also have more than one tasting room. One tasting room might be for club members, another might offer wines not available in the marketplace, and still another might serve the estate's more widely distributed bottles.

Wine drinkers can be nervous about their first winery visit. But their fears usually disappear as soon as they enter the tasting room. When you walk into a tasting room, you'll be greeted by a member of the tasting staff who will enthusiastically tell you about the winery and the wines. She may suggest a tasting order or hand you a menu organizing the available wines based on varietal, vintage, or appellation. If a tasting order isn't suggested to you, start with whites, advance to reds, and finish with sweet wines.

Message in a Bottle

You don't have to try all the wines. If you're a fan of a particular varietal, say Chardonnay, you may want to sample just those at each winery. This technique can help you learn how different vineyards, different vintages, and different winemakers affect taste. The strategy will give you a greater understanding of that varietal.

Only a small amount of wine—perhaps an ounce—will be poured into your glass. Keep in mind that you are in a tasting room, not a bar. Besides, these one-ounce tastings add up quickly. On the other hand, you may not want to drink the entire amount, preferring to move on to the next wine. Wineries understand this, which is why they should have spittoons available.

Pitchers of water should be available automatically. The water is also for rinsing your glass between wines or between types of wines, such as when you go from whites to reds. Just pour a little water into your glass, swirl it around, and dump it out in the bucket. Alternatively, you can drink the water to refresh your palate before the next wine. If you see a bowl of crackers on the counter, they're for cleansing your palate as well.

Once again, you will not offend the tasting room attendant if you spit or dump out wine. It's perfectly acceptable—and expected.

Tasting Room Etiquette

The temptation is to treat winery visits like big cocktail parties, but a more subdued attitude is best. Be respectful toward the people who are pouring (who are often the owners), toward winery property, and toward the other visitors.

Learning While Tasting

You are not going to like every wine you taste. Simply dump the unconsumed portion into the spittoon without making a disparaging remark. If you do not like a particular wine, the winemaker is not necessarily the one to blame. Everyone has his or her preferences.

You should never be afraid to discuss your impressions of the wines—politely, of course—with tasting room attendants. They are there to help you understand and appreciate what you are tasting, not pass judgment on you. Most winery personnel are trained to provide information and usually jump at the chance to talk about the wines. Their explanations, descriptions, and stories can add to your appreciation of their wines. They should be able to discuss the following subjects with you:

- Which grapes they grow in their own vineyards.
- Which wines are aged in barrels—and for how long.
- What have been the best vintages—and why.
- What foods would pair well with their wines.
- Which wine the winemaker is best known for.

Sometimes the winemaker will be available to answer questions. This depends on the size of the winery, the time of year, and whether the winemaker is busy making wine. Your chances are better at smaller wineries, where the winemaker produces the wine and also runs the tasting room. If she is there, ask her to sign one of the bottles you purchase.

Savvy Sipping

Remember the most important rule of picnicking at a winery: Always drink that winery's wine! They have welcomed you into their "house" and onto their property to enjoy yourself. It's just rude and tacky to take up their picnic space while sipping someone else's wine.

Spitting Is Allowed

When you visit several wineries in a day, an obvious concern is consuming too much alcohol. You can minimize both the amount and the effects.

- You don't have to taste every wine at every winery. You and your traveling companions can sample different wines. If one of you finds something really special, the rest of the group can try it too.
- Drink lots of water. It mitigates the dehydrating effects of alcohol. Pack plenty of bottled water for your trip and drink it often.
- Eat along the way. Start with a good breakfast and snack throughout the day. It helps to absorb the alcohol.

Rules of Two

Under ordinary circumstances, asking for a second taste of one particular wine is inappropriate. However, if you're sincerely interested in buying the wine, let the pourer know your intentions. When you've paid a tasting fee for one, it's perfectly okay to share your glass with a friend. It's also a way for the two of you to cut your alcohol consumption in half.

To Buy or Not to Buy

You are under no obligation to buy a bottle of wine at the tasting room, but there may be some good reasons to do so. Smaller production wineries have limited distribution, and their wines can be difficult—or impossible—to find on retailers' shelves. The only way to enjoy that coveted bottle at home might be to buy it either at the tasting room or from the website.

Message in a Bottle

It may seem illogical, but you'll often find wines selling for less at a wine store than at the winery. Because large retailers can get significant volume discounts, they can sell the wine at less than the list price suggested by the winery.

Some wineries, even high-production ones, intentionally restrict the availability of their finest bottles to the winery. That's where you can taste them, and that's where you can buy them. You can typically buy by the bottle or by the case (12 bottles). Wineries will often apply a case discount (and sometimes a half-case discount). It can be a case of one varietal or mixed.

Wine Clubs

Most wineries have mailing lists (and, increasingly, e-mail lists) to notify you about new releases that you can in turn order directly from the source. During your tasting, don't be surprised if your tasting room host mentions these lists as well as any wine clubs you might be eligible to join. When you join a club, you receive regular shipments of wine during the year. Read the fine print; the number of shipments and bottles per shipment vary from club to club. Here are other benefits you will likely enjoy as a club member:

- You get wines before they're released to the public.
- You receive a discount on wines.
- You get a discount on merchandise purchased from the winery.
- You may be invited to attend members-only special events.

Wine Country Dining

If an area of the world is renowned for its fine wines, that area will also likely attract talented chefs who create cuisines worthy of the wines around them. Many of the most visited wineries in the world have restaurants attached to them. Some American states or counties prohibit wineries from operating restaurants, but this had not stopped regions such as Napa and Sonoma from developing world-class cuisine. Wineries without restaurants might still have chefs, but they will only cook for private, corporate, or special winery events.

If you visit a famous wine region during the summer or autumn, you will need reservations to get seats at the more popular establishments. If you do get in on the evening of your choice, prepare to indulge. Many restaurants offer multicourse tasting menus complete with wine recommendations for each course. Don't be afraid to try new things, and certainly don't be intimidated by the sommelier. He or she is there to help.

Dining at exclusive restaurants gets expensive, but there are ways to save. For example, many wine-country restaurants allow you to bring bottles of wine with you to dinner. For what is called the corkage fee, the server will open that bottle for you and you can enjoy it with your meal. Some restaurants do not charge corkage fees at all. Since restaurants mark up wine prices significantly from their retail value, you might be better off not purchasing a bottle from the restaurant wine list, unless you see a rare gem you cannot do without.

Vino Veritas

The town of Yountville in the Napa Valley has around 3,000 year-round residents, yet this hamlet has more Michelin-starred restaurants per capita than any other city, town, or village in the world. The town's most famous restaurant is Thomas Keller's French Laundry.

Wine Tourism Resources

Every winery visit is a unique experience. As different as wine personalities are (with thousands of grapes and endless blending options—and effects of terroir), so too are winery profiles. A few generalities may be true for all visits, but each winemaking facility has a character all its own. Here are some online resources to guide you in planning your wine country adventure.

- Argentina: *www.argentinawinetourism.com*; *www.mendoza.com.ar*
- Chile: *www.winesofchile.org*
- France: *www.burgundy-wines.fr*; *www.bordeaux-tourisme.com/index_uk*
- Spain: *www.vibrantrioja.com*
- Italy: *http://tuscanblog.com*
- Australia: *www.southaustralia.com*; *www.margaretriver.com*
- South Africa: *www.wine.co.za*
- New Zealand: *www.wtn.co.nz*
- California: *www.landofwineandfood.com*; *http://napavalley.com*; *www.sonoma.com*; *www.sbcountywines.com*
- New York: *www.liwines.com*; *www.fingerlakes.org*
- Oregon: *www.oregonwine.org*
- Washington: *www.washingtonwine.org*; *www.facebook.com/winetourism*

CHAPTER 21

Wine and the Internet

The Internet has revolutionized the way people shop, date, exchange information, conduct research, and, of course, decide which wines to buy. Until very recently, the wine press was dominated by a few voices; now, thanks to the Internet, there are literally hundreds of ways to connect with fellow wine lovers, the wineries behind your favorite wines, and those who review wine for a living.

Visiting a Winery's Website

The most fundamental and perhaps obvious way to connect with a winery is through its website. Here you can learn about the wines—perhaps even download notes from the winemaker—view a calendar containing that winery's special events, sign up for the wine club, and view photos of the estate.

Winery websites are becoming more versatile as technology advances. Traditionally, if a winery offered tours or other paid programs, you could find out times and pricing from the website. Today, thanks to programs such as vinovisit.com, you can book that tour or that program without even leaving that winery's website.

A good winery website will also have easily identifiable links to that winery's social media outlets, including its blog, Facebook Fan page, and Twitter account. Thanks to these, interacting with a winery has never been easier.

Eat, Drink, Blog

One of the greatest innovations of the Internet is that it has allowed the average person to weigh in on matters as diverse as politics, health, religion, finance, and what to drink at night with your dinner. These contributions take the form of blogs, and now there are literally tens of millions of them in existence. Wine blogs constitute only a tiny fraction of that number, but their influence is immense.

Before the advent of wine blogging, most American wine lovers obtained their news and recommendations from three print sources: the *Wine Advocate*, *Wine Spectator*, and *Wine Enthusiast*. These periodicals are in no danger of folding, and they still influence wine buying habits around the world, but they are no longer the only game in town.

Pioneers of Wine Blogging

The earliest wine bloggers were motivated by a passion for wine as well as a desire to comment on wine-related issues the mainstream wine press either failed to cover or covered too one dimensionally. The powerful wine critics behind *Wine Enthusiast*, *Wine Spectator*, and the *Wine Advo-*

cate eventually established their own blogs, but now theirs were not the only voices.

Two of the earliest American wine blogs of note are Vinography (*www .vinography.com*), founded by Alder Yarrow, and Fermentation (*http:// fermentation.typepad.com*), founded by Tom Wark, both in 2004.

Yarrow writes that in 2003, he typed "wine blog" into Google and received zero results. That motivated him to establish Vinography, which now boasts more than 90,000 readers a month and includes content ranging from wine and restaurant reviews to an annual wine blog awards competition. Tom Wark focuses more on wine's place in popular culture, reviewing marketing strategies of wineries and industry trends.

Blogs can also act as platforms from which wineries promote events and give consumers a behind-the-scenes look at how their favorite wines came to be. Three California wineries in particular have practically raised blogging to an art form. Like Vinography and Fermentation, contributors to these winery blogs are united by a passion for wine, yet each blog has a voice as unique as the winery itself.

Savvy Sipping

There are more than seven hundred wine blogs on the Internet today. By the time you read this, that number will be obsolete.

Tablas Creek Vineyards, Paso Robles

Tablas Creek Vineyards began blogging in December 2005 (*www.tablas creek.typepad.com*). Tablas Creek is unique among California wineries in that it specializes in grapes from the Rhone region of France. Most wine drinkers are used to drinking wines made from Bordeaux grapes, including Cabernet Sauvignon, Merlot, and Malbec, whereas Rhone grapes include Syrah, Grenache, Mourvedre, and Roussanne. Tablas Creek not only uses its blog to market its wines and wine club; the blog also serves as an educational tool. Entries on these lesser-known Rhone grapes abound. Other entries recount with remarkable transparency the costs of planting a vineyard and the dining exploits of the national sales manager. With crystal clear photographs and perfect prose, the blog of Tablas Creek sets the bar very high.

St. Supery Winery, Napa Valley

St. Supery (*www.stsupery.com*) practically created the rules for how a winery can use the Internet to celebrate its wines and connect with its consumers. Their blog is only a single pillar of their online presence, but it just might be the sturdiest pillar of all. A casual glance at the blog invites two conclusions right away: St. Supery wants you to drink their wines with food, and they want you to interact with others about your experience. Recipes abound, such as Dungeness Crab Timbale and Pan Roasted Pork Tenderloin with Mango, Mint, and Lavender Salsa. The blog seamlessly incorporates the occasional video into the content, inviting fans to events at which St. Supery wines are the centerpiece. The idea is to connect with fellow wine lovers – hopefully lovers of St. Supery wines – and build relationships with them while building brand loyalty.

Message in a Bottle

Wine blogging has become such a force that in 2008 the first Wine Blogger's Conference took place. Three hundred wine bloggers converged in Walla Walla, Washington, for the 2010 event.

Jordan Winery and Vineyards, Alexander Valley

Jordan Winery (*http://jordanwinery.com*) was established in 1972 in northern Sonoma County. Their blog was activated somewhat recently, but they have made a major statement without really making much noise. The blog has a minimalist look and feel, but the content is immediately engaging. Practically every post has a superbly edited video in which the chef, winemaker, or vineyard manager shows you what's happening in the garden, in the barrel cellar, or in the vineyard during harvest. You don't read about it; you practically live it. Wine regions throughout the world have this allure about them, and Jordan Winery immerses you in that allure.

Social Media and Wine

When Facebook was founded in a Harvard dorm in 2004, serious wine blogs were just beginning to gain traction. Twitter arrived in 2006, when

Facebook had about 12 million active users. (Facebook now has 400 million active users.) Today, when most Internet users log on, one of their stops is a social media site. The ability to connect with people and companies all over the world has immediate appeal, and wine-related companies are quickly learning that utilizing social media intelligently can help them build brands, reach consumers on a more personal level, and hopefully sell some bottles. In the world of wine and social media, three innovators are leading the charge.

The Ripe Stuff

Which winery has the most Twitter followers?
At this writing, Eagles Nest Winery in San Diego, California, has the most Twitter followers: 32,447.

Gary Vaynerchuk and Wine Library TV

At this writing, Gary Vaynerchuk has 43,074 fans on Facebook and 851,397 followers on Twitter. If you enjoy wine and don't know who he is, you will.

Vaynerchuk discovered his passion for wine while working at his parents' liquor store in Springfield, New Jersey. As the wine buyer, he made it a point to sample every wine featured on his store shelves so that he could offer the best recommendations to his customers. Vaynerchuk's desire to connect with his current and future customers eventually led him in February 2006 to create video podcasts of himself evaluating a series of wines. He posted these podcasts on his website (*http://tv.winelibrary.com*).

Wine enthusiasts were immediately impressed with Vaynerchuk's enthusiasm and the fresh way he analyzed wines, a style vastly different from the somewhat dour seriousness of many of the wine critics at the time. One of his trademarks is spitting sampled wine into a bucket with New York Jets logos all over it, a jab at anyone who thinks that wine and snobbery go together.

Vaynerchuk didn't stop there. Soon he was all over Facebook and Twitter, further expanding his influence in the world of wine. His goals remained the same: to bring his passion for wine and his passion for helping people together. He now has his own consulting company, VaynerMedia, a book,

Crush It: Why Now is the Time to Cash in on Your Passion, and a lecture circuit that takes him all over the world.

In the first weeks of its release Vaynerchuk's first book *Crush It!* climbed to number one on the Amazon bestseller list for web marketing books. It also opened at number two on the *New York Times* bestseller list and number seven on the *Wall Street Journal* bestseller list.

Rick Bakas, Director of Social Media at St. Supery Winery, Napa Valley

With a name like Bakas, you are practically predestined to work in the wine business. His family name was originally spelled "Bacchus" (the Roman god of wine) before his great-grandparents changed the spelling. On his website, *www.rickbakas.com*, he claims an obsession with finding the perfect food and wine pairing, so it was only a matter of time before he ended up in wine country.

Bakas's business has always been branding. Before his foray into wine, he worked at Nike and created branding for NFL, NBA, and NCAA teams. In a business as competitive as wine, it is critical that a winery's brand message captures the public's attention because, quite simply, there are so many wineries fighting for your attention! St. Supery Winery in Napa Valley made headlines in 2009 when they hired Bakas as full-time director of social media, the first winery to create such a position.

Some wineries are seeing so much economic potential in utilizing social media that they are hiring social media directors. In Napa, a company called Vintank consults with wineries to help them get the most out of social media.

Creating content for Facebook, Twitter, and the blog merely scratches the surface of Bakas's program at St. Supery. Bakas also takes the tasting room on the road, hosting events at restaurants, retail stores, and wine festivals across the country that feature St. Supery wines. While being social, guests at these events use social media, especially Twitter, to broadcast their experiences to fellow wine enthusiasts, ideally St. Supery wine enthusiasts, around the world. These events became known casually as TweetUps, and they are taking the wine world by storm. Events such as these give St. Supery a unique firsthand glimpse into what consumers are thinking about their wines and wine in general.

In short, Rick Bakas's total command of food, wine and social media has made him and St. Supery Winery a force to be reckoned with. Whether it's posting a blog recipe that complements St. Supery's newly released Malbec or using YouTube to invite people personally to TweetUps, Bakas has all his bases covered.

Hardy Wallace and the "Really Goode Job"

In 2009 Sonoma County's Murphy-Goode Winery advertised a job opening that many people thought was a joke. The job title was "Lifestyle Correspondent," and the responsibilities included wine tasting, blogging, using Facebook and Twitter, and capitalizing on any other creative online tools to turn Murphy-Goode into a cutting-edge wine brand. The compensation? $10,000 a month for six months and free housing in the heart of wine country.

When wine lovers discovered that this was not a faux job, thousands of applications poured in. The final ten candidates were flown to California for interviews, and Hardy Wallace of Atlanta, Georgia, founder of the "Dirty South Wine" blog (*www.dirtysouthwine.com*), emerged victorious.

Hardy Wallace combines the passion and freshness of Gary Vaynerchuk with the technical skill of Rick Bakas, and throws in a sense of humor and creativity rarely encountered in the wine industry. By the end of his six months, Hardy had brought more than 5 million unique visitors to the Murphy-Goode website (*www.murphygoodewinery.com*), and more than 75 percent of the visitors to the Murphy-Goode tasting room mentioned the "Really Goode Job" promotion. Not bad for six months.

Two of Hardy's most intriguing exploits were not even wine-related, but they were strokes of genius. In September 2009 Hardy posted some blog photos suggesting that the house Murphy-Goode gave him to live in was haunted. He also used social media to promote his candidacy for Mr. Healdsburg 2010, a pageant recognizing the community's finest gentlemen.

Hardy no longer works for Murphy-Goode, but the winery and the industry as a whole will never be the same. Hardy taught the wine world something very important about social media: Be yourself! Rather than using social media solely to promote Murphy-Goode wines, Hardy used social media to recreate Murphy-Goode in his own image. Hardy did not stop being Hardy when he went to work at Murphy-Goode, and his authenticity was part of his success.

Vino Veritas

Another winery with its act together in the world of social media is King Estate, Oregon (*www.kingestate.com*), a certified-organic winery specializing in Pinot Gris and Pinot Noir. A touching March 2010 blog entry contains a photo gallery of employees and their kids picking daffodils to assemble into bouquets for the American Cancer Society.

Winery Social Media and You

The core values of the wine industry around the world are generosity and hospitality. Social media by its very nature embodies these two values: reaching out to others with useful information and inviting others to become part of what you are doing. If you wish to connect with a favorite winery using social media, here are some guidelines.

It's Easier Than You Think to Connect

The two most popular social media sites are Facebook and Twitter. You must have a Facebook and/or Twitter account to become fans or followers of wineries with presences on either one. Creating an account is free.

Use the Facebook search feature to find the winery with which you wish to connect. If more than one entry pops up, look for the fan page, which probably has the most followers anyway. Some enthusiasts have established group pages for their favorite wineries, but these are not always sources of reliable information.

For Twitter, go to *http://search.twitter.com* and search for your winery. You will get a list of recent tweets containing the winery's name. Look for tweets containing the @ symbol followed by the name of the winery you wish to follow. Click on that link. You will be sent to that winery's Twitter home page where you can become a follower and see all the official tweets from that winery.

Don't Be Afraid to Chat

Wineries want to get to know you! Don't be afraid to send tweets, tack Facebook posts on the walls of your winery's fan page, or post comments on the winery's blog. Good or bad, wineries want to know what you think. You will probably get a response within twenty-four hours from the manager of that winery's social media program. Just be civil, and you will get a civil response.

Becoming a Fan or Follower Has Benefits

Many wineries offer promotions exclusively for their Facebook and Twitter followers, ranging from wine discounts to invitations to special events.

Using the Internet to Find that Perfect Bottle

Shopping for wine can often be a stressful experience, especially when you go to a wine shop wanting a bottle of Chardonnay but see more than one hundred Chardonnays on the shelves. How can you be sure that you will like that $30 bottle? Thanks to the Internet, wine lovers can now shop with more confidence. Clearing houses of wine information have sprung up on the Internet, many of which have features that allow wine lovers to network with other wine lovers in an attempt to get the most bang for their wine buck in the marketplace.

CellarTracker

CellarTracker (*www.cellartracker.com*) is the brainchild of Eric LeVine, a former Microsoft employee whose passion for wine led him to create a rudimentary version of CellarTracker in 2003. The vision was simple: build a database of personal wine collections complete with notes about those wines, so that inquiring wine lovers and experienced wine collectors can connect and learn about a wine before buying or drinking it. By the end of 2009, CellarTracker boasted a database of more than 12 million bottles with 900,000 user tasting notes available.

As an example, suppose you are curious about the status of your bottle of 1982 Chateau Lafite. Perhaps you have a special event coming up and wonder if the bottle might finally be ready to drink. When you search for the wine on CellarTracker, any tasting notes submitted on the bottle will pop up along with a user score out of one hundred. Scores close to one hundred are good signs. You will also be able to click on a link to see what retailers lucky enough to have the bottle in stock are charging for it. An added benefit is that if you have the proper privileges, you can access the tasting notes of professional critics alongside the notes of general consumers. If 90 percent of the tasting notes recommend drinking the Lafite, then you have your answer.

CellarTracker did a massive site redesign for 2010. The new site looks quite a bit like Facebook, situating all tools in a more user-friendly style.

Snooth

CellarTracker's biggest competitor is Snooth (*www.snooth.com*), created in 2006 by former venture capitalist Philip James. Snooth also has a massive database of wines, but unlike CellarTracker, it has a massive database of user-submitted articles on topics as diverse as the country cooking of Ireland and the wines of Sauternes. Snooth is arguably the best single-stop online resource for wine education in the world.

Message in a Bottle

A superb example of a winery using social media to brand build is Judd's Hill Winery in Napa Valley. Visit *www.juddshill.com* and tune in to Judd's Enormous Wine Show to see what pirates and ukuleles have to do with great wine.

If you want to buy a bottle of Merlot for a party, but have no idea who makes the best Merlot for the money, you can simply search for Merlot in

Snooth. You will receive hundreds of recommendations, as well as links to articles on Merlot the grape. You can read reviews of the Merlots presented to you, as well as interact with the reviewers. Users can assign ratings to the wines, but these come in the form of stars, not numbers. Numbers, admittedly, give you a more exact idea of the wine's quality, but Snooth's sheer mass of information more than makes up for this. Even better, if you find a wine you like, Snooth allows you to connect with more than ten thousand wine retailers worldwide. You can discover in one click if the wine shop down the street from you has the wine you want and whether it charges what you feel like paying.

One of Snooth's greatest features is its food and wine pairing suggestions. For many of the wines in its database, Snooth will provide a link to a recipe at *www.myrecipes.com* that complements the wine in question. Therefore, if you know you want to drink a bottle of St. Supery Sauvignon Blanc that night, you can also take that perfectly matched scallop recipe with you when you go to the store.

CHAPTER 22

Careers in Wine

You know who you are. You have just returned from a week-long trip to Napa Valley or some other famous wine region, or perhaps you have just returned from a memorable three-hour dinner at which you helped consume the best bottle of wine you have ever had. The thought briefly crosses your mind, "I would sure love to quit my day job and wake up every day with grapevines out my bedroom window and my winery a few steps down the driveway." Then you see your mortgage statement on the kitchen table and the thought evaporates. Not so fast!

Before You Quit Your Day Job

The wine industry in all its facets is indeed fascinating, and those who work in it tend to be very passionate about what they do. Passion is an asset, because depending on your goals, you may have to work long hours with little pay in the early stages to achieve the financial security and leisure time you envision. You may also have to move. If you live in Alaska but have a burning desire to make Nebbiolo wines, you have to go to Italy!

Even for entry-level positions in the wine industry, competition can be fierce. If you wish to enter the wine industry from a completely unrelated field, you need to invest in some kind of wine education, ideally leading to a certification. Some suggestions follow. Such courses can help clarify which sector of the wine industry might be a good fit for you. Once you know where you want to go, you need to know what to expect in terms of pay, perks, and hurdles you might encounter along the way. Stay tuned for some advice.

As in most professions, education is critical. Who you know certainly does not hurt, but if you are at the cusp of a new wine career, it helps to have a degree or certification in wine under your belt, especially if you are saying farewell to an accounting firm. In some cases you do not even need to enroll at a college or university. Some wine societies will send course materials to your home, which you study before showing up at a designated location for an exam.

Message in a Bottle

Warren Winiarski, the founder of the legendary Stag's Leap Wine Cellars in Napa Valley, whose 1973 Cabernet Sauvignon bested its French counterparts at the 1976 Judgment of Paris tasting, does not have a winemaking degree. He learned the business as an apprentice at Souverain Cellars.

Going Back to College

If you desire to become a professional winemaker or vineyard manager but don't have the savings to drop everything and move to Bordeaux for a year for an unpaid apprenticeship, then enrolling at a college or university with viticulture (grape growing) and enology (winemaking) programs might be a good idea. Depending on your patience and interest, you can get associate through doctoral degrees at these places.

- **California** makes 90 percent of American wine, and most winemakers and vineyard managers in the state studied at either Fresno State University (*www.csufresno.edu*) or the University of California at Davis (*www.ucdavis.edu*). You could also study right in the heart of Napa or Sonoma! Napa County has Napa Valley College (*www.napavalley.edu*) and Sonoma County has Santa Rosa Junior College (*www.santarosa.edu*). Both offer associate degrees in viticulture, and your instructors might be local winemakers.
- **Oregon** has developed a superb reputation for Pinot Noir and Pinot Gris, and those who don't want to leave the state to learn how to grow it or make it can go to Oregon State University (*http://oregonstate.edu*).
- **Washington** makes the most wine after California. Walla Walla Community College (*www.wwcc.edu*) and Washington State University (*www.wsu.edu*) have superb programs.
- **New York State** makes more wine than people think, and Cornell University (*www.cornell.edu*) trains many of those winemakers. Cornell's Introduction to Wine class, taught by Stephen Mutkoski, has an enrollment of more than 700 students each term.

What If I Don't Want to Make Wine or Grow Grapes?

The wine industry is full of professionals who work neither in wineries nor vineyards. If you own a California winery, you need someone to sell your wine in New York City, and you will pay that person top dollar. If you manage a Michelin-starred restaurant with a wine list the size of a dictionary, you need someone to recommend wines to customers and to keep the list current. If jobs such as these appeal to you, wine education is still a must. Here are the major players in the world of wine certifications.

Court of Master Sommeliers

Founded in England in 1977 and established in America in 1987, the Court of Master Sommeliers (*www.mastersommeliers.org*) is the gold standard in education for restaurant wine service. Other organizations credential sommeliers, and these organizations often do an outstanding job, but the Court is most recognized internationally. Even if you choose not to work in a restaurant, this course is still a good investment. The Course offers four certification levels.

- **Introductory.** After two days of coursework, you sit for a written test on the world's major wine regions and wine service. A score of 60 percent is necessary to pass.
- **Certified.** If you pass the Introductory course, you can take a more difficult one-day exam that includes a blind-tasting component. Again, you must score 60 percent to pass and move on.
- **Advanced.** To prepare for the Advanced course examination, you must attend five days of courses. The exam stretches over two days and covers wine theory, service, and again, a blind tasting. The examiner sets six glasses in front of you, and you determine what they are. If you manage a score of 60 percent, you move on.
- **Master.** One of the most difficult wine exams in the world is the Master Sommelier exam, stretching over three days. The exam covers theory, service and tasting, but in this case the exam is oral. The successful candidate must score at least 75 percent on each section to pass.

At this writing, there are only 105 Master Sommeliers in North America. Fifteen of these professionals are women.

Society of Wine Educators

The Society of Wine Educators (*www.societyofwineeducators.org*) was founded in Washington D.C. in 1977 and is arguably the most popular certification for professionals working in wine distribution and wine retail. An advantage of this certification is that no coursework is required to sit for the two exams the Society offers. You study independently, with the help of a text, and then register for the exam.

- **Certified Specialist of Wine.** Candidates have one hour to pass a 100 question multiple choice exam. Seventy-five questions must be answered correctly to pass. There is no tasting component. One must pass this exam to move to the next level.
- **Certified Wine Educator.** The CWE is a vastly more difficult four-hour exam comprising 85 multiple choice questions, an essay, a tasting exercise in which you must identify eight wines from a list of ten possibilities, and another tasting exercise in which you must determine how eight wines are flawed or imbalanced. For the theory, 80 percent correct passes; for the tasting exercises, six correct out of eight pass. The Society added a teaching component in 2010.

Culinary Institute of America

The Culinary Institute of America (*www.ciaprochef.com*) is the most prestigious culinary school in the United States, and they have recently begun offering wine credentials through their Napa Valley campus. This program has two advantages: You get to study wine in the Napa Valley in state-of-the-art facilities, and your instructors are world-renowned wine writers and Master Sommeliers. The CIA, as it is playfully called, offers two certifications.

- **Certified Wine Professional Foundation Level 1.** This half-day exam consists of multiple choice questions and a blind tasting of three wines.
- **Certified Wine Professional Advanced Level 2.** This two-day exam consists of a written test and a blind tasting of nine wines. You don't have to take the foundation level exam to sit for the advanced level exam.

Message in a Bottle

Four of the instructors at The Culinary Institute of America's Napa Valley campus are Master Sommeliers.

Wine & Spirit Education Trust

This London-based Wine & Spirit Education Trust (*www.wset.co.uk*) is older than the Court of Master Sommeliers and only offers its courses in select U.S. locations. It focuses less on restaurant wine professionals and more on individuals working in wine marketing, sales and public relations. There are four levels of certification.

- **Foundation Certificate.** A one-day course concludes with a brief exam containing multiple choice questions and a food and wine pairing exercise.
- **Intermediate Certificate.** After three days of coursework, you take a fifty-question multiple choice exam on the third day covering foundational wine theory.
- **Advanced Certificate.** You take a more difficult exam on the fifth day of coursework. The exam includes theory and blind tasting.
- **Diploma in Wines and Spirits.** This two-year course of study concludes with an evaluation similar to a dissertation. You must have the Advanced Certificate to qualify for the Diploma.

Institute of Masters of Wine

With the Master Sommelier certification, the Master of Wine (*www.mastersofwine.org*) is the world's most elite wine designation. You must apply for admission, possessing at least the Advanced Certificate from the WSET. Candidates are evaluated over a period of two years before they sit for the notoriously difficult Master of Wine Examination. It consists of three parts:

- **Theory.** Candidates must submit four three-hour written papers on viticulture, winemaking and other relevant subject matter.
- **Practical.** You will sit for three separate twelve-wine blind tastings.
- **Dissertation.** You must submit an extended essay on a subject of personal interest relevant to your career goals.

There are fewer than 300 Masters of Wine in the world.

What Will You Do with that Certification?

By the time you have your wine credential, you probably know whether you want to make the wine, sell the wine, or talk about the wine in an educational setting. As you continue to focus your career goals, here are the most popular professions in the three prongs of the industry: making, selling, educating.

Winemaker

Winemakers do much, much more than taste wine out of barrels all day. Wouldn't that be nice? Some winemakers work at wineries which don't own their own vineyards, so these folks must decide which grapes to buy and use for their wines. Winemakers who have acres and acres of vines at their disposal must understand those vineyards intimately, deciding for example when to harvest the grapes. They decide how long to age the wine in barrels, which types of oak barrels to use, which blends the wines will assume, and when to bottle. If a fermentation tank springs a leak or the winery wishes to expand, the winemaker must respond to these issues.

It is true that winemakers get to attend lavish dinners, often with their wines at the center, and travel to exotic locations to learn about winemaking techniques and connect with other winemakers. However, winemakers experience the constant stress of dealing with nature, especially when frost or rain damages precious crops. In addition, there are precious few job openings for winemakers, but if you are good at what you do and patient, you can easily make $150,000 and up at the top of the profession.

Vino Veritas

Where can I find current job openings in the wine industry nationwide?
The best place to start is *www.winebusiness.com*, a database maintained by the Wine Communications Group, Sonoma, California.

Vineyard Manager

Vineyard managers are farmers, plain and simple. They need to know how to plant and replant a vineyard and deal with any pests or viruses that might give the grapevines a hard time. They need to anticipate when vineyard jobs need to be done and arrange to have a certain number of workers present for those jobs. They also work closely with the winemaker, especially as harvest draws near.

If you love drinking wine and working with your hands in the great outdoors, then this is the job for you. Vineyard managers do not show up at 9 and leave at 5. Your day can begin early and finish late, especially during harvest, as grapes are often picked in the early morning hours. At the top of this profession you can make six figures. To start, $40,000-$50,000 is reasonable.

Cellar Master

Larger wineries will have cellar masters. At smaller wineries, the winemaker is the cellar master. Cellar masters make sure the winemaker has everything he or she needs to make great wine. Thus, cellar masters should have degrees in winemaking. From training and overseeing winery staff to ordering equipment, the cellar master's role is critical.

Cellar masters often help the winemaker with blending, so you might get to taste and evaluate wines before they enter the bottle. Downsides to the job include long hours and physically demanding work. You could conceivably make $50,000-$60,000 as a seasoned cellar master.

Cellar Rat

The name is not glamorous, but this job is one of the best ways to get your foot in the door at a winery. You don't need a wine degree or certification, just a passion for wine and big muscles. Your responsibilities will be to clean out tanks, move barrels, drag hoses from place to place, and do whatever the cellar master tells you to do. You won't make much money, but you will learn the business from the ground up. Many famous winemakers began their careers as cellar rats.

Import/Export Manager

Ever wonder how that bottle of unpronounceable German wine ended up on the wine list at your favorite restaurant? An importer probably found it on a trip to Germany, brought it back to the U.S., and the restaurant wine director bought it from a distributor that an importer convinced to carry it. Importers are like talent scouts, always searching for the next big thing. To be successful as an importer, it helps to know one or two foreign languages. Comprehensive wine knowledge is also critical, so court the Court of Master Sommeliers or Culinary Institute of America.

Working long hours in the early stages will be necessary, but at the top, you can easily make six figures. Your endless days will be spent not only networking with winemakers in distant lands but also convincing distributors to pick up your newfound wine and pitch it to restaurants and wine shops.

Distributor

Given the organization of the U.S. wine market, wineries cannot sell their wines directly to retail stores and restaurants. They must go through distributors, or middlemen. To be successful as a distributor, you must have a keen awareness of which wines will sell in the marketplace. You will have literally thousands of wineries courting you for your business. You must also be cognizant of the web of state alcohol regulations. Thus, a degree in business and a certification from the Society of Wine Educators or Wine & Spirit Education Trust will serve you well. As distributors consolidate, the number of job openings will shrink, but if you get your foot in the door and pay your dues, you could see an annual salary of $100,000.

Vino Veritas

The largest distributor in the United States is Southern Wine and Spirits, which operates in twenty-nine states.

Sales Rep

Perhaps the most critical position at a winery after the winemaker and vineyard manager is the sales rep. These hardworking individuals convince restaurants, hotels, wine shops, and distributors to carry the wines they represent. In the brutally competitive wine marketplace, sales reps must tell the story of a winery or brand in an engaging way and develop relationships with buyers or potential buyers. Distributors also employ sales reps to present their portfolios to prospective customers.

Savvy Sipping

Gallo, the largest wine producer in the world, offers sales and management training to highly qualified college graduates.

At the beginning of your career as a sales rep, you will be poor and work long hours calling on accounts. Perks along the way include fine dining at restaurants you convinced to purchase your products, as well as trips to wineries whose wines you represent. In the long run, with some tenacity, patience, and of course talent, you can make a very good living, especially if you work in large markets such as Chicago, New York, and Los Angeles.

Sommelier/Restaurant Wine Manager

The title of sommelier has an air of glamour about it—the white-gloved gentleman carefully pouring the contents of a dusty old bottle into a crystal decanter and serving it gracefully. This image is not complete fantasy, but the sommelier or restaurant wine manager does occasionally have to perform unglamorous duties. Training servers, keeping the wine list updated, spending time tasting with sales reps, advising customers on which wines to buy—these tasks will find their way into your workday.

In order to make the most money and have the most career options, you should train to become a Master Sommelier through the Court of Master Sommeliers. This course trains you not just in wine regions and varieties but in the aesthetics of wine service. The Advanced Certificate at least should be a goal. If you do land a job at a wine-focused restaurant, you will get to taste beautiful wines and occasionally travel to the vineyards from which the wines originated. The major downside is a long workday. When people leave their jobs at 5 and head to your restaurant, your workday is just beginning.

Wine Shop Owner/Manager

Wine retail store owners and managers need a level of wine knowledge that would be expected from a sommelier. Customers will ask about food and wine pairing, which new wines they should buy, and how long they should cellar particular bottles. Like a sommelier, the wine store owner will also need to handle the sometimes mundane administrative tasks of keeping track of inventory, ordering, and training store associates. Wine store owners also need to be keenly aware of their communities, such that they don't stock their shelves with Chateau Margaux when the locals want Yellow Tail.

If this career path appeals to you, become a cashier or store clerk at a wine shop, and over time you will move up the ladder. You will learn the basics of customer service and immerse yourself in wine at the same time. You might also get to taste some really extraordinary bottles. You have the potential to make more money if you own or manage a chain of stores rather than a single store.

Wine Writer

For many, the prospect of becoming a wine writer is the ultimate wine job. You can work from home, fly around the world visiting out-of-the-way wine regions, and have wine samples sent to your home for review. The most successful wine writers, such as American Robert Parker and Englishman Hugh Johnson, certainly enjoy these perks, but the reality is that very few wine writers can support themselves entirely from their writing. Many work day jobs as they submit articles to magazine and newspapers, or book ideas to editors. Rejection of one's work is far more common than acceptance. The keys to success are to understand the wine business inside and out, know the major players, and have exceptional writing skills.

The wine writer plays a very important role in the industry as a whole. Wine columnists employed by national publications such as the *New York Times* and *Wine Spectator* reach millions of readers, educating them to become more discerning consumers of wine. Wines reviewed positively by wine writers can sell out quickly from stores and restaurants, making winemakers and sommeliers smile all the way to the bank.

Wine Educator

This is one of the broadest careers in the wine industry. Wineries need wine educators to work with visitors, whether they are in the trade or from the general public. Universities need professors to train the next generation of winemakers and vineyard managers. Culinary schools need instructors who can move easily between the worlds of wine and food as they shape future executive chefs.

You will need an advanced degree in your chosen field to reach the higher echelons of this career path. Master Sommeliers often teach in culinary schools. Winemakers with Ph.D.s in fermentation science will often work in higher education and conduct research that betters the industry as a whole. Good public speaking skills, good writing skills, and a passion for wine are essential is you wish to be a professional wine educator.

CHAPTER 23

Making Wine at Home

Any trip to a fabulous wine region such as Tuscany, Napa Valley, Mendoza, or Burgundy should be enough to make you want to drop everything and become a winemaker. While becoming a professional winemaker might not be an option, there is no reason why you cannot make wine at home. Your finished product will not be as transcendent as that bottle of Opus One you popped for your daughter's twenty-first birthday, but at least you can now officially call yourself a winemaker.

Advice Before You Begin

Home winemaking can be fun and challenging, and it may even turn into a lifelong hobby. Your expectations for the quality of the final product need to be realistic and based on how much time and, yes, money you put into the enterprise.

Message in a Bottle

There are as many as 750,000 home winemakers in the United States. In Sonoma County, California, home winemakers stage a grand tasting once a year and award medals to the best wines.

Before you start designing your wine labels, here are some extremely important issues to consider before you begin.

- **Make sure you have enough space.** If you plan to buy grapes and crush them yourself, you will need much more work space than if you buy grape concentrate from a brewing supply store. If you plan on the former, your garage is most logical base of operations. Depending on the size of your garage, you may have to park your car outside as you make your wine. Also, your work area must be somewhat cool and as clean as possible.

- **Decide how much money you want to spend.** Wineries spend millions of dollars on new equipment and on maintaining their existing equipment. This is not an option for most of us. If you are serious about establishing a home operation, you will have to spend several hundred dollars to acquire the most basic equipment. Again, if you plan to forego buying and crushing grapes, your costs will be considerably lower. It is also possible to rent home winemaking equipment.

- **Don't be afraid to fail.** Experience will be your most valuable teacher. If your first foray into home winemaking does not result in the most palatable wine, your next attempt will undoubtedly be more successful. Keep a journal as you make your wine, noting every step in the process, from the amounts of sulfur dioxide you add along the way to the type of yeast you use. Some techniques you will use again; others, you will discard.

- **Purchase a more detailed home winemaking guide.** The information in this chapter will allow you to produce a passable wine, but if questions or concerns spring up along the way, here are two excellent supplementary texts, both available from Amazon.com: Jon Iverson, *Home Winemaking Step by Step* and Daniel Pambianchi, *Techniques in Home Winemaking*.

Gathering the Equipment

Good wine is as good as the grapes used to make it, but without the right equipment, high-quality grapes will not have the chance to shine. Here is the most basic equipment to have on hand before you begin. You will need more of certain pieces depending on how much wine you plan to make.

- Grape crusher or destemmer (you can rent one for as little as $30)
- Plastic screen (colander) for filtering out grape solids during pressing (if crushing grapes)
- Basket press (again, only if starting from actual grapes)
- Primary fermenting vessel(s). These vary in size. The best are made of stainless steel, but cheaper options are food-grade plastic garbage cans with lids.
- Glass carboys, around five or so gallons in size. You will need these for wine racking and storage.
- Siphon
- Wine thief, for wine sampling and testing
- Stirring spoons or paddle
- Plastic tubing, at least ten feet
- Bottle brushes for cleaning
- Air locks for fermentation vessels
- Rubber stoppers for carboys
- Funnels
- Measuring cups
- Brix hydrometer (saccharometer)
- Regular thermometer
- pH test strips able to sustain readings below 3.7
- Bottles and closures

Any employee of a home brewing store will know what each of these is and how to locate them. You will also need to purchase certain wine additives, which are chemical in nature. Even if you decide not to crush your own grapes, these are critical.

- Acid blend (tartaric) for adjustments. These come in pill bottles or bags.
- Active dried yeasts (Prise de mousse)
- Yeast Nutrient, such as diammonium phosphate
- Potassium Metabisulfite powder for sulfur additions
- Sugar, in case you need to raise levels in must before fermentation
- Cleaning solution for hoses, carboys, bottles, etc. Everclear alcohol is a good option.

The following additives are optional, though recommended:

- Pectic enzymes, while the least critical of all the additives, do break down the structure of the grape creating more juice and a more clarified wine. Home wine makers add about one half-teaspoon pectic enzyme per gallon of fruit juice prior to starting fermentation.
- Grape tannin, which gives your red wine more structure, if needed.
- Malolactic fermentation culture, definitely not needed if you are making wine from a kit involving grape concentrate.

Once you have gathered the necessary equipment and additives, do not immediately start crushing your grapes. First, sterilize everything. Thanks to bacteria and other microbes, your home winemaking experiment can go horribly wrong before you even begin if your equipment is not clean.

Getting the Juice Out

You can certainly make good-tasting wine from jars of grape concentrate, but nothing compares to buying actual grapes and crushing them yourself. It is now possible to buy *Vitis vinifera* grapes in most states. If you live in New England, for example, you can buy California wine grapes from

American Wine Grape Distributors, based in Massachusetts, which imports grapes such as Merlot and Chenin Blanc.

Vino Veritas

The U.S. government regulates home winemaking. While you no longer need a permit to make wine at home—this requirement was lifted in 1979—it is still illegal for a household to produce more than 200 gallons (1,000 bottles) a year. It is also illegal to sell wine made at home, but this does not mean that you can't give bottles to friends.

Before you can decide how many grapes to buy, you need to decide roughly how much wine you want to make. A very rough but helpful conversion is that one gallon of juice can be pressed from about sixteen pounds of grapes. A half-ton of grapes will produce one barrel of wine.

Once you have your grapes, sort through them very carefully. If any grapes appear rotten or if any have slightly torn skins, remove them from the rest.

Now comes the most tedious part. If you have bunches of grapes, you must separate the grapes from the stems by hand. Sure, you could buy or rent a destemmer, but they are more expensive than crushers and presses. If you crush the grapes with the stems attached, you risk adding needless astringency and bitterness to your wine. So, invite some friends over, open up some bottles of somebody else's wine, and have a destemming party.

If red wine is your goal, then the grapes go into the crusher. For home winemakers, crushers will fit very easily over your fermentation vessel, whether steel or plastic. If you wish to make a white wine from a white grape, you could put the grapes directly into the press and squeeze, thus bypassing the crushing process. The key for any white wine is to minimize skin contact. Presses are designed to channel the precious juice into a container waiting right next to it.

Even if you decide to crush white grapes before pressing, you must still press the must (skins, juice, seeds) before you start fermentation. When pressing white whole grapes or freshly crushed white must, it's a good idea to place some kind of sieve over the juice-receiving container, as this will trap seeds and other grape matter from mixing with the juice. You want the white grape juice to be as clear as possible.

Preparing the Must for Fermentation

At this point, the freshly crushed must is extremely vulnerable to oxidation, white more than red. You must make your first sulfur addition. In addition, you must test the must for total acidity and sugar level (Brix) before beginning the all-important fermentation. Too little acidity and the must is fair game for microbial spoilage, and the wine will be flabby and lifeless. Too little sugar and the wine will not reach a respectable alcohol level.

Sulfur should be your first concern, however. Raise the total sulfur dioxide of your wine, whether white or red, to 50 ppm (mg/L) by adding *less than* a quarter teaspoon of powdered potassium metabisulfite. If your grapes look a little beat up, you could add as much as a quarter teaspoon, raising the level to 75 ppm. Use your stirring paddle to combine.

After you have added sulfur to your container of white juice, seal the container securely and leave it in a cool place. After at least twelve hours have passed, check the juice and you will see that even more grape matter has precipitated out of the wine and settled at the bottom of the container. Using your siphon and tubing, transfer the clarified juice directly into your fermentation vessel, which, ideally, should be composed of stainless steel.

Savvy Sipping

Any winemaker, whether working at home or in the winery, will be extremely careful not to add too much sulfur. Too much will not only kill the added yeast, which you need for fermentation, but create extremely unpleasant aromas.

Now, you must check the acid and sugar levels. For the former, follow the instructions in your acid test kit. For the former, your target pH should be no higher than 3.7. Use your pH test strips. Add your tartaric acid slowly, no more than a teaspoon at a time, to get to the correct reading. If your total acidity is too high, the yeast you need to add for fermentation will not function!

Next, check the sugar level using your hydrometer. A reading of 21° Brix means you can expect an alcohol level of 12 percent in your finished wine. The magic number is 0.575, which you multiply by the Brix reading to get your potential alcohol. If the sugar level is higher than you desire, you can add water to lower it, but check your acid levels again, because adding water affects acidity. If your sugar level is too low, you can add grape concentrate bit by bit until the desired level has been achieved. You can also dissolve one cup of pure cane sugar in one-third cup warm water to create a syrup, which you can also add in small amounts to achieve the desired Brix.

Savvy Sipping

Do not acidify with citric acid, an option which may be appealing at first due to its low cost. If you only use tartaric acid, you have a better chance of making a cleaner wine. If you acidify with citric acid before fermentation, the yeast can convert it into acetic acid, and your wine could be rendered undrinkable.

When you are ready to start fermenting, make sure that you do not fill your fermentation vessel to the very top. In fact, only fill about 80 percent of it. When fermentation begins, carbon dioxide in the form of foam will rise from the juice/must, and you don't want this to overflow. Also, if you are making red wine, you need room in the tank to punch down the cap.

Getting the Yeast Ready to Ferment

If only fermentation were as easy as dumping yeast into your juice or must! For the yeast to even work, the environment in which you choose to ferment needs to be warm, so if you live in North Dakota and wish to ferment in your garage in January, make sure your garage has a heater. Red wines should successfully ferment amidst temperatures ranging from 65° to 85° F, whereas for whites the temperature should be between 55° and 65° F.

When you went to the home brewing shop to buy your bag of yeast, you may have noticed that some yeast are better suited to dry red wine, others to dry white wine. If the yeast bag says Prise de Mousse, that will handle most home fermentations. If in doubt, check with a store employee.

The yeast cells also need food to function. Just like we need to have breakfast and lunch to get us through our workdays, yeast need certain nutrients to thrive, mainly nitrogen. Therefore, before you add the yeast to your juice/must, add approximately 12 ounces of diammonium phosphate (DAP) per 225 liters (one barrel) of juice/must you wish to ferment. The package will give you more detailed instructions about how much to add.

Finally, just like you can't work and sleep at the same time, you have to wake up your yeast before they can start fermenting. Always read the package before beginning, but here is a good strategy: In a sterile container, mix 10 grams of yeast with 100 ml of 102°F water. Wait 15 minutes, and add 100 ml of grape juice. Wait 15 more minutes, and add another 100 ml of grape juice. Once you see the mixture start to bubble, then you add the mixture to your fermenter full of juice/must.

Monitoring Fermentation

Once yeast nutrient has been added, add your activated yeast to your fermentation vessel. Yeast converts sugar into alcohol and carbon dioxide in the absence of oxygen, so make sure you cover your vessel. Make sure your cover is not so tight that carbon dioxide cannot escape. If your cover is too tight, your tank could explode!

During fermentation, you must perform the following three tasks:

- **Check the temperature several times a day.** If it is too hot or too cold, the yeast will not function. The yeast generates heat during fermentation, and temperatures of 90° F are typical. If you get sustained reading above 90°, take steps to cool the system, such as adding dry ice.
- **Check the Brix level.** Simply withdraw some juice/wine and use your hydrometer. Once the Brix reading reaches 0.5 degrees, the wine is dry (some grape sugars do not ferment).
- **Punch down the cap.** If you are making red wine, the released carbon dioxide will push the grape skins to the top of the fermentation vessel. If these are not broken apart and submerged, they will form a hard surface over the wine.

Because carbon dioxide is produced during fermentation, be sure you ferment in a well-ventilated space. If you do not take this precaution, then you or a loved one risks asphyxiation.

You may encounter a situation in which the yeast begin the process of fermentation and then suddenly stop before the wine is dry. This is symptomatic of a stuck fermentation, and while unfortunate, it does not necessarily mean you have to throw everything out and start over. Stuck fermentations usually take place when the temperature gets too high or the yeast run out of nutrients. Before you do anything else, take the juice/wine's temperature. If it is not too hot or too cold, try stirring with your paddle. If this does not restart fermentation, you still have options:

- Bring must temperature to about 68°F.
- Add another round of activated yeast.
- Add more diammonium phosphate (amount depends on how much wine you are making), or a composite nutrient addition such as Yeastex or Fermax.

If your goal is a sweeter red or white wine, you can stop fermentation yourself by lowering the temperature. The will preserve some of the grape's natural sugar in the finished wine. Again, a wine is dry when 0.1 degrees Brix has been achieved. An inexpensive Clinitest can be used to assess dryness.

Post-Fermentation Racking and Pressing

Once fermentation has ended for white wine, the wine needs to be removed from the fermentation tank. Its usual next step is a glass carboy or an oak barrel. Using your siphon and plastic tubing, rack as much of the wine as you can off of any remaining sediment and into your chosen container.

For red wine, leave the wine and skins together in the tank until the desired color has been reached. Rack the free-run wine off the skins and transfer the mass of skins, pulp, and seeds (pomace) to your press. Slowly squeeze out any remaining wine. Do not press too hard or you will fracture seeds. If you have decided not to invest in a press, put a sturdy sieve over a food-grade plastic trash can, place the pomace in the sieve, and use your hands to press out the remaining wine. (You might want to wear plastic gloves while you do this!)

Once you have pressed the pomace, the leftover skins make perfect composting material for your garden.

Once the wine is out of the fermentation tanks, you need to adjust sulfur dioxide levels once again. At this point, it might be worth preparing a 10 percent stock solution of potassium metabisulfite for your sulfur additions. It's quite easy to make: Just dissolve 100 grams of potassium metabisulfite in one liter of water. Here is a chart to help you determine how much of the solution to add to your wine:

Sulfur Dioxide Concentration (ppm)	10	20	30	40	50	75	100
	Added ml of 10 percent stock solution						
1 gallon wine	.66	1.3	2.0	2.6	3.3	4.9	6.6
10 gallons wine	3.3	6.6	9.9	13.1	16.4	24.6	32.9
50 gallons wine	32.9	65.7	98.6	131.4	164.3	246.4	328.6

Wine freshly racked out of its fermentation vessel should have its total sulfur dioxide levels adjusted to no more than 50 ppm. If you desire malolactic, or secondary, fermentation to occur, do not make a sulfur addition at this point. Also keep in mind that the lower the pH of the newly fermented wine, the less sulfur dioxide you need to add.

Once the wine is in its aging vessel, whether a carboy or a barrel, the wine will have to be racked again. Grape matter will continue to precipitate out of the wine, and since you want the clearest wine possible, you will have to pull the wine out, put it in a temporary container, clean out any sediment, and then return the wine to its original container. With each racking, test the sulfur dioxide levels. It is not necessary to add sulfur at each racking, but you must maintain 30 ppm free sulfur dioxide. Don't forget to taste the wine as it ages.

Malolactic (Secondary) Fermentation

Malolactic fermentation is the process by which the sharper malic acid is converted into the softer lactic acid through the influence of non-spoilage bacteria. Putting your red or white wine through this process might be desirable if the total acidity of your new wine is so high that wine is almost too tart to drink. In addition, malic acid is a food source for a spoilage bacteria, so getting the malic acid out of the system might be a good idea even if your wine does taste balanced.

Vino Veritas

A by-product of malolactic fermentation is diacetyl, a compound that creates a butterscotch or butter aroma in white wines. While diacetyl is present in red wines, its concentration is typically not high enough to be detected. The levels of diacetyl produced depend on factors ranging from the bacteria strain used to whether citric acid was used to acidify.

Malolactic fermentation can take place on its own, but adding a prepared culture will likely yield better results. Usually, malolactic starter cultures are packaged in such a way that one package is good for between five and ten gallons of wine. Once the amount of malic acid drops below .03 grams per liter, malolactic is finished and the wine can be aged further.

It is perfectly fine to rack your wine before malolactic fermentation has ended. The key is to keep your sulfur dioxide addition low enough such that malolactic fermentation can finish.

Getting Ready to Bottle

Once malolactic fermentation has ended and the wine has been clarified to your liking, you can begin to think about bottling. If you want your wine to exhibit oak influences, but you would rather not spend $1,000 on a new, sixty-gallon French oak barrel, you can purchase a pound of French oak chips for as little as $15. Submerge these chips in your carboy and sample the wine every few weeks until the desired flavor profile has been achieved. Adding from one to three grams of chips per liter of wine should work.

If you do wish to subject your wine to some degree of aging, make sure to store your carboys or barrels in cool, dark places and check the sulfur levels repeatedly. You can also still adjust the acidity at this stage if you desire.

Bottling and Enjoying

While the process of making wine is part of the fun, nothing beats drinking it. When the time comes to bottle, make sure your bottles are clean. If you choose to use corks, purchase the tapered variety, as these can be more easily inserted by hand. If you buy the corks in a sealed bag or from a reputable winemaking supply store, you do not need to sanitize them.

Vino Veritas

How do I know how many bottles I will need for my wine?
One gallon of wine will require about five standard sized (750 ml) bottles.

Before the corks go in, make your final sulfur dioxide addition of approximately 30 ppm. (Total sulfur dioxide levels should be no higher than 150 ppm.). Then use your siphon and tubing to move the wine from carboy or barrel to bottle. Be sure to leave no more than a half-inch between the bottom of the inserted cork and the wine.

If you choose to soak your corks before inserting them in the bottles, leave the bottles upright for about a week to give the corks time to dry. Then you can lay the bottles on their sides for storage. Homemade wines should not be aged for any significant duration. They should be consumed within a few months after bottling.

Pronunciation Guide

Albariño
ahl-bah-REE-nyoh

Alsace
ahl-SASS

Amarone
ah-mah-ROH-neh

Asti
AH-stee

Auslese
OWS-lay-zuh

Banyuls
bah-NYUHLS

Barbaresco
bar-bah-RESS-koh

Barbera d'Alba
bar-BEHR-ah DAHL-bah

Barbera d'Asti
bar-BEHR-ah DAH-stee

Bardolino
bar-doh-LEE-noh

Barolo
bah-ROH-loh

Beaujolais
boh-zhuh-LAY

Beerenauslese
BAY-ruhn-OWS-lay-zuh

Blanc de blanc
BLAHNGK duh BLAHNGK

Blanc de noir
blahngk duh NWAHR

Blauburgunder
BLOW-ber-guhn-der

Blaufränkisch
blow-FREHN-kish

Bollinger
BOHL-in-jer

Bordeaux
bor-DOE

Botrytis cinerea
boh-TRY-tihs sihn-EHR-ee-uh

Bourgogne
boor-GON-yuh

Brouilly
broo-YEE

Brunello di Montalcino
broo-NELL-oh dee mawn-tahl-CHEE-noh

Brut
BROOT

Cabernet Franc
ka-behr-NAY FRAHNGK

Cabernet Sauvignon
ka-behr-NAY SAW-vee-nyohn

Campania
kahm-PAH-nyah

Carmenère
kahr-meh-NEHR

Carneros
kahr-NEH-rohs

Cava
KAH-vah

Chablis
shah-BLEE

Champagne
sham-PAYN

Chardonnay
shar-doh-NAY

Château Cos d'Estournel
sha-TOH kaws dehss-toor-NEHL

Château d'Yquem
sha-TOH dee-KEHM

Château Gruaud-Larose
sha-TOH groo-oh lah-ROHZ

Château Haut-Brion
sha-TOH oh-bree-OHN

Château Haut-Bailly
sha-TOH oh bah-YEE

Château Lafite Rothschild
sha-TOH lah-FEET rawt-SHEELD

Château Lagrange
sha-TOH la-GRAHNZH

Château Latour
sha-TOH lah-TOOR

Château Margaux
sha-TOH mahr-GOH

Château Mouton-Rothschild
sha-TOH moo-TAWN rawt-SHEELD

Château Pétrus
sha-TOH pay-TROOS

Châteauneuf-du-Pape
sha-toh-nuhf-doo-PAHP

Chenin Blanc
shen-in BLAHNGK

Chianti
kee-AHN-tee

Chinon
shee-NOHN

Cinsault
SAN-soh

Clos de Vougeot
kloh duh voo-ZHOH

Cognac
KOHN-yak

Colheita
kuhl-YAY-tah

Condrieu
kawn-DREE-yuh

Copita
koh-PEE-tah

Corton-Charlemagne
kor-TAWN shahr-luh-MAHN-yuh

Côte de Beaune
koht duh BOHN

Côte de Nuit
koht duh NWEE

Côte d'Or
koht DOR

Côte Rôtie
koht roh-TEE

Côtes du Rhone
koht deu ROHN

Crianza
kree-AHN-zah

Cuvée
koo-VAY

Dolcetto
dohl-CHEHT-oh

Dosage
doh-SAHJ

Douro
DOO-roh

Doux
DOO

Eiswein
ICE-vine

Enology
ee-NAHL-uh-jee

Enophile
EE-nuh-file

Frizzante
freet-SAHN-teh

Fumé Blanc
FOO-may BLAHNGK

Gamay
ga-MAY

Gavi
GAH-vee

Gewürztraminer
guh-VURTS-trah-mee-ner

Grand cru classé
grahn kroo klah-SAY

Graves
GRAHV

Grenache
gruh-NAHSH

Grüner Veltliner
GROO-ner FELT-lee-ner

Halbtrocken
HAHLP-troe-ken

Hermitage
her-mee-TAHZH

Heurige
HOY-rih-guh

Kabinett
kah-bih-NEHT

Krug
KROOG

Lambrusco
lam-BROO-skoh

Languedoc-Roussillon
lahng-DAWK roo-see-YAWN

Loire
LWAHR

Mâcon Villages
mah-KAWN vee-LAHZH

Madeira
muh-DEER-uh

Malbec
mahl-BEHK

Médoc
may-DAWK

Meritage
MEHR-ih-tihj

Merlot
mehr-LOH

Méthode champenoise
may-TOHD shahm-peh-NWAHZ

Meunier
muh-NYAY

Meursault
mehr-SOH

Mis en Bouteille
mee zahn boo-TEH-yuh

Moët & Chandon
moh-EHT ay shahn-DAWN

Mosel
MOH-zuhl

Mourvèdre
moor-VEH-druh

Muscadet
meuhs-kah-DAY

Muscadine
MUHS-kuh-dihn

Muscat
MUHS-kat

Nebbiolo
neh-BYOH-loh

Nouveau
noo-VOH

Orvieto
ohr-VYAY-toh

Pauillac
poh-YAK

Penedès
pay-NAY-dahs

Perrier-Jouët
peh-RYAY zhoo-AY

Petit Verdot
puh-TEE vehr-DOH

Petite Sirah
peh-TEET sih-RAH

Picpoul
PEEK-pool

Pinot Blanc
PEE-noh BLAHNGK

Pinot Grigio
PEE-noh GREE-zhoh

Pinot Gris
PEE-noh GREE

Pinot Noir
PEE-noh NWAHR

Pinotage
pee-noh-TAHJ

Piper Heidsieck
PIPE-er HIDE-sehk

Pomerol
paw-muh-RAWL

Pommard
paw-MAHR

Pouilly-Fuissé
poo-yee fwee-SAY

Pouilly-Fumé
poo-yee few-MAY

Premier cru
preh-MYAY KROO

Primitivo
pree-mee-TEE-voh

Prosecco
praw-SEH-koh

Quinta
KEEN-tah

Riesling
REEZ-ling

Rioja
ree-OH-hah

Riserva
ree-ZEHR-vah

Sancerre
sahn-SEHR

Sangiovese
san-joh-VAY-zeh

Sauternes
soh-TEHRN

Sauvignon Blanc
SAW-vee-nyohn BLAHNGK

Sec
SAHK

Sekt
ZEHKT

Sémillon
seh-mee-YAWN

Semillon
SEH-meh-lon

Shiraz
shee-RAHZ

Soave
SWAH-veh

Sommelier
saw-muhl-YAY

Spätlese
SHPAYT-lay-zuh

Spumante
spoo-MAHN-tay

Syrah
see-RAH

Taittinger
that-teen-ZHEHR

Tastevin
taht-VAHN

Tavel
ta-VEHL

Tempranillo
tem-prah-NEE-yoh

Terroir
tehr-WAHR

Tinto
TEEN-toh

Trocken
TROH-kuhn

Valpolicella
vahl-paw-lee-CHEHL-lah

Verdelho
vehr-DEHL-yoh

Verdicchio
vehr-DEEK-yoh

Veuve Clicquot Ponsardin
vurv klee-KOH pawn-sahr-DAN

Vin de pays
van duh pay-YEE

Vinho Verde
VEEN-yoh VEHR-deh

Vino Nobile de Montepulciano
VEE-noh NAW-bee-lay dee
mawn-teh-pool-CHAH-noh

Vitis Vinifera
viht-ihs vihn-IF-uh-ruh

Viognier
vee-oh-NYAY

Vouvray
voo-VRAY

Weissburgunder
VISE-ber-guhn-der

Zinfandel
ZIHN-fuhn-dehl

Glossary

acidity
Naturally occurring acids in grapes that are vital components for the life, vitality, and balance of all wines.

aging
Maturing process of a wine to improve its taste.

alcohol
The major component in wine. Also known as ethyl alcohol.

appellation
The official geographical location where the grapes used in the wine are grown.

aroma
The smell of a wine.

astringent
The puckering sensation in the mouth attributable to the tannins and acids found in some wines.

austere
A tasting term that is used to describe young wines that have not yet developed a discernable aroma.

balance
A tasting term that describes how well a wine's components complement each other.

barrel
A container used to store or ferment wine.

big
This term is used to describe wines that are of full of flavor and with high levels of tannins, alcohol, and grape flavor extracts.

bite
A result of good levels of acidity (especially in young wines).

bitter
Unpleasant taste that registers at the back of the tongue.

blanc de blanc
A white wine—most often sparkling—made exclusively from white grapes.

blanc de noir
A white or slightly tinted wine—and usually sparkling—made exclusively from red grapes.

blend
The technique of mixing wines of different varieties, regions, and barrels from different years.

body
Perception of fullness or texture in the mouth due primarily to the wine's alcohol.

bottle aging
Allowing wine to acquire complexity, depth, and texture in the bottle.

bouquet
The combination of flowery and fruity aromas that come from the alcohols and acids in a wine.

breathe
Allowing air to mix with a wine to develop its flavor.

brut
Dry style of Champagne and sparkling wine.

capsule
The protective cover of tin, lead, aluminum, or plastic that is placed over the top of a bottle of wine to insulate the wine from outside influences.

Cava
The Spanish term for sparkling wines made using the traditional Champagne method.

character
A wine's features and style.

clarity
The appearance of wine that has no cloudiness.

clean
Wines that are straightforward and have no unpleasant odors or flavors.

cloudy
The opposite of clarity; wine that is visually unclear.

complex
Nuances of flavors of a wine often achieved with aging.

cork
The spongy material from the bark of the cork tree used to seal wine bottles.

corked
Wines that have the smell of wood dry rot resulting from a defective cork.

crisp
Wines with good acidity and taste without excessive sweetness.

cru
French term meaning "growth."

cuvée
Blend; in the production of Champagne, cuvée is the specific blend of still wines used as a base for Champagne.

decanting
Pouring wine from a bottle into a carafe or decanter.

depth
Wines with full-bodied, intense, and complex flavors.

disgorging
Removing sediment from a bottle of Champagne following secondary fermentation.

dry
Opposite of sweet. All the sugar from the grapes has been converted to alcohol during fermentation.

earthy
Flavors derived from the soil where the grapes have been grown.

enology
The study of wine and winemaking; also oenology.

extra dry
Champagne classification where there is a slight perception of sweetness.

fat
A big, soft, and silky wine that fills the mouth.

fermentation
The process that turns grape juice into wine. The enzymes in the yeast convert sugar into alcohol and carbon dioxide.

fining
Clarifying young wine before bottling to remove impurities.

finish
The aftertaste or impression a wine leaves after it's swallowed.

fortified wine
Wine whose alcohol content is increased by adding brandy or neutral spirits.

fruity
The flavor or aroma of fruits in wine.

hard
An abundance of tannin or acidity.

ice wine
Extremely sweet wines made from grapes that have been frozen on the vines prior to harvest; also called Eiswein.

late harvest wine
Wine made from ripe grapes left on the vine for periods in excess of their normal picking times, resulting in an extreme concentration of sugar.

lees
The sediment of yeasts and small grape particles that settle in the barrel as wine develops.

maceration
Technique of fermenting uncrushed grapes under pressure to produce fresh, fruity wine.

magnum
A bottle holding 1.5 liters or the equivalent of two standard bottles.

Meritage
Term used for both red and white American wines that are produced by blending traditional Bordeaux grape varietals.

nutty
A fine, crisp flavor often found in sherries and fine white wines.

oak
The flavor imparted to wine by barrel aging. It can be best described as a toasty or woodlike flavor. Sometimes a vanilla flavor will be imparted by fine oak to the wine.

oxidation
Exposure of wine to air, which causes chemical changes and deterioration.

pigeage
A French term for the traditional stomping of grapes by foot.

press
The piece of equipment used to gently separate grape juice from grape skins.

punt
The indentation at the base of a wine or Champagne bottle, which reinforces the bottle's structure.

reserve
A term without a legal definition in the United States but often used to designate a special wine.

richness
Rich wines have well-balanced flavors and intrinsic power.

sec
A term which, when applied to Champagne, describes a relatively sweet wine. Used in the context of still wines, the term means dry—without any residual sugar.

secondary fermentation
The process of converting still wine into Champagne that takes place in the bottle. In the production of still wines, the term is sometimes used in place of malolactic fermentation.

sommelier
French term for "wine waiter."

spumante
The Italian term for fully sparkling wines as opposed to those that are slightly sparkling—frizzante.

tannin
Substance found naturally in wine from the skin, pulp, and stalks. Tannins are responsible for the astringent quality found in wine, especially red wines. Tannins form the basis for the long life of wines and, while they can be overpowering in young wines, with bottle aging, they tend to become softer.

terroir
Literally "the soil." A French term referring to the particular character (aromas and flavors) of a given vineyard—or even a small part of that vineyard.

thin
Wines that lack fullness, depth, and complexity.

varietal
A wine named after the grape from which it is produced. In California, for instance, a wine labeled "Pinot Noir" must by law consist of at least 75 percent Pinot Noir grapes.

vineyard
The place where grapes are grown.

vinification
The process of making wine.

vintage
Harvest year of grapes and the resulting wines made from them. Ninety-five percent of the wine in a vintage-designated bottle must be from grapes harvested in that year.

viticulture
The practice (art, science, and philosophy) of growing grapevines.

woody
In most wines this is an undesirable condition indicating that there is a taint of some type from defective wood or an overuse of new oak.

yeast
Naturally occurring, single-celled organisms found on the skins of grapes that are the primary promoters of fermentation. In the fermentation process, yeast turns sugar into alcohol and carbon dioxide.

Index

We Have
EVERYTHING®
on Anything!

With more than 19 million copies sold, **the Everything® series** has become one of America's favorite resources for solving problems, learning new skills, and organizing lives. Our brand is not only recognizable—it's also welcomed.

The series is a hand-in-hand partner for people who are ready to tackle new subjects—like you!

For more information on the Everything® series, please visit *www.adamsmedia.com*

The Everything® list spans a wide range of subjects, with more than 500 titles covering 25 different categories:

Business	History	Reference
Careers	Home Improvement	Religion
Children's Storybooks	Everything Kids	Self-Help
Computers	Languages	Sports & Fitness
Cooking	Music	Travel
Crafts and Hobbies	New Age	Wedding
Education/Schools	Parenting	Writing
Games and Puzzles	Personal Finance	
Health	Pets	